The New York Times
COOKBOOK
FOR
SPECIAL
OCCASIONS

Books by Jean D. Hewitt

THE NEW YORK TIMES LARGE TYPE COOKBOOK,
New Revised Edition

THE NEW YORK TIMES MAIN DISH COOKBOOK

THE NEW YORK TIMES NATURAL FOODS COOKBOOK

THE NEW YORK TIMES HERITAGE COOKBOOK

THE FAMILY CIRCLE QUICK MENU COOKBOOK

JEAN HEWITT'S INTERNATIONAL MEATLESS COOKBOOK

The New York Times
COOKBOOK
FOR
SPECIAL
OCCASIONS

400 Recipes for Perfect Picnics •
Parties • Brunches • Buffets •
Romantic Dinners • Holiday
Meals • and other celebrations

JEAN HEWITT

Times
BOOKS

This book is dedicated to my husband.

Published by TIMES BOOKS,
The New York Times Book Co., Inc.
Three Park Avenue, New York, N.Y. 10016

Published simultaneously in Canada by
Fitzhenry & Whiteside, Ltd., Toronto

Library of Congress Cataloging in Publication Data

Hewitt, Jean.
    The New York times cookbook for special occasions.

    Rev. ed. of: The New York times weekend cookbook.
1975.
    Includes index.
    1. Cookery.   I. Hewitt, Jean.   New York times weekend
cookbook.   New York times.   III. Title.
IV. Title: Cookbook for special occasions.
TX715.H5746   1984   641.5'68   83-51166
ISBN 0-8129-6337-7 (pbk.)

Designed by Tere LoPrete

Manufactured in the United States of America

84 85 86 87 88   5 4 3 2 1

Contents

✝

Contents

SUMMER

FALL

Contents

Introduction

✁

Have you ever wondered which cookbook to look at when you've invited three couples to stop by for a light supper after a concert? *The New York Times Cookbook for Special Occasions* suggests serving champagne while the Torte di Spinaci (diced smoked pork chops, Parmesan and Ricotta cheeses in a spinach custard) you made early in the day is reheating. Lemon ice, also made ahead, is a super dessert ready to pull out of the freezer. The book builds confidence; you only need two dishes for a light supper.

There's a pound of noodles, a can of anchovies and some staples in the house and, on the spur of the moment, you ask old friends for pot luck. What will you serve? Your guests will be happy with Noodles with Anchovy Sauce, Italian bread or Melba toast, canned green bean and wax bean salad, Meringues with ice cream and chocolate or strawberry sauce or, if you have time, a Flan.

This book is arranged according to the seasons. In the fall, besides Treats for Halloween, there's a Make-Ahead Dinner for Six including Celery Root with Sour Cream, Chicken in Red Wine, Mushroom Salad and Fresh Fruit with Grand Marnier. Family menus for fall include Lima Bean Soup, Rice and Sausage Casserole, Tossed Salad and Deep-Dish Pear Pie. There are quick and easy dinners for anytime and any season, such as Chicken Livers with Cognac and Sherry, Broccoli, Cucumbers in Yogurt and Crème au Chocolat.

Summer and picnics are synonymous and a special occasions menu for toting includes recipes for Shrimp Sausalito, California-Style Rice Salad, Sandwiches-in-a-Loaf and fresh fruit. A hearty peasant-style buffet features Marinated Cod and Shrimp, Spinach Sauce with Fettucine, Chicken and Sausage, Fresh Fruit with Ricotta Sauce washed down with a Soave and Bardolino. Lunch Afloat in a No-Galley Boat is another picnic situation when sailors will praise Jackie's Scotch Eggs,

Caraway Potato Salad, Sweet and Sour Bean Salad, Sangria and William Greenberg's Sand Tarts.

Vegetarians are increasing in number and when you are expecting one or several at your table, there's help with a menu that includes Chilled Artichokes with Sunflower Seeds Vinaigrette, Clear Borscht, Sesame Seed Wafers, Vegetarian Coulibiac with Sour Cream Sauce, Broccoli Puree, Corn Relish, Bean Sprout and Citrus Salad on Watercress and Pumpkin Flan for dessert. Non-vegetarians will enjoy every bite too and may start to question why they think they have to eat meat at every meal.

Budget meals, sit down dinners, weekend guests, a dinner for two, holiday menus, cocktail parties and open house buffets are all covered with menus and recipes. And there's no rule that says you can't mix and match the seasons, as well as the individual recipes, to suit any occasion. Seeing the balance of dishes in one menu will help you plan other combinations, because good-quality ingredients prepared with love are a feast any time.

JEAN D. HEWITT

Westerly, R.I.

WINTER

After the Concert Buffet

Sunday concerts are a pleasant way to end a winter weekend in the city, especially if they are followed by a congenial buffet supper. However small the apartment, or limited the kitchen facilities, this simple meal to serve 12 can be finished off in the 30 minutes it takes to relax with an aperitif. Cushions on the floor can be the extra seating, and all the food can be eaten with only a fork. Individual paper soufflé cups solve the problem of not enough dishes for dessert.

Veal with Peppers*
Risotto*
Tossed Green Salad
Bert Greene's Lemon Mousse*
Verdicchio

VEAL WITH PEPPERS

4 *pounds boned shoulder of veal, cubed*	1 *cup chicken broth*
⅓ *cup flour*	1 *can (2 pounds 3 ounces) imported plum tomatoes*
Salt and freshly ground black pepper	¼ *cup tomato paste*
½ *cup olive oil*	1½ *teaspoons oregano*
¼ *cup butter*	2 *teaspoons basil*
4 *onions, sliced*	12–16 *Italian-style sweet green peppers*
4 *cloves garlic, finely chopped*	⅓ *cup chopped flat-leaf Italian parsley*
1½ *cups dry white wine*	1 *pound mushrooms, sliced*

1. Dredge the veal in the flour seasoned with salt and pepper. In a large, heavy porcelainized iron casserole or Dutch oven, heat the oil and butter.

2. Cook a few pieces of the meat at a time in the hot oil until browned on all sides. Drain on paper towels and keep warm. Repeat until all meat has been browned.

3. Add the onions and garlic to the oil left in the casserole and cook slowly until transparent. Add the wine and stir to loosen browned-on pieces.

4. Add the broth, tomatoes, tomato paste, oregano, basil and salt and pepper to taste. Bring to a boil. Add the browned meat pieces, cover and simmer until the meat is tender, about 1 hour.

5. Wash, halve, seed and cut the peppers into large chunks and add with the parsley and mushrooms to the cooked meat mixture. Cover and cook 10 minutes. Check the seasoning.

Yield: About 12 servings

Note: This dish can be prepared through step 4 early in the day, or even a day ahead, and held refrigerated for rewarming and continuing with step 5. The dish can be frozen at the end of step 4 or at the end of step 5.

RISOTTO

6 tablespoons olive oil	6 cups boiling chicken
6 tablespoons butter	broth
2 onions, finely	Salt and freshly
chopped	ground black pepper
2 cloves garlic, finely	to taste
chopped	2 packages (10 ounces
3 cups uncooked im-	each) frozen arti-
ported short-grain	choke hearts
Italian rice	(optional)

1. Heat the oil and butter in a heavy casserole and sauté in it the onions and garlic until transparent.

2. Add the rice and cook 10 to 12 minutes longer, stirring frequently.

3. Add the broth, salt and pepper. Bring to a boil, cover and cook slowly 25 minutes or until liquid is absorbed.

4. Cook the artichoke hearts according to package directions. Drain well. Halve each heart and add to the risotto.

Yield: 12 to 14 servings

Note: This dish can be prepared through step 2 early in the day. Short-grain Italian rice is available in Italian groceries.

BERT GREENE'S LEMON MOUSSE

6 lemons	2 teaspoons cornstarch
8 eggs, separated	½ cup Grand Marnier
3 cups granulated	3 cups heavy cream
sugar	6 tablespoons confec-
2 packages unflavored	tioners' sugar
gelatin	Toasted slivered
½ cup cold water	almonds

1. Grate the rind from the lemons and set aside. Squeeze juice and set aside.

2. Beat the egg yolks with the granulated sugar until the mixture is light colored and forms a ribbon when spooned back on itself.

3. Soften the gelatin in the cold water. Place over hot water and stir until gelatin is dissolved.

4. In a large bowl, combine the cornstarch with ⅓ of the lemon juice and stir until smooth. Add remaining juice, the lemon rind and gelatin and stir well. Add to the beaten egg mixture.

5. Turn mixture into a double boiler and cook over hot water until it thickens, stirring constantly. Add half the Grand Marnier and cook 1 minute longer. Do not allow to boil.

6. Chill the mixture until it begins to set.

7. Whip the cream with the remaining Grand Marnier and the confectioners' sugar until stiff. Beat the egg whites until stiff but not dry.

8. Fold the cream and egg whites into the lemon mixture and spoon into a soufflé dish, bowl or individual cups. Garnish with almonds.

Yield: 16 servings

Peanuts in the Meatloaf for Teenagers

In between the skating party and the record hop, the high school crowd is hungry, and they will charge through the house in search of food. Ask them to stay for dinner and surprise them with a peanut-stuffed meatloaf that is topped with homemade chili sauce and ringed with carrots and zucchini. Most teenagers will eat cole slaw, too, if they know there's pie in the freezer for later. The meatloaf can be assembled early in the day, the sauce made, vegetables cooked ahead and the slaw stashed away in the refrigerator. Make the lemon pie anytime there is an hour to spare because it will keep in the freezer for a week or longer.

*Stuffed Meatloaf**
Carrots and Zucchini
*Cole Slaw**
*Frozen Lemon Pie**

Stuffed Meatloaf

Stuffing

¼ cup butter
1 onion, finely chopped
1 clove garlic, finely chopped
1 cup chopped, unsalted raw peanuts or unsalted roasted peanuts (see note)
2 cups soft bread crumbs
1 teaspoon summer savory

1 rib celery with leaves, finely chopped
¼ teaspoon marjoram
Salt and freshly ground black pepper to taste
¼ cup chopped parsley
1 egg, lightly beaten
¼ cup chicken broth or water

Meat mixture

1 pound ground beef chuck
½ pound ground lean pork
½ pound ground veal
½ cup milk
1¼ teaspoons salt

Freshly ground black pepper to taste
1 egg, lightly beaten
½ cup fine dry bread crumbs
1 teaspoon worcestershire sauce

Sauce

2 tablespoons oil
1 onion, finely chopped
1 clove garlic, finely chopped
1 can (1 pound 1 ounce) imported plum tomatoes with basil

2 tablespoons tomato paste
¾ teaspoon salt
½ teaspoon thyme
2 tablespoons chopped, seeded hot chili pepper, or to taste

Garnish

> *Cooked carrots and*
> *zucchini slices*

1. To prepare stuffing, heat the butter in a small skillet and sauté in it the onion and garlic until tender. Turn into a large bowl.

2. Add the remaining stuffing ingredients and mix well.

3. Preheat oven to 375 degrees.

4. To prepare meat mixture, combine all the ingredients and blend with the fingers or a spoon.

5. On a piece of wax paper, flatten the meat mixture into a rectangle about 12 by 8 inches. Spread the stuffing evenly over the meat. Starting from the short end, roll the meat around the stuffing like a jellyroll. Place in a shallow roasting pan and bake 1 hour.

6. While the loaf is baking, prepare the sauce by heating the oil in the small skillet and sautéing in it the onion and garlic until tender.

7. Add remaining sauce ingredients, bring to a boil and simmer, uncovered, 10 minutes.

8. Arrange the loaf on a warm platter, spoon some of the sauce over and serve the remainder separately. Garnish with carrots and zucchini.

Yield: 6 servings

Note: Raw unsalted peanuts give the meatloaf a more subtle flavor than do roasted ones. Raw unsalted peanuts can be bought shelled and skinned or in the shell at most nut stores. Eight to 10 ounces of nuts in the shell give 1 cup of nutmeats.

COLE SLAW

¼ cup cider vinegar	4 cups shredded
¾ teaspoon dry	cabbage
mustard	1 carrot, shredded
2 eggs, lightly beaten	1 apple, cored and
1 cup light cream	diced
Salt to taste	½ cup seeded grapes
2 tablespoons sugar	¼ teaspoon celery seed
1 tablespoon butter	

1. Combine vinegar and mustard in the top of a double boiler and let stand 10 minutes.

2. Combine the eggs, cream, salt and sugar and whisk into the vinegar mixture. Cook, stirring, until mixture coats the spoon. Remove from the heat and swirl in the butter. Cool.

3. In a salad bowl, mix the cabbage, carrot, apple, grapes and celery seed. Pour the dressing over, toss and chill.

Yield: 6 servings

Frozen Lemon Pie

⅓ cup vanilla wafer crumbs	1 cup heavy cream
	⅓ cup lemon juice
3 eggs, separated	3 teaspoons grated
½ cup superfine sugar	lemon rind

1. Butter a 9-inch pie plate and sprinkle with ¼ cup of the vanilla wafer crumbs.

2. Beat the egg whites until foamy. Continue beating and gradually add the sugar, a tablespoon at a time, until the mixture is stiff and glossy.

3. Beat the egg yolks until thick and lemon colored. Fold in the egg white mixture. Beat the cream, lemon juice and rind together until stiff and fold into the egg mixture. Pour into the prepared pie plate.

4. Sprinkle with remaining crumbs and freeze the pie until it is solid.

Yield: 6 servings

End-of-the-Month Budget Special

❧

Good-tasting, inexpensive menus do not have to be dull. After a brisk walk in the park no one will realize he is eating a budget special. Lemon and coconut flavor the chicken with West African accents, and there's a creamy-light, warm rice pudding. The soup can be made up to the point of adding the watercress before you go out, and the chicken prepared through step 5. Cook the rice and set it aside to finish the pudding while the chicken is reheating and the zucchini sautéing. The Portuguese-style dinner will be on the table before the children fill up on snacks, and a discussion of Portuguese culture and cooking would be in order. The influence of Portugal's former African colony is reflected in the chicken dish.

Watercress Soup*
Chicken Mozambique*
Zucchini
Hearts of Lettuce Salad
Arroz Creme Pudim*

WATERCRESS SOUP

8–10 *small red-skinned*	¼ *cup olive oil*
or new potatoes,	2 *cups washed, dried*
peeled	*and trimmed water-*
1 *quart water*	*cress leaves*
Salt	

1. Cook potatoes in water with salt to taste in a covered saucepan until very tender. Do not drain.

2. Put the potatoes (water and all) through a food mill. Return to saucepan. The consistency should be that of a thin gruel. If necessary, add water.

3. Add the oil and bring the mixture to a boil. Add the watercress and cook 2 minutes. Check seasoning.

Yield: 6 servings

CHICKEN MOZAMBIQUE

2 *chickens (3½*	1 *cup grated fresh*
pounds each), left	*coconut, or 1 cup*
whole and trussed	*shredded unsweet-*
Juice and grated	*ened coconut*
rind of 2 lemons	*(available in health*
2 *cloves garlic, finely*	*food stores)*
chopped	1 *cup hot milk*
1½ *teaspoons salt*	1 *cup hot water*
Tabasco to taste	

1. Place chickens in a glass or enameled dish. Combine the juice, rind, garlic and salt. Add Tabasco and pour over the chickens, Marinate 2 hours at room temperature.

2. Mix the coconut and milk together and let stand 30 minutes. Force the mixture through a sieve, using a wooden spoon or pestle. Reserve the coconut-flavored milk.

3. Pour the hot water into the coconut pulp remaining and sieve again, reserving the liquid separately. Discard pulp.

4. Preheat oven to 350 degrees.

5. Place the chickens in a shallow casserole and bake 15 minutes. Pour the second, water-based coconut infusion over chickens and bake 45 minutes, basting 3 times.

6. Cook 30 minutes longer or until chicken is done. During this period, baste frequently with the coconut-flavored milk.

Yield: 6 to 8 servings

ARROZ CREME PUDIM

½ cup raw rice	1 cup milk
1 cup water	⅔ cup plus 2
½ teaspoon plus ⅛	tablespoons sugar
teaspoon salt	2 tablespoons flour
1 piece (2 inches)	2 eggs, separated
vanilla bean	2 tablespoons butter
Grated rind of 1	Cinnamon
lemon	

1. Wash the rice thoroughly with cold water and drain. Place rice, 1 cup water, ½ teaspoon salt, the vanilla bean and lemon rind in a saucepan. Bring to a boil, cover and simmer 20 minutes.

2. Remove from heat and let stand 10 minutes. Remove bean and stir rice.

3. Scald milk in the top of a double boiler. Mix ⅔ cup sugar with flour and whisk into milk. Cook, stirring, until mixture thickens.

4. Lightly beat the egg yolks, add a little hot milk mixture and return to pan.

5. Cook until mixture thickens slightly. Stir in the butter. Set aside.

6. Beat egg whites with remaining ⅛ teaspoon salt until they form peaks. Add remaining 2 tablespoons sugar and continue beating until stiff. Stir rice into custard mixture. Fold in whites and pour into lightly buttered deep platter, about 11 by 14 inches. Sprinkle with cinnamon. Serve at room temperature.

Yield: 4 to 6 servings

Ski Buffet

Dedicated skiers such as Bonny Birnbaum hate to spend a moment's daylight away from the slopes during a skiing weekend. Mrs. Leonard Birnbaum has a home six miles from Catamount ski area that is open house for fellow ski enthusiasts all winter long. The freezer is her biggest helper for keeping ingredients and finished dishes ready for last-minute preparation. The cooking and freezing of the main dish may have been done in her Manhattan apartment and the frozen food toted to the country in an insulated container. Mrs. Birnbaum's ski buffet menu below will serve eight hungry people or as many as ten or twelve if half a ham or a smoked Canadian bacon roast is added.

*Jane's Coeur**
*Chicken and Shrimp Casserole**
*Dilled Rice and Noodles**
*Frozen Mousse Izarra**
*Aunt Lil's Cookies**

JANE'S COEUR

½ pound Cheddar
cheese, grated, at
room temperature
¼ pound blue cheese,
at room temperature
½ pound cottage
cheese
1 teaspoon salt

1 teaspoon worcester-
shire sauce
1 cup heavy cream
Dash cayenne
pepper
Apple slices or fresh
raw vegetables

1. Cream the Cheddar and blue cheeses together. Add the cottage cheese, salt, worcestershire, cream and cayenne and mix.

2. Pour into a cheesecloth-lined colander or conical sieve and allow to drain several hours, or until no more liquid comes from the mixture.

3. Invert the mixture onto a serving dish and serve with apples or vegetables.

Yield: About 8 servings

CHICKEN AND SHRIMP CASSEROLE

⅓ cup butter
2 tablespoons oil
2 broiler-fryer chickens (3 pounds each), cut into serving pieces
3 onions, finely chopped
1 clove garlic, finely chopped
½ cup port wine
1 teaspoon basil
1 cup tomato sauce (preferably home-made)
Salt and freshly ground black pepper to taste
1 pound shelled, de-veined, raw shrimp
3 tablespoons chopped parsley

1. Heat the butter and oil in a heavy casserole or large, deep skillet. Brown the chicken pieces in it on all sides. Add the onions and garlic and cook until they wilt.

2. Stir in the port, basil, tomato sauce, salt and pepper. Bring to a boil, cover and simmer until the chicken is tender, about 35 minutes.

3. Add the shrimp and parsley and cook 8 minutes longer.

Yield: 8 servings if served alone, 10 to 12 if smoked Canadian roast or ham is included.

Note: The entire dish can be frozen or, preferably, freeze at end of step 2 and add shrimp and parsley to thawed and reheated dish and cook 8 minutes.

DILLED RICE AND NOODLES

2 tablespoons butter
1 cup very fine, soup-style egg noodles
1 cup raw rice
2 cups chicken broth
Salt and freshly ground black pepper to taste
½ cup snipped fresh dill weed

1. Melt the butter in a heavy casserole. Add the noddles and cook over medium heat, stirring constantly, until they are golden brown, but do not allow the butter to burn.

2. Add the rice and cook a few minutes longer.

3. Add the chicken broth, bring to a boil, cover and simmer very gently about 20 minutes or until liquid has been absorbed.

4. Season with salt and pepper and stir in the dill.

Yield: 6 servings

FROZEN MOUSSE IZARRA

6 egg yolks
½ cup sugar
1 cup heavy cream
¼ cup Izarra green,
 an imported liqueur
 (or creme de
 menthe)

Green food coloring
(optional)
Small candy canes
(optional)

1. Beat the egg yolks and sugar together until very pale and thick. Beat in the cream and Izarra. Continue to beat until mixture is light and fluffy.

2. Add a few drops green food coloring to make the mixture pale green. Pour into a 1-quart mold or bowl, and freeze. If there is a little mixture over, freeze it for a taster.

3. Dip the frozen mousse briefly into warm water. Place a cold platter over the mousse and invert to unmold. Freeze again. Stick candy canes into top of dessert and around base if desired.

Yield: 6 servings

AUNT LIL'S COOKIES

¾ pound softened
 butter
2 egg yolks
1 cup sugar
3 cups flour
 Chocolate bits
 (optional)

Candied cherries,
cut into eighths
(optional)
Pecan or walnut
halves (optional)

1. Beat the butter together with the egg yolks. Gradually beat in the sugar and continue beating until mixture is light and fluffy.

2. Stir in the flour and mix well. Chill the mixture until it can be handled easily.

3. Preheat oven to 350 degrees.

4. Either place teaspoonsful of the mixture on an ungreased cookie sheet or, with floured hands, make small balls of the mixture and place on the sheet.

5. Decorate the tops with chocolate bits, cherry pieces or nuts if desired. Bake about 12 minutes or until cookies are lightly browned at the edges.

Yield: About 6 dozen cookies

Candlelight
Midnight Supper

✕

Champagne, candlelight and midnight repasts do not have to be reserved for New Year's Eve. When there's an occasion to celebrate, or someone special to entertain, and a no-work day following, a late supper is romantic and old-fashioned enough for a hostess to wear a flowing chiffon gown and create an art-deco setting. Culinary offerings should be light, sophisticated and sparse. Caviar is the ultimate accompaniment to the Piper-Heidsieck or Bollinger Brut and needs no recipe or cooking, just money. But, smoked salmon is an alternate luxury tidbit that can be stretched with fish stock and cream into a smooth, delectable dish for eight to ten special friends to nibble on with champagne. A sliver of Hungarian chocolate cake, with more champagne, will make a fitting ending. The salmon mousse and the cake can be made a day ahead.

Piper-Heidsieck or Bollinger Brut
Smoked Salmon Mousse à la Caravelle°*
Hungarian Chocolate Cake°*

SMOKED SALMON MOUSSE À LA CARAVELLE

1 *pound smoked salmon*	*Red food coloring (optional)*
1 *recipe fish velouté (recipe below)*	*Yellow food coloring (optional)*
Juice of ½ lemon	½ *cup heavy cream, whipped*
1 *recipe fish aspic (recipe below)*	*Flowers cut from carrots or egg-white slices*
Freshly ground white pepper to taste	*Stems and leaves cut from leek greens*

1. Grind the smoked salmon and fish velouté through the finest blade of a meat grinder. The mixture should be very fine and smooth. If it is not, the mixture should be forced through a fine sieve.

2. Beat in the lemon juice and ¾ cup of the cooled, but not set, aspic and add pepper. Add a drop of red and a drop of yellow food coloring, if desired, and fold in the whipped cream.

3. Spoon the salmon mousse mixture into a 1-quart metal mold or bowl. If space permits, pour a thin layer of aspic over. Chill the mold 4 hours or overnight.

4. Chill a serving platter (silver is traditional).

5. Set the mold briefly in warm water or hold a towel wrung out in hot water over the surface of the mold and turn out onto the chilled platter.

6. Decorate the top with aspic-dipped carrot or egg-white flowers with stalks and leaves cut from leeks. Gently spoon partly thickened aspic over them to cover mousse and decorations with a thin layer. Chill. Chill remaining aspic.

7. Remove excess aspic drippings from the platter, wipe it clean and surround the mold with finely chopped chilled aspic. Serve each slice of salmon mousse with a little of the chopped aspic.

Yield: 8 to 10 servings

Fish Stock

3 pounds fish heads and bones	1 rib celery, quartered
1 quart water	1 carrot, quartered
1 cup dry white wine	1 bay leaf
1 small onion	1 teaspoon salt
1 sprig parsley	½ teaspoon black peppercorns

Place all ingredients in a heavy saucepan. Bring to a boil, cover and simmer 20 minutes. Strain.

Yield: About 5 cups

Fish Velouté

2 tablespoons butter	¾ cup strained fish
¼ cup flour	stock (recipe above)

1. In a small saucepan, melt the butter. Stir in the flour and cook 1 minute.

2. Gradually blend in the fish stock. Bring to a boil, stirring, until the mixture thickens. Cook, still stirring, 2 minutes.

Yield: About ¾ cup

Fish Aspic

4 cups strained fish stock, approximately (recipe above)	3 egg shells, crushed
	2 tablespoons unflavored gelatin
3 egg whites, lightly beaten	¼ cup cold water

1. Place the stock, egg whites and shells in a saucepan. Soften the gelatin in the cold water and add.

2. Gradually bring the mixture to a boil, stirring often. Allow to simmer gently until liquid clears. Pour through a sieve lined with wet flannel.

Yield: About 4 cups

HUNGARIAN CHOCOLATE CAKE

10 *egg yolks*
⅔ *cup sugar*
10 *tablespoons butter*
8 *ounces bittersweet*
   or German sweet
   chocolate

1 *cup very finely*
   ground pecans (see
   note)
8 *egg whites*
¾ *cup apricot*
   preserves
⅔ *cup chopped pecans*

1. Preheat oven to 350 degrees.
2. Grease and flour an 8-inch springform pan.
3. In a large bowl, mix together the egg yolks and sugar. Stir occasionally, but do not beat, to dissolve the sugar while assembling the remaining ingredients.
4. In the top of a double boiler, place the butter and chocolate. Set over hot water and heat gently until the mixture is smooth.
5. Stir the melted chocolate mixture into the egg yolk and sugar mixture until blended.
6. Remove 1 cup of the mixture and set aside to use as a frosting for the cake.
7. Fold the ground pecans into the mixture remaining in the bowl. Beat the egg whites until stiff but not dry. Stir ¼ of the egg whites into the nut mixture. Gently fold in the remaining whites. Pour the mixture into the prepared pan and bake 50 to 60 minutes or until the center feels springy to the touch.
8. Set the pan on a rack to cool and gently ease a spatula around the edge so that the cake falls evenly as it cools. When cool, remove the sides of the pan. Transfer the cake to a serving dish or compote. Slice into 2 layers and spread the preserves over the bottom layer. Replace the top layer.
9. If the frosting mixture is not stiff enough to spread, refrigerate 20 to 30 minutes. Using a small spatula, frost the top and sides of the cake with the mixture. Pat the chopped nuts around the edges. Refrigerate until served. The cake can be made a day ahead, but should be stored in the refrigerator.

Yield: 8 to 10 servings

Note: This is best done in a Mouli grater or nut grinder; the texture should be as fine and fluffy as flour.

Something Regal for the Holidays

If you're bored with turkey, don't like goose and think duck is for the birds, but you still yearn for stuffing, a stuffed crown roast of lamb is festive enough for any holiday-season dinner party. Stuffed crown roast of lamb is expensive but it takes less time to cook than the average turkey, is easier to carve and, with eight at table, there won't be any leftovers. Ring the serving platter with stuffed squash, toss a salad, add an appetizer and an unusual dessert, such as the cassis soufflé, and few restaurants could compete chez vous. Kir, the white wine and cassis mixture, would be ideal as an aperitif, followed by a Pommard or Nuits-Saint-Georges with the lamb and a fine Sauternes with dessert.

Kir*
Oyster Beignets with Horseradish Sauce*
Stuffed Crown Roast of Lamb*
Baked Squash with Peas and Spinach*
Tossed Salad
Cheese
Cassis Soufflé*

KIR

1 cup chilled, dry,
white Burgundy
wine
½ ounce (more, or less,
to taste) crème de
cassis

1 small twist lemon
rind (optional)

Combine the ingredients in a large wine glass.
Yield: 1 serving

OYSTER BEIGNETS WITH HORSERADISH SAUCE

About 12 large
oysters (8 ounces),
shucked
1 cup flour
½ teaspoon sugar

1 cup milk
¼ cup butter
4 eggs
Oil or fat for deep-
frying

Sauce

¾ cup chili sauce
¼ cup ketchup
¼ cup very finely
chopped celery
1 tablespoon lemon
juice

1 tablespoon horse-
radish, or to taste
½ teaspoon salt
1–2 drops Tabasco

1. Drain the oysters very well and chop finely. The juice can be
added to a fish stew or soup.
2. Sift the flour and sugar into a bowl.
3. Place the milk and butter in a sauce pan and heat to boiling,
stirring to melt the butter. Add the flour mixture all at once and stir
over medium heat until the mixture leaves the sides of the pan
clean. Remove from the heat.
4. Beat in the eggs, one at a time, very well and continue to beat
until a stiff batter is formed. Add the oysters and mix well.
5. Drop the mixture by teaspoonsful into deep fat or oil heated to
350 degrees. Fry until golden and done, about 5 minutes. Drain on
paper towels and keep warm while frying remainder.

6. Meanwhile, combine all the sauce ingredients and chill. Serve the sauce as a dip for the beignets.

Yield: About 10 appetizer servings.

STUFFED CROWN ROAST OF LAMB

1 small eggplant	8 Greek olives, pitted
Salt	and chopped
Boiling salted	¼ teaspoon cinnamon
water	¼ teaspoon ground
1 crown roast of	cardamom
lamb (6 pounds,	¼ cup golden raisins
16 chops)	(optional)
2 cloves garlic,	⅓ cup chopped
slivered	walnuts
Freshly ground	¼ teaspoon chopped
black pepper	parsley
2 tablespoons oil	1 teaspoon grated
1 onion, finely	lemon rind
chopped	8 cooked artichoke
1 pound ground lean	hearts, fresh, frozen
lamb	or canned, drained
1½ cups cooked rice	and halved
1 rib celery, finely	Crab apples
chopped	

1. Peel the eggplant and cut into ½-inch-thick slices, sprinkle with salt and let stand 10 minutes. Rinse under running water. Cut into 1-inch chunks. Cook in boiling salted water until barely tender; drain.

2. Make incisions into the inside of the crown roast and insert the garlic slivers. Season inside and out with salt and pepper.

3. Preheat oven to 350 degrees.

4. Heat the oil and sauté in it the onion until tender and golden. Add the ground lamb and cook, stirring, until lightly browned.

5. Add the drained eggplant, the rice, celery, olives, cinnamon, cardamom, raisins, walnuts, parsley and lemon rind to the ground lamb. Season the mixture with salt and pepper to taste.

6. Spoon ¾ of the mixture into the crown roast cavity, arrange the halved artichoke hearts over the surface and pile up the remain-

ing stuffing. Wrap the ends of the frenched chop bones with small pieces of aluminum foil and set the roast on a rack in a shallow roasting pan.

7. Roast 1¼ hours, or until cooked to the desired degree of doneness. Let stand 10 minutes in a warm place before carving like a pie. Remove foil and decorate alternate bones with crab apples.

Yield: 8 servings

BAKED SQUASH WITH PEAS AND SPINACH

4 acorn or small butternut squash
Salt and freshly ground black pepper to taste
¼ cup butter
¼ cup light brown sugar (optional)

1⅓ cups hot cooked peas
1½ cups hot cooked chopped spinach
⅓ cup sour cream
⅛ teaspoon grated nutmeg

1. Preheat oven to 350 degrees.
2. Wash the squash and halve each. Remove the seeds and place squash cut side down in a shallow baking dish. Pour in enough water to barely cover the bottom of the dish.
3. Bake 45 minutes or until barely tender.
4. Turn squash cut side up, season with salt and pepper, dot with butter, sprinkle with brown sugar, if desired, and bake 15 minutes longer.
5. Fill 4 squash halves with peas. Mix the spinach with sour cream, nutmeg, salt and pepper and use mixture to fill the other 4 halves. Reheat in oven.

Yield: 8 servings

CASSIS SOUFFLÉ

1 *package plus 1 teaspoon unflavored gelatin*	*Crème de cassis (see note)*
¼ *cup water*	*Red food coloring*
4 *eggs, separated*	1 *cup heavy cream, whipped*
½ *cup sugar*	2 *egg whites*
⅛ *teaspoon salt*	*Crystallized violets*

1. Soak the gelatin in the water 5 minutes.
2. Fold a strip of aluminum foil in half lengthwise. Secure it with string around the outside of a 1-quart soufflé dish so that a collar is formed above the dish. Lightly oil the dish and the inside of the foil collar.
3. Place the egg yolks, sugar, salt and softened gelatin in the top of a double boiler. Set over hot water and beat with a wire whisk over medium heat until the mixture is thick, creamy and light in color. The gelatin dissolves and the mixture resembles thick zabaglione. Do not allow mixture to boil.
4. Remove top of double boiler from stove and beat in 1¼ cups cassis. Add 2 or 3 drops of red food coloring to give a deep rosy hue. Turn mixture into a large bowl and chill until it begins to thicken, stirring several times so that it thickens evenly.
5. When mixture is the consistency of thick custard sauce, fold in the whipped cream.
6. Beat the 6 egg whites until stiff and glossy. Do not allow them to become dry. Stir ⅓ of the beaten whites into the cassis mixture. Fold in the remaining whites.
7. Spoon or pour the mixture into the prepared soufflé dish.
8. Chill several hours or overnight. Remove the foil collar and garnish soufflé with crystallized violets. Serve in dessert dishes, with a tablespoon of cassis poured over if desired.

Yield: 6 to 8 servings

Note: Nonalcoholic cassis syrup may be substituted.

Bread-Baking Marathon

❦

Chances are there is someone you know who has a reputation as a bread baker. It could be the young bachelor across the hall who took baking classes, or someone's mother, or grandmother, who has been doing it for years. Persuading an expert to oversee a one-day baking marathon, when friends and neighbors would gather in the largest kitchen available and actually get the feel of dough and learn not to be afraid of cooking with yeast, should not be too difficult.

If the cook-in starts early enough the first loaves could be ready for a cheese, wine and bread lunch. Here are three recipes for healthful, good-tasting loaves to try or to pass out to the day's students as a postgraduate course.

*Honey and Egg Bread**
*Cracked Wheat Bread**
*Soy Protein Bread**

HONEY AND EGG BREAD

1 package dry active
  yeast or 1 cake
  compressed yeast
1¾ cups lukewarm
  water
½ cup eggs, raw at
  room temperature
¼ cup shortening or
  margarine
½ cup honey
½ cup nonfat dry
  milk solids
1 teaspoon salt
6–7 cups unbleached
  white flour
  Melted butter or
  margarine

1. Dissolve the yeast in ¼ cup of the lukewarm water. Stir in the eggs, shortening or margarine, the honey, dry milk solids, salt, remaining water and enough of the flour to make a batter that can be beaten.

2. Beat 3 minutes with an electric beater or 75 strokes by hand. Work in enough of the remaining flour to make a dough that can be kneaded.

3. Turn dough onto a board and knead until smooth and satiny, about 10 minutes. Place in a lightly greased bowl, grease the top of the dough with shortening, cover and let rise until doubled in bulk, about 1 hour.

4. Punch the dough down. Knead briefly. Divide in half and shape into loaves. Place in greased 9-by-5-by-3-inch loaf pans, cover and let rise until doubled in bulk, about 1 hour.

5. Preheat oven to 350 degrees.

6. Bake 40 minutes, or until loaves sound hollow when tapped on the bottom. Brush with melted butter or margarine for a soft crust. Cool on a rack.

Yield: 2 loaves

CRACKED WHEAT BREAD

5 cups lukewarm
  water
3 packages dry active
  yeast
2 cups cracked wheat
  (sold in health food
  stores as cereal)
2 eggs, lightly beaten
½ cup light brown
  sugar

1 tablespoon salt
2 cups nonfat dry
  milk solids
¼ cup melted butter
1 cup soy granules
½ cup wheat germ
8–9 cups unbleached
  white flour
Cornmeal
½ cup sesame seeds

1. Place the water and yeast in a large bowl and stir to dissolve. Add the cracked wheat and set aside for 1 hour.

2. Reserve 2 tablespoons beaten eggs. Combine remaining eggs with sugar, salt, dry milk solids, butter, soy granules and wheat germ. Stir in the cracked wheat mixture and mix very well.

3. Add the flour cup by cup until you have a dough that is soft enough to knead. It will be a little sticky at first.

4. Turn onto a lightly floured board and knead until the dough is smooth and elastic and loses its stickiness, about 10 minutes.

5. Place dough in a buttered bowl; turn to butter the top. Cover with a damp towel and clear plastic wrap and set in a warm place to rise until doubled in bulk, about 1 hour.

6. Punch the dough down and divide into 4 pieces. Shape into round loaves, or shape and fit into 4 greased 8½-by-4½-by-2½-inch loaf pans or make some round and some loaf-shape. Set round loaves on greased and cornmeal-dusted baking sheets.

7. Brush loaves with reserved egg, sprinkle with sesame seeds, cover and let rise in a warm place until doubled in bulk, about 45 minutes.

8. Preheat oven to 350 degrees.

9. Bake the loaves 45 minutes or until the loaves sound hollow when tapped on the bottom. Cool on a rack.

Yield: 4 loaves

Soy Protein Bread

1¾ cups boiling beef broth	1 tablespoon salt
½ cup (1½ ounces) dehydrated, un-flavored, textured, soy (vegetable) protein granules or bits	2 packages dry active yeast
	½ cup milk
	½ cup light molasses
	⅓ cup butter or margarine
8–9 cups unbleached white flour	1 egg, at room temperature

1. Combine ¾ cup boiling beef broth and the textured soy protein granules and set aside.

2. In the large bowl of an electric mixer, thoroughly mix 2 cups flour, the salt and undissolved dry active yeast.

3. Combine the milk, remaining broth, the molasses and butter or margarine in a saucepan and heat over low heat until very warm, about 120 to 130 degrees on a thermometer. The fat does not have to melt.

4. Gradually add the liquid mixture to the dry ingredients and beat 2 minutes at medium speed.

5. Add the egg, soaked *or* rehydrated soy protein granules (from step 1) and 1 cup flour. Beat at high speed 2 minutes. Stir in enough of the remaining flour to make a stiff dough.

6. Turn onto a lightly floured board and knead until smooth and elastic, about 10 minutes. Place in a greased bowl; turn to grease the top. Cover and let rise in a warm place until doubled in bulk, about 1¼ hours.

7. Punch dough down, divide in half and roll each half into a 14-by-9-inch rectangle. Beginning at 9-inch end, roll each as for a jellyroll. Pinch seam to seal.

8. Place seam side down and press down ends with heel of the hand and fold underneath. Place, seam side down, in greased 9-by-5-by-3-inch loaf pans. Cover and let rise until doubled in bulk, about 1¼ hours.

9. Preheat oven to 375 degrees.

10. Bake on lowest rack position 40 to 45 minutes or until bottom sounds hollow when tapped. Remove from pans and cool on a rack.

Yield: 2 loaves

Come for Dessert and Coffee

Friends in town on Friday night? Invite them over for dessert and coffee about nine o'clock. By then you will have had a chance to adjust from the hectic week, put on comfortable clothes and listen to music. The espresso ricotta cheesecake and good luck cookies were made the night before. All that is left to do is to put on the pot of espresso and set out the bottle of Sambucca and you'll be a hostess who doesn't miss any of the conversation or the plans for the rest of the weekend.

Espresso Ricotta Cheesecake*
Good Luck Cookies*
Espresso and Sambucca

Espresso Ricotta Cheesecake

24 little packages (48
   single cookies)
   amaretti, hard
   Italian macaroons
½ cup graham
   cracker crumbs
½ cup melted butter
1½ tablespoons un-
   flavored gelatin
3 tablespoons cold
   water
½ cup sugar

1 cup hot, double-
   strength espresso
   coffee (see note)
2 containers (15
   ounces each)
   whole-milk ricotta
   cheese
1 teaspoon vanilla
2 cups heavy cream
   Dash of cinnamon
2 tablespoons toasted,
   sliced almonds

1. Preheat oven to 400 degrees.

2. Unwrap the amaretti and crush with a rolling pin until very fine. Reserve ½ cup of crumbs.

3. Transfer remaining crumbs to a bowl, add the graham cracker crumbs and stir in the butter. Press the mixture against the bottom, and halfway up the sides, of a greased 10-inch springform pan.

4. Bake the crumb crust 5 minutes. Cool.

5. Sprinkle the gelatin over the cold water and allow to soften. Stir soaked gelatin and the sugar into the hot espresso and stir to dissolve completely. Allow to cool slightly.

6. Add the ricotta cheese and beat until smooth. Stir in the vanilla. Whip 1 cup of the cream until stiff and fold into the cheese mixture.

7. Pour half the mixture into the cooled crust, sprinkle with reserved crumbs and top with remaining cheese mixture. Chill several hours or overnight.

8. Loosen around the sides of the crust with a spatula, and remove the spring from sides. Set the cheesecake and metal base on a serving plate.

9. Whip the remaining cream with the cinnamon and pipe with a star tube, or spoon, into mounds around the edge of the cake. Sprinkle cream with the almonds.

Yield: 10 servings

Note: Double-strength espresso coffee is made using 6 tablespoons ground espresso coffee to a cup of water. If an espresso maker is not available, use a regular coffee maker.

Good Luck Cookies

½ cup butter
1 cup sugar
1 egg
¼ cup molasses
2 cups flour
2 teaspoons baking
soda

¼ teaspoon salt
1 teaspoon cinnamon
¾ teaspoon ground
ginger
¾ teaspoon ground
cloves

1. Cream butter and sugar together and beat in egg and molasses.

2. Sift together the flour, baking soda, salt, cinnamon, ginger and cloves.

3. Stir dry ingredients into butter mixture.

4. Chill dough 1 hour or until it can be handled easily.

5. Preheat oven to 375 degrees.

6. Form dough into 1-inch balls and place on a greased baking sheet. Bake 10 to 12 minutes.

Yield: About 3 dozen cookies

Open House Sunday, Three to Six

✖

Fitting one more party into the holiday schedule is often difficult, but an informal open house is a friendly way to exchange greetings of the season with friends, family and neighbors, and include the children too. Punch bowls garnished with fruits and colorful ice rings are the best way to dispense both alcoholic and nonalcoholic beverages to a crowd. Offer a selection of savoury and sweet tidbits set on an attractively decorated buffet or dining room table and no one will have to work during the party.

Stone Fence Punch*
Open House Punch*
Chili Doughnuts with Guacamole Sauce*
Black Walnut Cakes*
Kisses*
Fanny Pierson Crane's Spice Krinkles*
Holiday Cake*

━━━━━◆•◆━━━━━

STONE FENCE PUNCH

1 *bottle (⅘ quart) applejack*
1 *quart sweet cider*
1 *quart chilled soda water*

Orange slices studded with whole cloves

Pour applejack, cider and soda over ice cubes in a punch bowl. Stir. Garnish with orange slices.

Yield: About 24 servings

Open House Punch

1 pound superfine sugar	1½ cups peach brandy
2 cups lemon juice	Block of ice or decorated ice ring
1 bottle (⅘ quart) light rum	2 quarts chilled soda water or spring
1 bottle (⅘ quart) cognac	water, or to taste

1. In a punch bowl, dissolve the sugar in the lemon juice. Add the rum, cognac and peach brandy.

2. Just before serving, add the ice and the soda water or spring water.

Yield: About 20 servings

Chili Doughnuts with Guacamole Sauce

Chili

2 tablespoons oil	1 tablespoon cumin
1½ small onions, finely chopped	½ teaspoon salt
1 clove garlic, finely chopped	⅛ teaspoon cayenne pepper
¾ pound lean ground beef	3 tablespoons tomato paste
2 tablespoons chili powder	

Doughnuts

2 cups flour	2 eggs
½ teaspoon salt	¼ cup oil
3 teaspoons baking powder	Fat or oil for deep-frying
¾ cup milk	

1. To prepare chili, heat the oil in a heavy skillet and sauté in it the onions and garlic until tender.

2. Add the ground beef and cook, stirring, until meat loses its red color. Add the remaining ingredients and cook, stirring, until well blended, about 3 to 5 minutes. Cool. Drain off excess grease or liquid.

3. To prepare doughnuts, sift together the flour, salt and baking powder. Add the milk, eggs and ¼ cup oil and beat until smooth.

4. Fold in 1 cup of the cooled, drained chili. Check the consistency of the mixture by making a trial doughnut in deep fat heated to 375 degrees.

5. Using a ½-inch plain piping tube and a large pastry bag, pipe a doughnut ring, about 2 inches in diameter, onto a greased slotted spoon and lower gently into the fat. If dough is too stiff, stir in more milk, and if dough is too thin to retain its shape, whisk in a small quantity of flour.

6. Cook ½ minute on each side and drain on paper towels. Alternately, the mixture can be dropped by teaspoonsful into the hot fat to give solid "doughnuts."

7. Serve hot with guacamole sauce (recipe below).

Yield: About 2 dozen doughnuts, depending on size

Guacamole Sauce

2 tablespoons chop-
    ped onion
1 large tomato,
    skinned and halved
3 tablespoons lemon
    juice
2 tablespoons olive
    oil
1 tablespoon mayon-
    naise
    Salt and freshly
    ground black
    pepper to taste

1 ripe avocado,
    peeled, pitted and
    diced
1 tablespoon chop-
    ped, canned hot
    chili peppers, or
    to taste
1½ tablespoons chop-
    ped cilantro (also
    called fresh cori-
    ander or Chinese
    parsley), or parsley

1. Place the onion, half the tomato, 1 tablespoon lemon juice, the oil, mayonnaise, salt and pepper in an electric blender container. Blend until smooth.

2. Dice the remaining tomato half and combine in a bowl with the avocado, chili peppers, cilantro and the remaining lemon juice. Add the pureed mixture. Toss to mix well.

Yield: About 2 cups

Black Walnut Cakes

Cakes

½ cup shortening
1 cup light brown sugar
1 egg, lightly beaten
1 teaspoon vanilla
1½ cups flour

½ teaspoon baking soda
½ teaspoon salt
1 cup chopped black walnuts

Frosting

¼ cup maple syrup
¼ cup butter
½ teaspoon maple flavoring

2½ cups confectioners' sugar, approximately

1. Preheat oven to 375 degrees.
2. To prepare cakes, cream the shortening and sugar together until light and creamy. Beat in the egg and vanilla.
3. Sift together the flour, baking soda and salt and stir into sugar mixture. Stir in black walnuts. Drop by teaspoonsful onto greased baking sheets and bake 12 to 15 minutes.
4. To prepare frosting, heat the syrup. Add butter and stir until it melts. Stir in flavoring and enough confectioners' sugar to make a spreading consistency.
5. Frost tops of the cooled cakes.

Yield: About 30 cakes

Kisses

3 egg whites
1 teaspoon vanilla
¼ teaspoon cream of tartar

⅛ teaspoon salt
1 cup sugar

1. Preheat oven to 275 degrees.
2. Beat the egg whites, vanilla, cream of tartar and salt together until soft peaks form. Slowly beat in sugar until a stiff glossy meringue forms.
3. Drop from teaspoons onto ungreased baking sheets and bake 45 minutes or until kisses are fairly dry.
4. Shut off the oven, open the door and leave the kisses in until they are dry and crisp.

Yield: 3 to 4 dozen kisses

FANNY PIERSON CRANE'S SPICE KRINKLES

¾ cup softened butter	2 teaspoons cinnamon
1 cup light brown sugar	2 teaspoons ground ginger
1 egg, lightly beaten	¾ teaspoon ground cloves
¼ cup molasses	
2¼ cups flour	¼ teaspoon salt
2 teaspoons baking soda	2 tablespoons sugar

1. Cream the butter and brown sugar. Beat in the egg and molasses. Sift together the remaining ingredients except the sugar and stir into the batter.
2. Wrap the mixture in wax paper and chill 2 hours or overnight.
3. Preheat oven to 375 degrees.
4. Break off or cut, pieces of dough big enough to form into balls the size of walnuts. Dip tops in sugar and set 3 inches apart on a baking sheet. Bake 10 to 12 minutes or until set but not hard. For a festive look, the cookies can be decorated while hot from the oven by pressing each one with a wooden butter print mold. Cool on a rack.

Yield: 36 to 40 cookies

HOLIDAY CAKE

1 cup butter
1½ cups sugar
2 teaspoons grated
  lemon rind
1 teaspoon vanilla
3 eggs
3¾ cups flour

3 teaspoons baking
  powder
1 teaspoon salt
⅓ cup milk
1 cup chopped
  candied fruits
½ cup chopped
  almonds

1. Preheat oven to 350 degrees.

2. Cream ¾ cup of the butter with 1 cup of the sugar until light and fluffy. Beat in the rind and vanilla.

3. Beat in the eggs, one at a time, very well. Sift together 3 cups of the flour, the baking powder and salt. Stir in the sifted dry ingredients alternately with the milk until batter is just smooth.

4. Cut remaining butter into remaining flour. Stir in the remaining sugar, the candied fruits and almonds.

5. Spoon alternate layers of the cake batter and the crumb-fruit mixture into a greased 10-inch tube pan, using ⅓ of the mixture at a time, starting with batter and ending with crumbs. Bake 50 minutes, or until done.

Yield: 12 to 16 servings

Après-Ski for a Crowd

✣

Sharing a ski hut on weekends cuts costs and is fun if the group is congenial and no one gets saddled with much more than scrambling eggs or making coffee. You came to ski. Line up a volunteer each week to make and tote homemade soup in a thermos and a couple of casseroles to reheat. For the woman or man, willing to put time and effort into the assignment, here's a recipe for cannelloni with homemade pasta. The cannelloni has two fillings and two sauces. If your reaction is that no one spends that much time in the kitchen even for friends, then substitute store-bought manicotti, make one filling and use only the tomato sauce, canned if you really must.

Split Pea Soup°
Cannelloni°
Crusty Hot Garlic Bread
Tossed Green Salad
Fresh Fruit

————————◆ ◆◆ ◆————————

SPLIT PEA SOUP

3 cups green split peas	6 carrots, sliced
4½ quarts water	Salt and freshly ground black pepper to taste
1 large smoked ham bone with meat removed, or 3 smoked ham hocks	9 chorizos (Spanish-style sausages) or Italian sausages, sliced
3 onions, sliced	

1. Wash and pick over the peas and place in a saucepan with the water, ham bone, onions, carrots, salt and pepper. Bring to a boil, cover and simmer 1½ to 2 hours or until tender.

2. Remove the bone. Force the mixture through a sieve or a food mill into a clean saucepan. Meanwhile, fry the sausage slices until browned and cooked. Add with 3 tablespoons of the sausage fat to the soup and reheat. Check the seasoning and consistency. Add extra water if the soup is too thick.

Yield: 18 servings

CANNELLONI

1 recipe ricotta filling (recipe below)
1 recipe pasta dough, cut into cannelloni, cooked, cooled and drained as directed (recipe below)
1 recipe tomato sauce (recipe below)

⅔ cup freshly grated Romano or Parmesan cheese
1 recipe meat filling (recipe below)
1 recipe béchamel (recipe below)
1 recipe meat sauce (recipe below)

1. Preheat oven to 375 degrees.

2. Spread the ricotta filling over about 24 of the cooked and cooled cannelloni, leaving a ½-inch border all around. Roll from the short end.

3. Spread a thin layer of tomato sauce over the bottom of a shallow baking dish (about 13 by 9 by 2 inches). Arrange the cannelloni in a single layer over the sauce and cover with remaining tomato sauce.

4. Sprinkle with ⅓ cup of the grated cheese.

5. Spread remaining cannelloni (24 to 30) with the meat filling mixed with ½ cup of the béchamel, leaving a ½-inch border all around.

6. Roll from the short end. Spread a thin layer of meat sauce over the bottom of a shallow baking dish.

7. Arrange cannelloni in a single layer over the sauce. Spread remaining meat sauce over the cannelloni. Pour remaining béchamel over and sprinkle with remaining cheese.

8. Bake both dishes 25 minutes or until bubbly hot. The surface of meat-filled cannelloni can be browned under a preheated broiler if desired.

Yield: About 18 servings

Ricotta Filling

2 *pounds fresh spin-ach or 2 packages (10 ounces each) frozen chopped spinach*	⅔ *cup freshly grated Romano or Parmesan cheese*
1 *pound ricotta*	⅓ *cup chopped parsley*
3 *eggs, lightly beaten*	2 *teaspoons salt*
	½ *teaspoon freshly ground black pepper*

1. If using fresh spinach, wash it and cook until just wilted in the water clinging to the leaves. Drain very well, chop and cool. If using frozen spinach, cook according to package directions. Drain very well and cool.

2. Add remaining ingredients and mix well.

Yield: About 5 cups

Pasta

3 *cups flour*	2 *teaspoons olive oil*
¾ *teaspoon salt*	1 *tablespoon warm water, approximately*
3 *large eggs*	

1. Place the flour and salt in a pile on a board. Make a well in the center. Break the eggs into the well. Add the olive oil and 1 tablespoon water.

2. With the fingers, mix the liquids together and then gradually draw the flour in to make a ball of dough. Add more water as necessary. Cover with an upturned bowl and allow to rest 10 minutes.

3. On a lightly floured board, knead the dough until very smooth and pliable. Cut into eighths and roll out each piece paper thin. Cut the rolled dough into 3-by-4-inch rectangles. Alternately, the dough can be worked and rolled in a pasta machine and then cut by hand.

4. Bring 6 quarts of salted water to a boil. Place a bowl of cold water beside the stove and spread out clean kitchen towels.

5. Drop 6 rectangles of pasta into the boiling water and cook 30 seconds after the water returns to the boil. Remove with a slotted spoon and drop into the cold water. Remove with a slotted spoon from the cold water and arrange in a single layer on the towels. Repeat with remaining pasta.

Yield: About 50 cannelloni for stuffing

Tomato Sauce

¼ cup olive oil
2 cups chopped onions
1 cup chopped carrots
2 cloves garlic, finely chopped
1 can (2 pounds 3 ounces) Italian plum tomatoes

Salt and freshly ground black pepper to taste
1 teaspoon oregano
2 tablespoons chopped fresh basil, or 1 teaspoon dried

1. In a large kettle, heat the olive oil and sauté in it the onions, carrots and garlic until transparent.

2. Add remaining ingredients, bring to a boil and simmer 20 minutes.

Yield: About 5 cups

Meat Filling

2 tablespoons olive oil
2 small onions, finely chopped
2 cloves garlic, finely chopped
1½ pounds ground veal shoulder or ground, boned and skinned raw chicken
½ pound mushrooms, chopped

1 cup soft bread crumbs
⅔ cup freshly grated Parmesan or Romano cheese
1 egg
Salt and freshly ground black pepper to taste
¼ cup chopped parsley
½ teaspoon thyme

1. Heat the oil and sauté in it the onions and garlic until translucent.

2. Add the veal or chicken and the mushrooms and cook, stirring, until veal loses its pinkness or chicken looks opaque.

3. Stir in remaining ingredients and cool.

Yield: About 5 cups

Béchamel

6 *tablespoons butter*	¼ *teaspoon grated*
6 *tablespoons flour*	*nutmeg*
Salt and freshly	2 *cups milk*
ground white	1 *cup light cream*
pepper to taste	

Melt the butter and blend in the flour. Add salt, pepper and nutmeg. Gradually stir in the milk and cream. Bring to a boil, stirring. Cover and cook very gently 10 minutes.

Yield: About 3 cups

Meat Sauce

3 *tablespoons olive oil*	1 *cup chopped canned*
¼ *cup finely chopped*	*Italian plum toma-*
onion	*toes with liquid*
1 *small clove garlic,*	*Salt and freshly*
finely chopped	*ground black pepper*
8 *ounces lean ground*	*to taste*
round of beef	

1. Heat the oil in a small skillet and cook the onion in it until golden. Add the garlic and beef. Cook, stirring, until meat loses its pink color, but do not allow to brown.

2. Add the tomatoes, salt and pepper and bring to a boil, stirring. Simmer, uncovered, 25 minutes.

Yield: About 3 cups

A Jug of Wine,
A Loaf of Bread...

On a winter weekend when the snow is falling and the kids are sledding in the park, a warm kitchen beckons to the amateur and experienced cook. It is a perfect time to bake a batch of bread and invite new neighbors to share a jug of wine and help themselves from a cheese board. The smell of yeast dough cooking is the best welcome to any home. And, give them a loaf to take home.

Ezekiel's Bread*
Cornell Whole Wheat Bread*
Russian Black Bread*
Brie
Vacherin Gruyère
Boursault
California Zinfandel (Sebastiani)

Ezekiel's Bread

¼ cup soy flour
¼ cup millet flour
½ cup small pearl barley, ground in a Moulinex coffee and nut grinder
½ cup red split lentils, ground as above
3 cups boiling water
2 teaspoons salt
2 tablespoons olive oil or sunflower seed oil

2 packages dry active yeast
½ cup lukewarm water
½ cup molasses or honey
2 cups stone-ground whole wheat flour
2 teaspoons dried dill weed
5½ cups unbleached white flour, approximately
Melted butter

1. In a bowl, mix together the soy flour, millet flour, barley and lentils. Gradually stir in the boiling water. Add salt and oil and stir until smooth. Set aside to cool to lukewarm.

2. Dissolve the yeast in the lukewarm water and stir with the molasses, whole wheat flour and dill into the cooled mixture.

3. Stir in enough of the unbleached flour to make a soft dough that can be kneaded. Turn out onto a lightly floured board, cover with a towel and let rest 10 minutes.

4. Knead the dough until smooth and satiny, about 10 minutes. Add flour as necessary to prevent sticking. Place the dough in a clean, greased bowl, cover with a damp towel and set in a warm place to rise.

5. When the dough has doubled in bulk (after about 1¼ hours), punch it down, cover and let rest 10 minutes. Knead briefly and form into two loaves. Set in two greased 9-by-5-by-3-inch loaf pans. Brush the top surfaces with melted butter, cover and let rise until doubled in bulk and rounded on top, about 1 hour.

6. Preheat oven to 350 degrees.

7. Bake the loaves 55 to 60 minutes or until loaves sound hollow when tapped on the bottom.

Yield: 2 loaves

Note: Unusual ingredients for this bread are available in health food stores.

CORNELL WHOLE WHEAT BREAD

2 cups lukewarm
water
2 packages dry active
yeast
¼ cup dark molasses
¼ cup light brown
sugar
1 egg
4½ cups whole wheat
flour, approximately

½ cup full-fat soy
flour
¾ cup nonfat dry
milk solids
3 tablespoons wheat
germ
2 teaspoons salt
Melted butter

1. Place the water, yeast, molasses and sugar in a bowl and let stand 5 minutes.

2. Beat in the egg and 3½ cups whole wheat flour. Beat the mixture 3 minutes with an electric beater or 1,000 strokes by hand.

3. Mix together the soy flour, dry milk solids, wheat germ and salt. Work the dry ingredients into the yeast mixture and add enough remaining whole wheat flour to make a dough that can be kneaded.

4. Knead the dough until it is smooth and satiny, about 10 minutes. Place in a clean, greased bowl, grease the top of the dough, cover and let rise in a warm place until doubled in bulk, about 1 hour.

5. Punch dough down, cover and let rest 10 minutes. Divide in half and shape each half into a loaf. Place in greased 8-by-4½-by-2½-inch loaf pans. Cover and let rise in a warm place until doubled in bulk, about 30 minutes.

6. Preheat oven to 350 degrees.

7. Bake loaves about 1 hour or until they sound hollow when tapped on the bottom. Brush tops with melted butter for a soft crust and cool on a rack.

Yield: 2 loaves

Russian Black Bread

4 *cups unsifted rye flour*	2 *packages dry active yeast*
1 *teaspoon sugar*	3 *cups water*
2 *teaspoons salt*	¼ *cup vinegar*
2 *cups whole bran cereal*	¼ *cup molasses*
2 *tablespoons caraway seeds, crushed*	1 *ounce (1 square) unsweetened chocolate*
2 *teaspoons powdered instant coffee*	¼ *cup butter*
½ *teaspoon fennel seeds, crushed*	3 *cups white flour, approximately*
	1 *teaspoon cornstarch*

1. Combine the first 8 ingredients in a large bowl.

2. Place 2½ cups of the water, then the vinegar, molasses, chocolate and butter in a saucepan and heat to lukewarm. Butter and chocolate need not be completely melted.

3. Stir the liquid mixture into the dry ingredients and mix well. Add enough flour to make a soft dough.

4. Turn onto a lightly floured board, cover with a bowl and let rest 15 minutes. Knead the dough until it is smooth and elastic, about 15 minutes.

5. Place in a clean, greased bowl; turn to grease dough. Cover and set in a warm place to rise until doubled in bulk, about 1 hour.

6. Punch dough down. Divide in half. Shape each half into a ball about 5 inches in diameter. Place each in a greased 8-inch layer pan. Cover and let rise in a warm place until doubled in bulk, about 1 hour.

7. Preheat oven to 350 degrees.

8. Bake loaves 45 to 50 minutes or until done. Meanwhile, combine the cornstarch and remaining water in a saucepan. Heat, stirring, until mixture thickens; cook 1 minute.

9. Brush hot mixture over baked bread, return to the oven and bake 2 to 3 minutes or until glaze is set. Cool on a rack.

Yield: 2 loaves

Cocktail Party for Thirty People

꙳

The large cocktail party for a couple dozen people or more is a happy solution to seeing a lot of friends at least once a year. The choice of potables depends on personal preference, budget and the availability of an efficient bartender. Getting away from the dips and dunks and offering more appetizing fare shows it is a special occasion. And, by serving a few tasty, substantial tidbits, guests do not have to dash to the nearest hamburger place or restaurant when they leave.

*Maria Pais's Shrimp Pockets**
*Chicken Drums**
*Onion-Cheese Tarts**
*Pastelillos**

Maria Pais's Shrimp Pockets

Dough

1½ cups water	1½ cups flour
2 tablespoons butter	1 teaspoon salt

Filling

3 tablespoons olive oil	Salt and freshly ground black pepper to taste
1 large onion, finely chopped	2 tablespoons chopped parsley
1 pound raw shrimp, shelled, deveined and finely chopped	2–3 cups dry bread crumbs
4 eggs, lightly beaten	Fat or oil for deep-frying

1. To prepare dough, place the water and butter in a saucepan and heat to boiling. Add the flour and salt all at once, stirring vigorously over low heat until the mixture forms a ball of dough and leaves the sides of the pan clean. Cover dough and let cool to room temperature.

2. Meanwhile, to prepare filling, heat the olive oil and sauté in it the onion until tender and lightly browned.

3. Add the chopped shrimp and cook, stirring, 2 to 3 minutes or until the shrimp turn pink.

4. Stir in 2 eggs and the salt and pepper; cook, stirring, until eggs are just set. Turn the mixture into a bowl. Stir in the parsley and let cool to room temperature.

5. Knead the cooled dough on a lightly floured board until smooth and elastic. Divide into half. Roll out one half until it is very thin.

6. Cut out circles of dough 2 to 3 inches in diameter. Place ½ teaspoon of filling on each circle, moisten edges with water and fold over to make a turnover. Pinch edges to seal.

7. Coat the turnovers with the remaining eggs, roll in the bread crumbs and fry, a few at a time, in the fat or oil heated to 355 degrees, until golden, about 3 minutes.

8. Drain on paper towels and serve hot or cold. Repeat with second half of dough and remaining filling. The pockets can be

made ahead, refrigerated and then heated and crisped in a 400-degree oven before serving.

Yield: About 80 bite-size pockets

CHICKEN DRUMS

1 cup finely chopped
cooked chicken
¼ cup finely chopped
celery or fennel
1 tablespoon grated
onion
1 tablespoon finely
chopped green
pepper
1 tablespoon chopped
parsley

Mayonnaise
Salt and freshly
ground black pepper
to taste
6 thin slices white
bread or challah
(sliced lengthwise)
½ cup well-toasted
chopped almonds

1. Combine the chicken, celery or fennel, onion, green pepper and parsley in a bowl. Stir in enough mayonnaise to moisten.
2. Season with salt and black pepper.
3. Spread half the bread or challah slices with the chicken mixture. Top with remaining slices and, using a 1½-inch plain cutter, cut 4 rounds from each sandwich.
4. Brush the cut edge with, or roll in, mayonnaise and then in the nuts. Hold refrigerated until serving time.

Yield: 12 hors d'oeuvre

ONION-CHEESE TARTS

2 cups flour
Salt
⅔ cup butter
3 eggs, lightly beaten
1½ cups finely
chopped onions
3 tablespoons oil
2½ tablespoons Dijon
mustard

1 cup grated Gruyère
cheese
⅔ cup heavy cream
Freshly ground
black pepper
⅛ teaspoon grated
nutmeg

1. Place flour, ¼ teaspoon salt and the butter in a bowl. Using a pastry blender or fork, break up the butter into the flour until mixture resembles coarse oatmeal.
2. Add 1 egg and enough water to make a dough. It should hold together and be pliable but not sticky or damp. With the heel of the hand, push the dough against the board in a 6-inch sweep.
3. Gather dough up with spatula; knead into a ball. Chill well.
4. Meanwhile, sauté the onions very slowly in the oil until tender and golden. Set aside.
5. Roll out the pastry to ⅛-inch thick. Place dough over 8 tart tins 3 inches wide by 2½ inches deep. Bang rolling pin over edges of tins to cut dough to fit.
6. With a ball of extra dough, press dough down into each tin. Ease pastry up and over the edges slightly because it will shrink in cooking. Press well to the sides of the tins. Chill.
7. Preheat oven to 400 degrees.
8. Brush chilled tart shells with the mustard. Distribute the onions and ¾ of the cheese among the tins. Bake 12 minutes or until the pastry is set.
9. Mix together remaining eggs, the cream, salt and pepper to taste and the nutmeg. Spoon into the partly baked tarts. Sprinkle with remaining cheese. Bake 15 minutes longer or until set.

Yield: 8 appetizer servings or 4 luncheon entrée servings

PASTELILLOS

Pastry

2 cups *flour*	¼ cup *softened butter*
1 teaspoon *salt*	2 *egg yolks*
½ teaspoon *baking soda*	¼ cup *cold water, approximately*

Filling

1 *pound lean pork or boned chicken*	3 *tablespoons oil*
2 *ounces smoked ham*	2 *tablespoons tomato paste*
1 *teaspoon salt*	½ *cup water*
¼ *teaspoon freshly ground black pepper*	1 *teaspoon drained capers*
¼ *teaspoon oregano*	2 *tablespoons raisins*
1 *clove garlic, finely chopped*	8 *pitted black olives, chopped*
1 *small onion, finely chopped*	2 *hard-cooked eggs, chopped*
2 *teaspoons vinegar*	*Fat or oil for deep-frying*
1 *bay leaf*	
2 *tablespoons chopped parsley*	

1. To prepare pastry, place flour, salt and baking soda in a bowl. Mix together butter and egg yolks and stir into flour mixture. Stir in enough water to make a dough.

2. Wrap dough in wax paper and refrigerate at least 1 hour.

3. To prepare filling, grind the pork or chicken and the ham together. Add salt, pepper, oregano, garlic, onion, vinegar, bay leaf and parsley.

4. Heat the oil in a heavy skillet. Add meat mixture and cook until well browned, stirring constantly. Add tomato paste and ½ cup water. Stir well. Cover and cook 25 minutes.

5. Add capers and raisins and cook 5 minutes. Add olives and eggs and mix again. Set aside to cool.

6. To make the pies, roll out one-quarter of the dough ⅛-inch thick on a lightly floured board.

7. Cut into 2-inch squares. Place a teaspoon of the cooled meat mixture in center of a square. Moisten edges with water. Top with a second square. Press edges to seal.

8. Continue until all pastry and filling are used.

9. Heat fat or oil to 375 degrees and fry the pastelillos, a few at a time, until they are golden, about 3 minutes. Drain on paper towels. Serve hot or warm.

Yield: About 4 dozen

We'll Spend a Weekend with You on our Way South

✢

Spending time with friends you may only see once a year to catch up on what has happened is more important than bang-up fancy meals that exhaust hosts and guests alike. Make it simple and re-laxed and they won't wish they had stayed in a motel. And, there's a better chance you'll see them again soon.

FRIDAY NIGHT
(something for any time guests arrive)

*Mushroom Appetizer**
*Mary's Portuguese Soup**
*Maple Ice Cream**

SATURDAY BREAKFAST

Grapefruit
Sautéed Chicken Livers and Scrambled Eggs
Farmhouse Coffeecakes (made ahead and frozen)*

SATURDAY LUNCH

*Vegetables with Salsa Verde**
Crusty Bread
*Two-Tone Chocolate Mousse** (made early Friday)*

SATURDAY DINNER

*Ruth's Fricassee de Volaille**
Herbed Pilaf
Avocado Salad
*Frozen Lemon Soufflé** (made ahead)*

SUNDAY BRUNCH

Sliced Oranges
*Stewed Mushrooms over Toast Points**
*Grace Chu's Broccoli Flowerets with Water Chestnuts**

SUNDAY DINNER

*Clay-Roasted Stuffed Leg of Lamb**
White Beans Provençale
Cucumber Salad
*Individual Cream Cheese Cakes** (made ahead and frozen)*
or
*Jeremy's Apple Butter Crunch**

MUSHROOM APPETIZER

2 pounds tiny button
  mushrooms
2 cups boiling water
2 cups chopped celery
¼ cup chopped
  scallion
1 clove garlic, finely
  chopped
6–8 anchovy fillets,
  chopped
⅓ cup pitted and
  sliced ripe olives

¼ cup sliced stuffed
  green olives
2 tablespoons chopped
  parsley
1 tablespoon chopped
  fennel green
½ cup olive oil
1 tablespoon wine
  vinegar
  Boston lettuce cups

1. Rinse the mushrooms. Cut stems even with caps. Discard the stems or reserve for another recipe. Place the caps in a saucepan with the water. Cover and simmer 5 minutes. Drain and rinse under cold water. Pat dry with paper towels and place in a bowl.

2. Add all remaining ingredients except lettuce cups. Toss thoroughly. Chill well and serve in lettuce cups.

Yield: 10 to 12 appetizer servings

MARY'S PORTUGUESE SOUP

1 cup red kidney
beans, picked over
and washed
1 cup California pea
beans, picked over
and washed
1 boneless chuck beef
pot roast (3 pounds)
Salt and freshly
ground black pepper
2 tablespoons oil

3 onions, sliced
3–4 chourico (Portu-
guese sausage) or
chorizo (Spanish
sausage)
4 cups shredded
cabbage
3–4 cups small broccoli
flowerets
1 pound fresh spinach,
roughly shredded

1. Place the beans in a bowl, cover with cold water and let soak overnight.

2. Sprinkle the meat generously with salt and pepper and, with the fingers, rub the seasoning in. Cover meat and let stand in the refrigerator overnight or up to 3 days.

3. Heat the oil in a large, heavy casserole or kettle, add the meat and brown quickly on all sides. Add the onions and 6 cups water, bring to a boil, cover and simmer slowly about 1 hour.

4. Drain the beans and add to the casserole. Bring to a boil, cover and simmer 45 minutes or until meat and beans are tender. Remove meat, dice finely and return to casserole.

5. Add the chourico or chorizo and cook 5 minutes. Stir in the cabbage and cook, covered, 5 minutes; stir in the broccoli and cook, covered, 5 minutes; add the spinach and cook, covered, 3 minutes. Check seasoning and add salt and pepper if necessary.

Yield: 10 to 12 servings

MAPLE ICE CREAM

4 cups maple syrup
1⅓ cups water
¼ cup flour
4 eggs, separated
¼ teaspoon salt
4 cups heavy cream

2 teaspoons vanilla
Maple flavoring to
taste (optional)
2 teaspoons lemon
juice

1. Heat the maple syrup to just below the boil. Gradually blend the water into the flour to make a smooth paste and whisk in the hot syrup.

2. Return the mixture to the saucepan and cook, stirring constantly, until mixture thickens. Beat the egg yolks lightly with the salt and pour in some of the hot mixture. Return to the saucepan and cook, stirring, until mixture thickens slightly, but do not allow to boil.

3. Stir in the cream, vanilla, maple flavoring, if desired, and lemon juice. Chill the mixture.

4. Pour the chilled mixture into the can of an ice cream freezer (the can should be no more than ¾ full) and follow the manufacturer's instructions until the mixture is partly frozen; it should take about 15 minutes.

5. Beat the egg whites until stiff but not dry and add to mixture. Continue to freeze until cranking becomes difficult or motor slows. Remove the dasher, replace cover with cork in the hole or transfer the ice cream to plastic containers and ripen for 1 to 2 hours or until serving time in a mixture of 4 parts crushed ice to 1 part rock salt. Or, the containers may be placed in the home freezer. The ice cream should be removed from the home freezer for a while before serving.

Yield: About 5 cups

Note: Most ice cream freezers will operate efficiently when alternate layers of 4 cups crushed ice and ⅓ cup rock salt are used. Adding 1 cup of water will start the ice melting.

Basic Dough for Farmhouse Coffeecakes

4½ cups flour, approximately
  mately
 2 packages dry active
  yeast
 ½ teaspoon grated
  nutmeg
 ½ cup milk

½ cup water
½ cup sugar
¼ cup oil
 2 teaspoons salt
 2 teaspoons grated
  lemon rind
 2 eggs

1. Place 2 cups flour, the dry yeast and the nutmeg in the bowl of an electric mixer.

2. Heat the milk, water, sugar, oil and salt together to lukewarm, stirring to dissolve the sugar.

3. While beating at medium speed, add the lemon rind and milk mixture to the flour mixture. Beat in the eggs. Add another cup flour and beat 1 minute.

4. Remove the bowl from the mixing machine and, with a wooden spoon, beat in enough remaining flour to make a medium-stiff dough. Turn onto a lightly floured board and knead until smooth and satiny, about 8 minutes.

5. Place the dough in a clean, greased bowl. Turn to grease all sides, cover and let rise in a warm place until doubled in bulk, about 1 hour.

Yield: Basic dough for 1 mincemeat coffeecake or 2 lemon loaves (recipes below).

Mincemeat Coffeecake

1 recipe basic dough
 (recipe above)
1 cup mincemeat
1½ cups sugar

1½ teaspoons grated
 nutmeg
¾ cup melted butter

1. To shape the mincemeat coffeecake, punch the dough down and divide into thirds. Cover and let stand 10 minutes.

2. Divide each third into 16 pieces and roll each piece into a ball. Spread half the mincemeat over the bottom of a well-buttered 10-inch tube pan.

3. Mix the sugar with the nutmeg. Dip half the balls in the melted butter and then in the sugar mixture and arrange neatly over the mincemeat.

4. Spread the remaining mincemeat over the balls and top with the remaining balls dipped in butter and then in the sugar mixture. Cover and let rise in a warm place until doubled in bulk, about 1 hour.

5. Preheat oven to 375 degrees.

6. Bake 40 to 45 minutes or until done. Let cool in the pan 2 minutes and then invert onto a serving plate. Serve warm.

Yield: 10 servings

Lemon Loaves

1 recipe basic dough (see page 58)	2 tablespoons lemon juice
⅓ cup plus 2 tablespoons butter	½ cup chopped pecans
1¼ cups sugar	¼ cup flour
4 teaspoons grated lemon rind	

1. To shape the lemon loaves, punch the dough down and divide in half, cover and let stand 10 minutes.

2. Roll half the dough into a 10-by-16-inch rectangle. Cut into 4 rectangles, 5-by-8 inches each. Melt ⅓ cup of the butter and brush 1 rectangle with the butter.

3. Combine 1 cup of the sugar, the lemon rind, juice and nuts. Sprinkle ⅛ of the sugar mixture over the buttered rectangle. Top with a second rectangle and repeat buttering and sprinkling with the sugar mixture. Repeat with the remaining 2 rectangles to give a stack of 4.

4. Cut the stack in 4 strips lengthwise. Fit into a well-greased or Teflon-coated 9-by-5-by-3-inch loaf pan, cut sides up, side by side.

5. Roll out the remaining dough, shape as above and place in a second loaf pan.

6. Combine the flour, remaining sugar and remaining butter to make a crumbly topping. Sprinkle over the loaves. Cover and let rise in a warm place until doubled in bulk, about 30 minutes.

7. Preheat oven to 400 degrees.

8. Bake 30 to 35 minutes or until done. Serve warm.

Yield: 2 loaves

Vegetables with Salsa Verde

½ pound green beans, trimmed, cooked whole and drained

½ bunch broccoli, broken into flowerets, cooked and drained

3 cups small new potato balls, boiled until barely tender and drained

1 pound fresh lima beans, shelled, cooked and drained

3 cups sliced carrots, cooked and drained

2 cups sliced zucchini, cooked and drained

6 hard-cooked eggs, shelled and quartered

⅓ cup olive oil

3 cloves garlic, halved lengthwise

½ cup finely chopped flat-leaf Italian parsley

½ cup finely chopped fresh spinach leaves

½ cup chopped watercress

½ teaspoon salt

¼ teaspoon freshly ground black pepper, or to taste

¼ cup dry white wine

¼ cup heavy cream

1. Arrange the hot vegetables in an attractive design, alternating dark and light ones, on a large platter. Garnish with the egg quarters.

2. Heat the oil and brown the garlic pieces in it until crisp. Remove the garlic and chop finely and return to the oil along with the remaining ingredients. Stir to mix.

3. Bring to a simmer while stirring, cook 2 minutes and pour over the vegetables. Serve lukewarm.

Yield: 6 to 8 servings

Two-Tone Chocolate Mousse

1 cup light brown sugar	4 eggs, separated
¼ cup water	⅓ cup orange juice
1 envelope unflavored gelatin	¼ teaspoon salt
1 package (6 ounces, 1 cup) semisweet chocolate bits	1 cup heavy cream, whipped

1. In a saucepan, combine ½ cup brown sugar, the water and gelatin. Mix well and cook over low heat until gelatin is dissolved.

2. Meanwhile, melt the chocolate bits over hot water.

3. Beat the egg yolks lightly. Gradually beat the gelatin mixture, egg yolks and orange juice into the melted chocolate. Continue beating until mixture is light. Remove from hot water.

4. Remove and reserve ½ cup of the chocolate mixture.

5. Beat the egg whites and salt together until mixture forms soft peaks. Gradually beat in the remaining brown sugar and continue beating until mixture is stiff and glossy. Fold into the bulk of the chocolate mixture. Fold in the whipped cream.

6. Spoon the mixture into 8 individual ramekins, soufflé cups or custard cups. Divide reserved chocolate mixture over top of each. Chill several hours.

Yield: 8 servings

Ruth's Fricassee de Volaille

3½ tablespoons butter	8 small white onions
1 frying chicken (3–3½ pounds), cut into serving pieces	½ pound small mushrooms, halved or quartered
¾ cup chopped onion	1 cup heavy cream
⅓ cup flour	½ cup chicken broth
Salt and freshly ground black pepper	2 tablespoons lemon juice
1¼ cups dry white Burgundy	1 tablespoon chopped parsley

1. Heat 2 tablespoons butter in a heavy skillet, add the chicken pieces and brown on all sides. Add the chopped onion, cover and simmer 10 minutes.

2. Mix together the flour, 1 teaspoon salt and ¼ teaspoon pepper.

3. Sprinkle the mixture over the chicken and turn to coat each piece. Mix extra flour mixture into the pan liquid. Cover and simmer 3 minutes longer.

4. Turn the chicken again, add the white Burgundy and bring to a boil. Cover and simmer for about 30 minutes or until the chicken appears to be tender.

5. Meanwhile, in a separate skillet, melt remaining butter and sauté the white onions in it for 5 minutes, turning frequently. Add the mushrooms and cook about 3 minutes longer.

6. Add onion mixture to the chicken during the last 10 minutes of the cooking.

7. Stir ¾ cup of the cream into the chicken mixture in the skillet. Check the seasoning. Bring to a boil. Transfer the chicken pieces to a warm platter and arrange the onions and mushrooms so that they surround the chicken.

8. Add the chicken broth to the skillet and cook, stirring, until mixture thickens. Pass through a sieve into a clean saucepan.

9. Bring to a boil and stir in the remaining cream. Pour over the chicken. Before serving, sprinkle the chicken with the lemon juice and the chopped parsley.

Yield: 4 servings

Note: Recipe can be doubled.

Frozen Lemon Soufflé

1 envelope unflavored
    gelatin
¼ cup cold water
6 egg yolks
1 cup sugar
⅔ cup lemon juice
1 tablespoon grated
    lemon rind

4 egg whites
1½ cups heavy cream,
    whipped
1 pint large fresh
    strawberries, dipped in sugar, or
    thawed frozen
    strawberries

1. Soften the gelatin in the water.

2. Beat the egg yolks and sugar together until very thick and light colored. Stir in the lemon juice.

3. Transfer to the top of a double boiler or heavy pan and cook over low heat or hot water until slightly thickened. Do not allow to boil.

4. Stir in the softened gelatin and the lemon rind. Cool until the mixture is the consistency of unbeaten egg white.

5. Beat the egg whites until stiff but not dry and fold into the cooled lemon mixture. Fold in the cream.

6. Slowly pour the mixture into a 1- or 1½-quart soufflé dish or mold and freeze until solid.

7. Unmold or serve directly from the soufflé dish, with strawberries.

Yield: 6 servings

STEWED MUSHROOMS OVER TOAST POINTS

6 slices bacon, chopped
4 scallions, chopped
1 pound mushrooms, sliced
Salt and freshly ground black pepper to taste
⅛ teaspoon grated nutmeg

2 tablespoons chopped parsley
1½ tablespoons flour
¼ cup heavy cream
¾ cup chicken broth
4 slices toast, cut into triangles

1. Sauté the bacon in a heavy skillet until crisp. Remove the bits and reserve.

2. Sauté the scallions 2 minutes in the bacon fat remaining in the skillet.

3. Add the mushrooms and cook 3 minutes or until barely tender. Do not overcook. Add salt, pepper, nutmeg and parsley.

4. Sprinkle with the flour and gradually stir in the cream and the chicken broth. Bring to a boil and cook, stirring, until mixture thickens. Spoon over the toast triangles and sprinkle with reserved bacon bits.

Yield: 4 servings
Note: Recipe can be doubled.

Grace Chu's Broccoli Flowerets with Water Chestnuts

¼ cup peanut oil
1 large bunch fresh
broccoli to yield 4
cups flowerets
2 teaspoons salt

1 teaspoon sugar
½ cup cold water
½ cup sliced water
chestnuts

1. Heat the oil in a wok or skillet. Add the flowerets and stir-fry for about 2 minutes. Add the salt and sugar. Mix well.

2. Add the water, cover and cook over medium heat for 5 minutes or until water is almost absorbed. Mix in water chestnuts and serve.

Yield: 8 servings

Clay-Roasted Stuffed Leg of Lamb

1 leg of lamb (6–7
pounds), boned and
ready for rolling,
and at room tem-
perature (the boned
leg will weigh 4–5
pounds)
Juice of 1 lemon
3 cloves garlic, finely
chopped
⅓ cup chopped parsley
6–8 anchovy fillets

⅓ cup chopped pitted
ripe olives
1 teaspoon rosemary
½ teaspoon freshly
ground black
pepper
3 tablespoons pine
nuts
Olive oil
8 small white onions
4 carrots, quartered
Flour (optional)

1. Season or soak the clay pot according to manufacturer's instructions.

2. Spread the lamb, skin side down, on a board. Sprinkle with the lemon juice.

3. Mash the garlic, parsley and anchovies together in a mortar with a pestle until they form a paste. Mix in the olives, rosemary and pepper and spread the mixture over the center of the lamb.

4. Sprinkle the pine nuts over the stuffing and roll the lamb to enclose the mixture and make a neat bundle that will fit the clay pot. Rub lamb roll with olive oil.

5. Place the roll in the pot, using a parchment paper liner *only if manufacturer's instructions require.* Scatter the onions and carrots around. Cover the pot and place in a cold oven.

6. Set temperature indicator at 400 degrees and turn the oven on. Bake 1¼ hours for pink lamb or 1½ to 1¾ hours for well done.

7. If desired, the pan juices can be thickened with 1 tablespoon of flour for each cup of liquid.

Yield: 8 to 10 servings

Note: A boned butt-half of a leg of lamb can be prepared, using half the stuffing and vegetable ingredients.

INDIVIDUAL CREAM CHEESE CAKES

3 packages (8 ounces each) cream cheese, at room temperature
1 cup plus 3 table-spoons sugar
2 teaspoons vanilla
4 eggs
1 tablespoon finely grated lemon rind
⅓ cup graham cracker crumbs
⅛ teaspoon cinnamon
2 cups sour cream
Glacéed orange slices

1. Preheat oven to 300 degrees.

2. Cream the cheese with 1 cup sugar and 1 teaspoon vanilla until light and fluffy. Beat in the eggs one at a time, beating well after each addition.

3. Stir in the lemon rind. Mix crumbs with the cinnamon. Sprinkle about ½ teaspoon crumb mixture in each of 28 paper soufflé cups that hold about ⅓ cup and measure approximately 2¼ inches in diameter and 1½ inches deep. Place cups on cookie sheets.

4. Fill each cup ¾ full with the mixture and bake 30 minutes.

5. Combine the sour cream and the remaining sugar and vanilla. Remove cookie sheets from the oven and spread cakes with sour cream topping. Bake 15 minutes longer. Cool.

6. Store in the refrigerator for several days or freeze on trays; or pack into plastic bags and store in the freezer. Thaw if necessary and remove paper cups before garnishing with orange slices.

Yield: 28 cakes

JEREMY'S APPLE BUTTER CRUNCH

½ cup butter
1 cup sugar
¾ cup flour
6–7 tart green apples,
peeled, cored and
sliced

½ cup water
1 tablespoon grated
lemon rind

1. Preheat oven to 350 degrees.

2. Cream the butter and sugar together until very light and fluffy. Gradually work in the flour and set aside.

3. Place the apples in a 10-inch pie plate or fluted ceramic quiche pan. Add the water and lemon rind.

4. Pinch off walnut-size pieces of dough, flatten into 1½-inch patties and place overlapping on top of apples. Bake 1 hour or until top is browned and apples tender.

Yield: 6 servings

Semiformal Preholiday Dinner Party for Eight

🙢

Times when there was help in the kitchen are a memory, and it takes extra thought to cook and serve a formal, seated dinner without spending ages in the kitchen after guests arrive. In the menu below, the escabèche and mousse-torte can be made early in the day and held in the refrigerator. The ducks go into the oven before the appointed hour for aperitifs and need no attention until it's time to carve. The broccoli mixture can be made, poured into the mold and left ready to go in with the ducks for the last 45 minutes of the roasting time. With salad ingredients washed and crisp, the egg minced, and dressing chilling, individual salad plates are fixed quickly at the last minute. Bon appétit.

*Escabèche with Mushrooms**
*Stuffed Ducks**
*Broccoli Mold**
Mimosa Salad (Boston lettuce and minced egg)
*Maida Heatter's Chocolate Mousse-Torte**
Espresso

Escabèche with Mushrooms

1½ pounds flounder fillets	1 clove garlic, crushed
⅓ cup lime juice	2 canned hot chili peppers, seeded and chopped, or 1 fresh
½ cup flour	
1 teaspoon salt	
¼ teaspoon freshly ground black pepper	1 bay leaf
¼ cup oil	1 cup white vinegar
1 cup chopped onions	¼ teaspoon ground cumin
½ pound mushrooms, sliced	Lemon wedges

1. Soak the fish in the lime juice for 10 minutes. Drain. Dip in the flour mixed with the salt and pepper.

2. Heat the oil in a heavy skillet, add the fish and cook quickly on both sides until lightly browned. Arrange the fish in a shallow dish.

3. Sauté the onions until wilted in the oil remaining in the skillet. Add the mushrooms and cook 3 minutes longer.

4. Add the garlic, chili peppers, bay leaf, vinegar and cumin and bring to a boil. Pour over the fish. Cool. Cover and chill several hours or overnight. Serve with lemon wedges.

Yield: 8 appetizer servings

Stuffed Ducks

2 cups shelled filberts	Salt and freshly ground black pepper to taste
½ cup butter	
½ cup chopped onion	
1 cup chopped celery	1 tablespoon chopped parsley
2 cups cored and chopped apples	
1 orange	½ teaspoon rosemary, crushed
1 lemon	
2 eggs, lightly beaten	⅛ teaspoon mace
½ cup dry white wine	2 ducks (4–5 pounds each), cleaned and oven-ready
4 cups soft bread crumbs	

1. Preheat oven to 275 degrees.

2. Spread the filberts in a shallow pan and toast in the oven about 20 minutes, or until tender and the skins start to crack. Place the nuts in a clean towel and roll back and forth to remove skins. They do not have to be eliminated completely.

3. Heat ¼ cup of the butter in a skillet and sauté in it the onion and celery until tender.

4. Combine the filberts, onion mixture and apples in a large bowl. Grate and add the rind from the orange and lemon. Remove the white skins and discard. Section both orange and lemon and add to the bowl. Increase oven heat to 425 degrees.

5. Stir in eggs, wine, crumbs, salt, pepper, parsley, rosemary and mace. Toss to mix and use to stuff both ducks. Truss and place on a rack in a shallow roasting pan.

6. Melt remaining butter and brush over ducks. Roast 30 minutes. Reduce oven heat to 375 degrees and continue cooking 60 minutes. Reduce oven heat to 350 degrees, put broccoli mold (recipe below) in oven and cook 45 minutes longer or until mold is set and ducks no longer drip pink liquid when pierced in the thigh.

Yield: 8 servings

BROCCOLI MOLD

1 bunch broccoli, well trimmed, flowerets broken into small pieces Boiling salted water	3 eggs, lightly beaten ⅓ cup grated Swiss cheese 1 teaspoon salt
¼ cup chicken broth 3 tablespoons butter ¼ cup chopped scallions 3 tablespoons flour 1 cup sour cream	¼ teaspoon freshly ground black pepper ½ teaspoon grated nutmeg ¼ cup finely chopped toasted almonds

1. Place the broccoli in a saucepan and cover with boiling salted water. Cover, bring to a boil and boil rapidly about 8 minutes or until broccoli is crisp-tender. Drain well.

2. Preheat oven to 350 degrees.

3. Chop broccoli finely and add the chicken broth.

4. Melt the butter, add the scallions and sauté until tender. Stir in the flour and cook, stirring, 1 minute.

5. Blend in the sour cream and cook, stirring constantly, until thick, but do not allow to boil. Remove from the heat and stir in the eggs.

6. Stir in the broccoli mixture and remaining ingredients and turn into a well-greased 5-cup ring mold. Set in a shallow pan of boiling water and bake 45 minutes or until a silver knife inserted in the center comes out clean.

7. Let stand 5 minutes. Run a knife around the edges and unmold onto a warm platter.

Yield: 6 to 8 servings

Maida Heatter's Chocolate Mousse-Torte

8 ounces (8 squares) semisweet chocolate
1 tablespoon instant coffee powder
¼ cup boiling water
8 eggs, separated
⅔ cup sugar

2½ teaspoons vanilla
⅛ teaspoon salt
Fine dry bread crumbs
1½ cups heavy cream
¼ cup sieved confectioners' sugar

1. Preheat oven to 350 degrees.

2. Place the chocolate in the top of a double boiler over hot, not boiling, water. Dissolve the instant coffee powder in the boiling water and add to the chocolate. Cover and let stand over very low heat. Stir occasionally with a wire whisk. When the chocolate is almost melted, remove the top of the double boiler and whisk mixture until smooth.

3. Meanwhile, beat the egg yolks until thick. Gradually beat in the sugar until the mixture is thick and lemon colored.

4. Gradually beat the chocolate into the yolk mixture.

5. Beat in 1 teaspoon of vanilla.

6. Beat the egg whites and salt together until stiff but not dry. Stir ¼ of the whites into the chocolate mixture. Gently fold in the remaining whites until blended.

7. Dust a well-buttered 9-inch pie plate with fine dry bread crumbs. Fill plate with part of the mousse mixture so that it just

comes level with the edge. Bake 25 minutes. Turn off the oven heat
and leave in the oven 5 minutes longer.

8. Remove and cool for 2 hours on a wire rack. As the cooked
mousse cools, it sinks in the middle to form a pie shell.

9. Meanwhile, cover and refrigerate the remaining uncooked
mousse. When the shell has cooled, fill with the chilled uncooked
mousse, mounding it up like a pie filling. Chill 2 to 3 hours.

10. Beat the cream, remaining vanilla and the confectioners'
sugar together until stiff. Spread over the pie or, using a piping bag
and star tube, make a lattice pattern over the top of the pie.

Yield: 8 servings

Holiday Buffet Supper

Depending on the calendar, Christmas Eve may coincide with a weekend, or it may not, but a trim-the-tree get-together on the weekend before the holiday is an opportunity to sit around the fire and relax with family and friends. Cold fruit soup is a traditional Scandinavian holiday dish and it looks attractive in a glass serving bowl ready to ladle into mugs or bowls. Set the chafing dish with the creamed scallops on the hearth, or buffet, and have a dish of sherbet scoops ready in the freezer. Serve them in punch cups, with demitasse spoons.

*Cold Fruit Soup**
*Creamed Scallops**
Rice
Sherbet
*Orange Cookies**

Cold Fruit Soup

- ½ *cup dried apricots, quartered*
- ¾ *cup dried pitted prunes, quartered*
- 6 *cups water*
- 1 *orange, peeled and sectioned*
- ½ *lemon, cut into 3 wedges*
- 1 *cinnamon stick*
- 1¼ *cups sugar*
- 3 *tablespoons quick-cooking tapioca*
- 1 *can (1 pound) pitted sour red cherries with juice*
- *Salt to taste*
- ¾ *cup toasted walnut halves, coarsely chopped*

1. In a saucepan, combine the apricots, prunes, water, orange sections, lemon wedges and cinnamon stick and let stand 30 minutes.

2. Bring to a boil. Stir in remaining ingredients except walnuts. Simmer, stirring occasionally, about 12 minutes. Remove lemon wedges and cinnamon stick. Add walnuts and chill. Serve cold.

Yield: 6 servings

CREAMED SCALLOPS

1 cup dry white wine	1 teaspoon dry mustard
1 cup water	1 tablespoon Dijon mustard
1 small onion, halved	
1 rib celery with leaves, diced	1¼ cups heavy cream
	6 tablespoons butter
3 sprigs parsley	4 tablespoons flour
½ bay leaf, crumbled	Juice of 1 lemon
¼ teaspoon thyme	Freshly ground white pepper to taste
8 black peppercorns	
Salt to taste	
2 pounds scallops, quartered if large sea scallops	1–2 cups cooked, drained carrots, peas and tiny onions
3 egg yolks	Chopped parsley

1. In a heavy skillet, combine the wine, water, onion, celery, parsley, bay leaf, thyme, peppercorns and salt. Bring to a boil, cover and simmer 10 minutes. Add scallops and simmer 5 minutes.

2. With a slotted spoon, remove scallops. Keep warm in a small amount of the broth. Strain remaining broth and boil if necessary to reduce to make 2 cups. Reserve.

3. Mix together the egg yolks, mustards, and heavy cream. Set aside.

4. Melt the butter, blend in the flour and cook 3 minutes. Do not allow to brown. Gradually blend in the reserved broth. Bring to a boil while stirring and cook, continuing to stir, for 5 to 10 minutes. Stir in the egg-cream mixture and cook until slightly thickened, but do not allow to boil. Remove from heat and stir in lemon juice, salt and white pepper.

5. In a hot serving dish, combine the drained scallops and vegetables. Pour the sauce over all and sprinkle with chopped parsley.
Yield: 6 servings

ORANGE COOKIES

2¼ *cups flour*
½ *teaspoon salt*
½ *cup sugar*
½ *cup shortening*
2 *egg yolks, well beaten*
2 *tablespoons orange juice*

1 *tablespoon grated lemon rind*
1 *egg white, lightly beaten*
¼ *cup finely chopped blanched almonds*

1. Preheat oven to 350 degrees.
2. Sift the flour, salt and 6 tablespoons of the sugar into a bowl. With 2 knives, a pastry blender or the fingertips, work the shortening into the dry ingredients as though making pastry.
3. With a fork, stir in the egg yolks, orange juice and lemon rind. Gather into a ball of dough. Roll out on a lightly floured board to ¼ inch thick. Cut with a cookie cutter and place on a greased baking sheet.
4. Brush with the egg white. Mix together the remaining sugar and the nuts and sprinkle over cookies.
5. Bake 10 minutes or until lightly browned around the edges.
Yield: About 30 cookies

Accommodating the Latest Utility Bill

The weekend after receiving the biggest utility bill in history is not the time for celebrating or entertaining. Budget meals seem more to the point, and here is a plan that will not compound the situation but will tempt lagging appetites. None of the menus or dishes need an apology; they are imaginative and they taste good.

FRIDAY DINNER

Fish Ratatouille*
Boiled Potatoes
Chocolate Pie*

SATURDAY BREAKFAST

Scrambled Eggs
Yogurt Granola Bread*

SATURDAY LUNCH

Cornmeal Gnocchi with Tomato Sauce*

SATURDAY DINNER

*Lentil and Sausage Casseroles**
Cole Slaw
Baked Bananas
*Honey and Nut Custard**

SUNDAY BRUNCH

*Linda Kondabjan's Gâteau aux Pommes de Terre**
*Mushroom Cream Sauce**

SUNDAY DINNER

*Chicken Wings Provençale**
Rice
Broccoli
*Apples Alaska**

———————— ◆•◆ ————————

FISH RATATOUILLE

¼ cup oil
½ cup finely chopped onion
½ clove garlic, finely chopped
1 small eggplant, peeled and diced
2 medium-size zucchini, sliced ¼ inch thick

2 large tomatoes, skinned and chopped
2 tablespoons chopped parsley
Salt and freshly ground black pepper to taste
2 teaspoons drained capers
1½ pounds cod fillets

1. Heat the oil in a heavy skillet and sauté in it the onion and garlic until tender but not browned. Add the eggplant and zucchini and cook 5 minutes.

2. Add the tomatoes, cover and simmer 10 minutes.

3. Preheat oven to 350 degrees.

4. Stir the parsley, salt, pepper and capers into the vegetable mixture. Arrange the fish in a buttered baking dish. Spoon the eggplant mixture over and bake 25 minutes or until fish flakes easily.

Yield: 6 servings

Chocolate Pie

4 ounces German sweet chocolate	⅛ teaspoon salt
¼ cup butter	2 eggs
1 can (13 ounces) evaporated milk	1 teaspoon vanilla
1½ cups sugar	1 unbaked 9-inch pie shell
3 tablespoons cornstarch	½ cup chopped pecans or walnuts (optional)

1. Preheat oven to 375 degrees.

2. Melt the chocolate with the butter over low heat, stirring until blended. Remove from the heat and gradually blend in the evaporated milk.

3. Mix sugar, cornstarch and salt together thoroughly. Beat in eggs and vanilla.

4. Gradually blend in the chocolate mixture. Pour into the pie shell. Sprinkle with nuts.

5. Bake 45 to 50 minutes or until top is puffed and browned. If it starts to overbrown, cover with aluminum foil. Pie will be soft when taken from the oven but will become firm on cooling.

Yield: 8 to 10 servings

YOGURT GRANOLA BREAD

2 cups unsifted whole wheat flour	1½ cups plus 1 tablespoon water
1 cup granola with fruit and nuts, either homemade or store-bought	1 cup plain yogurt
	½ cup orange marmalade
½ cup wheat germ	¼ cup light molasses
2 tablespoons toasted sesame seeds	2 tablespoons butter or margarine
2 teaspoons salt	4½–5½ cups unbleached white flour
2 packages dry active yeast	1 egg, lightly beaten

1. In the large bowl of an electric mixer, mix the whole wheat flour, granola, wheat germ, sesame seeds, salt and undissolved dry yeast.

2. Combine 1½ cups water, the yogurt, orange marmalade, molasses and butter or margarine in a saucepan. Heat over low heat until liquids are very warm, about 120 to 130 degrees on a thermometer. The fat does not need to melt.

3. Gradually add the hot liquid ingredients to the dry ingredients and beat 2 minutes at medium speed. Stir in enough unbleached flour to make a soft dough.

4. Turn dough onto a lightly floured board and knead until smooth and elastic, about 10 minutes. Place in a greased bowl; turn to grease the top. Cover and let rise in a warm place until doubled in bulk, about 1 hour.

5. Punch dough down, divide in half and shape each piece into a smooth round ball. Place on greased baking sheets. Cover and let rise in a warm place until doubled in bulk, about 1 hour.

6. Preheat oven to 375 degrees.

7. With a razor blade or sharp knife, cut slashes in the top of the loaves. Combine egg and remaining 1 tablespoon water and use to brush loaves. Bake 40 to 45 minutes or until loaves sound hollow when tapped on the bottom. Cover with aluminum foil if they start to overbrown. Cool on a rack.

Yield: 2 loaves

CORNMEAL GNOCCHI WITH TOMATO SAUCE

1½ cups yellow corn-
   meal
1½ teaspoons salt
2 cups cold water
2 cups milk, scalded
1 onion, finely
   chopped
1 clove garlic, finely
   chopped
½ cup melted butter

2 eggs, lightly beaten
½ cup grated
   Gruyère cheese
2 tablespoons chop-
   ped parsley
¼ cup freshly grated
   Parmesan cheese
2 cups warm tomato
   sauce, preferably
   homemade

1. Mix the cornmeal, salt and water together in the top of a double boiler. Stir in the milk and cook over boiling water until mixture thickens and comes to a boil, about 15 minutes. Stir frequently.

2. Meanwhile, cook the onion and garlic in 2 tablespoons of the butter until tender but not browned. Add to the cooked cornmeal mixture.

3. Beat in the eggs and cheese and pour or spread mixture into a greased pan or dish so that mixture is about ½ inch thick.

4. Cool mixture to room temperature. Cut the mixture into squares, diamond shapes or rounds and arrange, slightly overlapping, in a greased, heatproof dish.

5. Pour the remaining butter over, sprinkle with the parsley and Parmesan cheese and heat under a preheated broiler until thoroughly heated and lightly browned on top. Serve tomato sauce separately.

Yield: 6 servings

LENTIL AND SAUSAGE CASSEROLES

¾ pound Italian sweet
    sausage, sliced
¼ pound Italian hot
    sausage, sliced
2 onions, chopped
1 small clove garlic,
    finely chopped
½ bay leaf
½ teaspoon oregano
3 cups beef broth or
    chicken broth
2 tablespoons wine
    vinegar

½ pound lentils,
    picked over and
    washed
1 cup drained Italian
    plum tomatoes
1 cup sliced zucchini
    Salt and freshly
    ground black pepper
    to taste
    Freshly snipped fen-
    nel greens or
    chopped parsley

1. In a heavy skillet, sauté the sausage slices until done. Remove with a slotted spoon and set aside.

2. In the fat remaining in the skillet, sauté the onions and garlic until tender but not browned. Add the bay leaf, oregano, broth, vinegar and lentils. Bring to a boil.

3. Cover the skillet and simmer 15 minutes. Add the tomatoes, zucchini, salt and pepper and cover. Continue simmering until the lentils and zucchini are tender but still retain their shape, about 15 minutes. Return sausage to the skillet and reheat.

4. Serve in individual casseroles and sprinkle with fennel or parsley.

Yield: 4 servings

HONEY AND NUT CUSTARD

3 eggs
2 cups milk
¼ cup honey
    one-inch piece
    vanilla bean

¼ cup freshly ground
    unhomogenized nut
    butter (almond, pea-
    nut or cashew)
⅛ teaspoon grated
    nutmeg

1. Preheat oven to 325 degrees.
2. Place all the ingredients except the nutmeg in an electric blender. Blend at high speed 15 seconds. Pour into an oiled 3-cup baking dish. Sprinkle with nutmeg.
3. Set dish in a pan with 1 inch of hot water in it. Bake 1 hour or until a silver knife inserted near the edge of the custard comes out clean.

Yield: 4 servings

LINDA KONDABJAN'S GÂTEAU AUX POMMES DE TERRE

2 pounds potatoes, scrubbed
Boiling salted water
¼ cup plus 3 tablespoons butter
1¼ cups grated Swiss or Gruyère cheese
2 eggs, lightly beaten
Salt and freshly ground black pepper to taste
1 pound fresh spinach, washed, or 1 package (10 ounces) frozen chopped
1½ tablespoons flour
¾ cup milk

⅛ teaspoon grated nutmeg
¼ pound mushrooms, sliced
2 ounces prosciutto or ham, finely chopped
2 ounces provolone cheese, finely chopped
2 ounces mozzarella cheese, grated
¼ cup dry bread crumbs
¼ cup freshly grated Parmesan cheese
Mushroom cream sauce (recipe below)

1. Cook the potatoes in boiling salted water to cover until tender.
2. Preheat oven to 400 degrees.
3. Drain potatoes, peel and force through a ricer or sieve into a bowl. Add ¼ cup butter, the Swiss or Gruyère, the eggs, salt and pepper.
4. Cook the fresh spinach 4 minutes in the water clinging to the leaves. Drain well and chop. Cook the frozen spinach according to package directions. Drain well.

5. Melt 1½ tablespoons butter in a small saucepan. Blend in the flour and gradually stir in the milk. Bring to a boil, stirring until mixture thickens. Season with salt, pepper and nutmeg. Stir in the spinach.

6. Heat the remaining 1½ tablespoons butter in a skillet, add the mushrooms and cook briefly. Add to the spinach mixture and stir in the prosciutto or ham, the provolone and mozzarella.

7. Mix together the crumbs and Parmesan. Butter a 9-inch-square baking dish. Sprinkle with some of the crumb-cheese mixture. Spread half of the potato mixture over the bottom of the prepared dish. Top with the spinach mixture and cover with remaining potato mixture. Sprinkle with remaining crumb-cheese mixture. Bake 30 minutes or until well browned. The gâteau can be turned out or served in squares directly from the dish, with the sauce spooned over.

Yield: 6 servings

Mushroom Cream Sauce

¼ cup butter	1½ cups milk
¼ pound mushrooms, diced	Pinch grated nutmeg
2 shallots, finely chopped	Salt and freshly ground black pepper to taste
3 tablespoons flour	

1. Melt the butter in a saucepan, add the mushrooms and shallots and cook until tender. Blend in the flour and gradually stir in the milk.

2. Bring to a boil, stirring. Add nutmeg, salt and pepper and cook 1 minute.

Yield: About 2 cups sauce

CHICKEN WINGS PROVENÇALE

2 pounds chicken wings
1 large clove garlic, slivered
Salt and freshly ground black pepper to taste
Juice of ½ lemon
1 tablespoon butter
2 tablespoons olive oil
1 onion, finely chopped
⅓ cup dry white wine
2 cups chopped, skinned and seeded fresh tomatoes, or canned Italian plum tomatoes
1 tablespoon tomato paste
4 anchovy fillets, mashed to a paste
1 tablespoon chopped fresh basil, or ½ teaspoon dried
½ teaspoon thyme
8–12 black olives
2 tablespoons chopped fresh parsley

1. Remove the wing tips for use in stocks or soups. Insert the slivers of garlic under the skin of the wings.

2. Season the wings with salt and pepper and sprinkle with lemon juice.

3. Heat the butter and oil in a large skillet, add the wings and brown on both sides. Add the onion and cook until it is golden.

4. Add the wine and cook, stirring, until reduced to a tablespoon or two of liquid.

5. Add the remaining ingredients except the parsley, bring to a boil and simmer 15 minutes, or until wings are tender.

6. Transfer the wings to a warm platter and keep warm. Reduce the sauce by boiling, uncovered, until it is the desired consistency. Season with salt and pepper.

7. Spoon some of the sauce over the wings, sprinkle with the parsley and serve the remaining sauce separately.

Yield: 4 servings

APPLES ALASKA

¼ cup sugar	2 tablespoons cognac
1½ cups water	1 tablespoon chopped
2 two-inch lengths	pecans, almonds or
lemon rind	walnuts
4 medium-size (about	2 egg whites
2½ inches) Red	⅛ teaspoon cream of
Delicious or Rome	tartar
Beauty apples	⅓ cup superfine sugar
¼ cup raisins	4 slivers crystallized
2 tablespoons diced	ginger or angelica
glacéed fruits	for stems

1. Heat the sugar, water and lemon rind together in a skillet just big enough to hold the 4 apples. Stir until the sugar dissolves. Cover and boil gently 10 minutes.

2. Meanwhile, core and peel the apples. Set in the syrup, cover and simmer gently until tender when tested with a toothpick, about 15 minutes. Do not overcook.

3. Mix together the raisins, glacéed fruits, cognac and nuts and set aside while apples cook.

4. Using a slotted spoon, remove the apples, drain on paper towels and then transfer to a baking sheet lined with parchment paper or unglazed brown paper. Add 1 tablespoon syrup from the skillet to the raisin mixture and use to stuff the apples, piling it up on top. The apples may be finished off with the meringue immediately for an all-hot dessert, or they can be cooled, chilled and then covered with meringue.

5. Preheat oven to 300 degrees.

6. Place the egg whites in the bowl of an electric mixer and beat until frothy. Add the cream of tartar and beat until stiff. Gradually beat in the superfine sugar until mixture is very stiff and glossy.

7. Spoon the mixture into a pastry bag fitted with a plain or star tube and pipe the meringue in spirals around the apples, starting at the base and covering them completely.

8. Bake about 20 minutes or until very lightly browned.

9. Place the slivers of ginger or angelica to form the stems of the apples. Serve immediately.

Yield: 4 servings

Weekend
Sour Dough Bread

More and more people are baking their own bread for any number
of reasons: economy, taste, satisfaction, relief from tensions and just
for the fun of it, as well as to make inexpensive, but highly accept-
able, gifts. Successful sour dough bread is the ultimate in most
bread bakers' repertoire, and those who only have time, or facilities,
available on weekends are discovering that the starter, after its
weekly rejuvenation, keeps well in the refrigerator and that it takes
only a short while of actual stirring, kneading and baking to produce a batch of good-tasting loaves. The important activity goes on
all by itself during the several risings. Begin a starter one weekend
and enjoy the first loaves the next.

Sour Dough Bread*

SOUR DOUGH BREAD

Starter

    2 cups warm water   2 cups unbleached
    1 package dry active   white flour
       yeast

To replenish starter

    1 cup warm water   1 cup unbleached flour

Sour dough bread

1 cup starter
2 cups warm water
6 cups unbleached
   flour, approximately
1 package dry active
   yeast

2 teaspoons salt
Cornmeal
1 egg, lightly beaten
1 tablespoon water

1. First weekend: To prepare starter, stir the water and yeast together until the yeast dissolves. Stir in the flour and place mixture in a 3-quart plastic, glass or ceramic bowl. Cover tightly and set in a warm place for 48 to 60 hours or until the mixture has stopped bubbling and there is a liquid layer on top and a definite sour-fermenting smell. Store in the refrigerator.

2. Second weekend and each succeeding one: Remove 1 cup of the starter and set aside. To replenish the starter remaining in the bowl, add 1 cup warm water and 1 cup flour, mix, cover and set in a warm place until the liquid forms on top again. Store in the refrigerator for the next weekend.

3. To prepare bread, place the reserved cup of starter in a large bowl. Add 1 cup of the warm water and 2 cups flour. Mix well, cover and let stand overnight.

4. Next day, dissolve the yeast in another cup of warm water and add to the mixture from above (step 3), along with salt and enough remaining flour to make a dough that can be kneaded. Knead in an electric mixer with a dough hook, or by hand on a lightly floured board until smooth.

5. Put the dough in an ungreased bowl, cover and let rise until doubled in bulk. The slower the rising, the more sourness is developed. This can be done in a warm place in 2 hours.

6. Punch down the dough. Divide in half and shape each into a round or long loaf. Place on greased and cornmeal-sprinkled baking sheets or in greased 9-by-5-by-3-inch loaf pans. Let rise until doubled in bulk, about 1 hour.

7. Preheat oven to 450 degrees.

8. Brush the loaves with the egg combined with the tablespoon of water. Bake for 25 minutes or until loaves sound hollow when tapped on the bottom.

Yield: 2 loaves

Dining Vegetarian-Style

Concern for the world's hungry, high-priced meats, experimenting with alternate lifestyles, or vegetarians coming for dinner are but a few of the reasons why it is time to experiment with meatless meals. Discover that combining grains and beans or peas and making full use of eggs and dairy foods can deliver all the essential nutrients in good-tasting dishes.

*Chilled Artichokes with Sunflower Seeds Vinaigrette**
*Clear Borscht**
*Sesame Seed Wafers**
*Vegetarian Coulibiac with Sour Cream Sauce**
*Broccoli Puree**
Corn Relish
*Bean Sprout and Citrus Salad on Watercress**
*Pumpkin Flan**
Apple Cider

CHILLED ARTICHOKES WITH SUNFLOWER SEEDS VINAIGRETTE

8 *medium-size arti-
chokes*
1 *lemon, halved*
Boiling salted water
2 *cups safflower, pea-
nut or corn oil*
¼ *cup lemon juice*
2 *tablespoons wine
vinegar*
1 *tablespoon finely
chopped shallot or
scallion*

2 *teaspoons chopped
sour pickles
(optional)*
¼ *cup chopped parsley*
1 *clove garlic, crushed*
2 *tablespoons sun-
flower seeds, finely
chopped*
*Salt and freshly
ground black pepper
to taste*

1. Trim the artichokes, including the tips of the leaves, and rub all cut surfaces with a lemon half. Cut off the top third of each artichoke. Open up the center leaves, turn artichokes over and press down to make leaves open further.

2. Using a sturdy spoon, scrape out the choke and surrounding yellow leaves and discard. Sprinkle inside of artichokes with lemon juice from the lemon half used to rub cut surfaces (step 1). Arrange the artichokes in a kettle so that they are wedged together.

3. Add boiling salted water to cover. Squeeze the remaining half lemon over, cover and cook 30 minutes or until tender. Drain upside down. Chill.

4. Meanwhile, combine the remaining ingredients in a jar. Shake well and chill. To serve, arrange artichokes on individual plates. Remove garlic clove and spoon some of the dressing into each artichoke.

Yield: 8 servings

CLEAR BORSCHT

1 *large onion, finely*
  chopped
2 *ribs celery, diced*
1 *white turnip, diced*
2 *carrots, diced*
2 *cups shredded cab-*
  bage
2 *quarts vegetable*
  broth or water

8 *raw beets, peeled*
  and diced
Salt and freshly
  ground black pepper
  to taste
Sour salt or lemon
  juice to taste
2 *cooked beets, cut*
  into julienne strips

1. Place the onion, celery, turnip, carrots, cabbage and broth in a large kettle. Bring to a boil, cover and simmer 30 minutes.

2. Add the diced raw beets, salt and pepper. Cover and simmer 20 minutes. Strain the broth into a clean saucepan. Add sour salt or lemon juice and the julienne strips of beets. Reheat and check the seasoning.

Yield: 8 servings

SESAME SEED WAFERS

¼ *cup sesame seeds*
1 *cup flour*
¼ *teaspoon salt*
  Pinch cayenne

3 *tablespoons butter*
1 *egg yolk*
Ice water

1. Toast the sesame seeds in a skillet over low heat, stirring frequently, or in a 300-degree oven 15 minutes. Cool.

2. Preheat oven to 350 degrees.

3. Place the flour, salt and cayenne in a bowl. With the fingertips, work in the butter until the mixture resembles coarse oatmeal. Add the cooled seeds, the egg yolk and enough ice water to make a dough.

4. Roll out the dough ¼-inch thick on a floured board and cut into 2-inch rounds. Place on an ungreased cookie sheet and bake 15 minutes or until light golden. Cool on a rack.

Yield: About 18 wafers

VEGETARIAN COULIBIAC WITH SOUR CREAM SAUCE

Coulibiac

4 tablespoons butter
1½ cups chopped
  onions
1 pound mushrooms,
  chopped
2 large ribs celery,
  finely chopped
2½ cups cooked soy-
  beans (see note)
3 cups cooked brown
  rice
1 cup raw cashews,
  chopped
⅓ cup snipped fresh
  dill weed
¼ cup chopped
  parsley

1 tablespoon salt
½ teaspoon freshly
  ground black
  pepper
2 eggs, lightly beaten
¾ pound phyllo
  pastry
½ pound unsalted
  butter, melted
Fine, unflavored,
  dry bread crumbs
4 hard-cooked eggs,
  quartered length-
  wise

Sauce

¼ cup butter
1 cup finely chopped
  onions
2 tablespoons flour
2 cups sour cream,
  at room tempera-
  ture

Vegetable broth or
  milk
1 tablespoon snipped
  fresh dill weed
Salt and freshly
  ground black pep-
  per to taste

1. To prepare coulibiac, melt the butter in a large heavy skillet and cook the onions in it until tender, but not browned. Add the mushrooms and celery and cook over high heat until the liquid has evaporated.

2. Stir in the soybeans, brown rice, cashews, dill, parsley, salt, pepper and eggs. Mix well and check seasoning.

3. Preheat oven to 375 degrees.

4. Place the phyllo pastry on a damp towel and cover with a second damp towel. Take one sheet of the pastry and place on a third damp towel. Keep remaining dough covered. Brush the sheet of pastry with melted butter and sprinkle very lightly with dry

bread crumbs. Place a second sheet of phyllo pastry over the first, brush with melted butter and sprinkle with crumbs. Repeat this step until there are 10 to 12 sheets in a stack.

5. Pile half of the soybean mixture along the long side of the stack about 3 inches from the edge and leaving 1 inch at either side. Arrange 2 sliced eggs along the top of the pile. Using the towel as an aid, roll the filling in the pastry to make a strudel-like roll, tucking in the sides.

6. Roll the coulibiac onto an ungreased baking sheet, preferably one with an edge. Brush with melted butter. Cover with a damp towel. Repeat the procedure with the remaining phyllo pastry and soybean filling.

7. Bake the rolls 35 minutes or until crisp and well browned. Let stand 5 minutes before cutting into thick slices.

8. Meanwhile, to prepare sauce, melt the butter and cook the onions in it very slowly until they are golden brown and very tender. This will take 20 minutes.

9. Sprinkle with the flour, stir in the sour cream and bring to a boil, stirring. Thin the mixture with broth or milk until mixture is of sauce consistency. Add dill, salt and pepper and serve with the coulibiac.

Yield: 8 to 10 servings

Note: One cup of dried soybeans makes 2½ to 3 cups when cooked. After soaking overnight in the refrigerator, cook beans in a pressure cooker with water to cover and ¼ cup oil for 20 minutes, or without oil in a covered saucepan for 2 to 3 hours until tender.

BROCCOLI PUREE

2 bunches broccoli, broken into small flowerets	Salt and freshly ground black pepper to taste
Boiling salted water	⅛ teaspoon grated nutmeg
2 large potatoes, quartered	Heavy cream (optional)
2 tablespoons butter	

1. Cook the broccoil in boiling salted water until tender. Drain and force through a food mill.

2. Cook the potatoes in boiling salted water until tender. Drain

and force through a food mill or potato ricer. Mix the two pureed vegetables.

3. Beat in the butter, salt, pepper, nutmeg and a tablespoon or 2 of cream if necessary to correct the consistency. Reheat.

Yield: 8 servings

BEAN SPROUT AND CITRUS SALAD ON WATERCRESS

⅔ cup safflower oil
¼ cup lemon juice
¼ teaspoon dry mus-
  tard
  Salt and freshly
  ground black pepper
  to taste
1 bunch watercress,
  washed and chilled

2 grapefruit, sec-
  tioned and sections
  quartered
4 oranges, sectioned
  and sections halved
3 cups fresh bean
  sprouts

1. Combine the oil, lemon juice, mustard, salt and pepper. Chill.
2. Arrange watercress on 8 plates. Top with grapefruit and orange pieces and bean sprouts.
3. Just before serving, spoon the chilled dressing over.

Yield: 8 servings

PUMPKIN FLAN

½ cup sugar
¾ cup light brown
  sugar
½ teaspoon cinnamon
½ teaspoon ground
  ginger
¼ teaspoon grated
  nutmeg
¼ teaspoon salt
1 cup cooked pump-
  kin puree (see
  note)

1½ cups light cream
  or half-and-half
5 eggs, lightly beaten
1 teaspoon vanilla
½ cup heavy cream,
  whipped
  Candied ginger,
  diced (optional)

1. Preheat oven to 350 degrees.

2. Place the ½ cup sugar in a small heavy skillet, set over medium-low heat and cook, stirring, until the sugar melts and turns a caramel color. Do not overcook. Pour into a 9-inch pie plate, rotating to cover bottom.

3. In a large bowl, combine the brown sugar, cinnamon, ground ginger, nutmeg and salt. Stir in the pumpkin puree.

4. Mix together the light cream, eggs and vanilla and pour into the pumpkin mixture. Mix well. Pour into the prepared pie plate. Set in a pan of hot water and bake 1 hour and 10 minutes, or until a knife inserted near the middle comes out clean.

5. Cool on a rack. Chill thoroughly. To serve, loosen around the edges and turn out onto a serving plate or compote. Using a pastry bag and star tube, decorate the flan with whipped cream. Garnish with candied ginger if desired.

Yield: 8 servings

Note: One small pumpkin, baked until tender, will yield 2 cups of puree and enough seeds to toast in the following manner. They are great as a snack.

Heat a heavy skillet over medium heat. Add the seeds with 1 or 2 tablespoons of safflower oil and cook, stirring constantly, until lightly browned. Watch carefully, they burn easily. Sprinkle with salt.

SPRING

Japanese Menu (For All Diets)

Mary Sue is on another diet, John has to watch his cholesterol, and Marie and Tony are taking that advanced Chinese cooking course. And, they are all coming to dinner Saturday night expecting to eat like birds but hoping for miracles. Set the scene with tatami mats, bonsai trees and Japanese flower arrangements and serve sashimi on earthenware trays and the miso soup in lacquered bowls. Oh yes— remember to leave the shrimp off John's dish. And, keep the calorie figures handy to prove it is possible to count calories and still enjoy a complete dinner (941 calories per person).

*Sashimi (178)**
*Miso Soup (25)**
*Yakitori (290)**
*Rice (204)**
*Daikon Salad (50)**
*Pears Poached in Wine (194)**
Warm Sake for Nondieters
Green Tea for All (0)

NOTE: The calorie counts which appear in parentheses throughout this section are based on U.S.D.A. Composition of Foods, Handbook No. 8.

Japanese ingredients are available in Oriental food shops.

SASHIMI (Raw Fish Appetizer)

6 large shrimp in the
shell (156)
Boiling water
1¼ pounds boneless,
skinned striped
bass or halibut
(595)
1 can (1 ounce)
wasabi, horseradish
powder (18)
1 piece (3 ounces)
daikon, Japanese
white radish (12)

1 large carrot (27)
1 cucumber, peeled
and seeded (12)
¾ cup plus ⅓ cup
shoyu, Japanese
soy sauce (200)
3 tablespoons sake,
rice wine (24)
⅓ cup white vinegar
(9)
1 lemon, halved (15)
6 leaves flat-leaf
Italian parsley

1. Insert a bamboo skewer through each shrimp to keep them straight. Cook in boiling water 1 minute. Drain, shell and devein.

2. Slice fish at a slight angle into pieces ¼ inch thick by about 1½ to 2 inches wide.

3. Mix wasabi with just enough water to make a stiff paste.

4. Cut the daikon, carrot and cucumber into slivers $\frac{1}{16}$ inch wide by 3 inches long. Mix together.

5. Mix the ⅓ cup shoyu with sake, vinegar and juice from half a lemon. Divide among 6 little dishes.

6. Slice the remaining lemon half very thinly. Quarter each slice. To serve, place pile of vegetable slivers on each dish. Top with fish slices, lemon garnish and shrimp. Add ball of wasabi and parsley leaf.

7. Divide remaining ¾ cup choyu among 6 small dishes. To eat with chopsticks, mix wasabi to taste in the shoyu and use it and the sake mixture to dip the fish into before eating.

Yield: 6 servings (1068); 178 calories per serving

MISO SOUP

Water
1 piece (2 inches square) kombu, dried kelp
¾ cup dried, shaved fish flakes (katsuobushi)
2 tablespoons dark (aka) miso paste (60)

2 tablespoons light (shiro) miso paste (60)
3 tablespoons shoyu, Japanese soy sauce (19)
2 tablespoons finely chopped green scallion (2)
1 mushroom, thinly sliced

1. Heat 1½ quarts water to boiling. Wash the kombu and add to the pan. Remove after 2 seconds with slotted spoon. Add fish flakes, turn off heat and let stand one minute, then strain through 2 thicknesses of cheesecloth. Reserve broth. Retain solids to make more broth.

2. Blend the miso with enough water to make a paste. Stir in some of the hot broth, return to the pan, add shoyu and reheat, but do not boil. Serve garnished with scallion bits and a slice of mushroom.

Yield: 6 servings (141); 25 calories per serving

YAKITORI

¾ cup sake, rice wine (156)
¼ cup mirin, sweet cooking sauce (268)*
¾ cup shoyu, Japanese soy sauce (124)
3 thin slices fresh ginger, finely chopped

6 whole, boned and skinned chicken breasts, cut into 1½-inch cubes (1159)
54 pieces (1½ inches long) scallions (33) Kona sansho, Japanese pepper, to taste

1. Combine sake, mirin, shoyu and ginger in a bowl. Add the chicken and marinate 20 to 30 minutes.
2. Thread the chicken and scallion pieces onto small bamboo skewers which have been soaked in water. Brush with the marinade and broil 4 inches from the flame about 4 minutes a side, brushing frequently with the marinade.
3. Heat some of remaining marinade to spoon over skewers when served. Sprinkle with kona sansho.

Yield: 6 servings (1790); 290 calories per serving

RICE

1½ cups uncooked Japanese rice (1224)	2¼ cups water

Rinse the rice well under cold running water. Place rice in a saucepan with the 2¼ cups water, bring to a boil, cover and cook over medium heat 10 minutes. Reduce heat to very low and cook 10 minutes longer. Let stand 5 minutes.

Yield: 6 servings (1224); 204 calories per serving

DAIKON SALAD

1 pound daikon, Japanese white radish, grated (67)	¼ cup white vinegar (10)
1 teaspoon grated fresh ginger root	2 tablespoons sugar (109)
2 tablespoons toasted sesame seeds, ground to a paste (80)	1 tablespoon soy sauce (6)
	⅛ teaspoon salt
	1 bunch watercress (30)

1. Squeeze the daikon to remove excess moisture. Combine remaining ingredients except watercress and pour over daikon. Toss.
2. Arrange watercress in 6 bowls and top with a pile of daikon.

Yield: 6 servings (302); 50 calories per serving

* Calorie count based on sugar.

PEARS POACHED IN WINE

½ cup red wine (84)
½ cup sugar (381)
1 cinnamon stick,
 broken in pieces
1 strip (2 inches)
 lemon rind

4 whole cloves
6 medium-size Bosc
 pears, halved,
 peeled and cored
 (700)

Heat the wine, sugar, cinnamon, lemon rind and cloves together
to boiling. Boil 2 minutes. Add 2 or 3 pear halves at a time and
cover and poach until tender, about 10 minutes. Remove pears and
boil syrup until it measures about ½ cup. Pour over pears and chill.
 Yield: 6 servings (1165); 194 calories per serving

Sweetmeats for Passover

✣

The week before the traditional Passover ceremonies begin is a busy one for Jewish homemakers. Special cleaning must be done, Passover dishes unpacked and the carefully regulated menus planned to observe the dietary restrictions of the eight-day holiday. Daughters and daughters-in-law can learn the rituals in the home and the kitchen by watching Mama. Several days before the start of the holiday they can help prepare many of the sweetmeats, perhaps reserving the last Sunday before Passover for this happy task.

*Chocolate Nut Squares**
*Orange Marmalade Bars**
*Fruit Candy**
*Candied Grapefruit (or Orange) Peel**

——————— •◆• ———————

CHOCOLATE NUT SQUARES

2 ounces pareve bittersweet chocolate	¼ cup matzo cake meal
¼ pound pareve margarine	2 tablespoons potato starch
3 eggs	1 teaspoon liqueur
1 cup sugar	½ cup chopped nuts

1. Preheat oven to 350 degrees.
2. Melt chocolate and margarine together over low heat.

3. Put eggs and sugar into a bowl and beat until very light and fluffy.

4. Sift together the matzo cake meal and potato starch. Add the dry ingredients alternately with the chocolate mixture to egg mixture, beginning and ending with dry ingredients.

5. Stir in the liqueur and nuts. Pour mixture into a greased 9-inch-square pan. Bake 25 minutes. Cool in the pan and frost with frosting (recipe below). Refrigerate. Cut in squares and serve at room temperature.

Yield: 25 squares

Frosting

3 ounces pareve bitter-   ¼ pound pareve mar-
sweet chocolate   garine
3 tablespoons strong
coffee or liqueur
used in the squares

1. Place chocolate and coffee or liqueur in the top of a double boiler over hot water. Stir until melted and smooth.

2. Remove top of double boiler from heat and beat in the margarine, 1 tablespoon at a time, making sure that it is blended in well before adding the next tablespoon. Cool slightly before using to frost.

Yield: About 1 cup

ORANGE MARMALADE BARS

¼ cup pareve mar-   1 cup orange juice
garine   ⅓ cup orange marma-
1 cup sugar   lade or strawberry
1 cup matzo cake   preserves
meal   1 teaspoon cinnamon
½ cup plus 1 table-   ¼ cup chopped nuts
spoon potato starch   1 tablespoon melted
2 eggs   pareve margarine

1. Preheat oven to 350 degrees.

2. Cream the ¼ cup margarine and ¾ cup of the sugar together until light and fluffy.

3. Sift together the matzo cake meal and ½ cup potato starch and add to the margarine mixture. Stir gently until smooth.

4. Beat together the eggs and orange juice. Add to the cake meal mixture, stirring gently. Pour half the batter into a greased 9-inch-square pan lightly sprinkled on the bottom with potato starch.

5. Spoon marmalade or preserves over and top with remaining batter. Combine cinnamon, nuts, melted margarine and remaining sugar and sprinkle over top of batter. Bake 30 to 35 minutes. Cool in the pan. Cut in squares.

Yield: 16 squares

FRUIT CANDY

½ *pound pitted prunes*
¼ *pound golden raisins*
½ *pound dried apricots*
¼ *pound candied orange peel (recipe below)*
¼ *pound candied grapefruit peel (recipe below)*
¼ *pound pareve bittersweet chocolate, melted*
1 *tablespoon brandy*
Sugar

1. Grind together the prunes, raisins, apricots and orange and grapefruit peels. Add chocolate and brandy and work with the hands to mix.

2. Roll into logs, cut into 1-inch slices and roll into balls. Roll in sugar and store in a dry place.

Yield: 2 pounds

CANDIED GRAPEFRUIT (OR ORANGE) PEEL

4 *grapefruit or 6 oranges*
⅓ *cup lemon juice*
2 *cups plus 2 tablespoons sugar, approximately*

1. With a potato peeler, remove the thin yellow skin if using grapefruits. This is not necessary with the oranges.

2. Score the fruit in 8 sections and remove the peel. Use pulp in fruit compote. Place peel in a saucepan and cover with water. Bring

to a boil and boil 5 minutes. Drain. Cover with fresh water and boil 5 minutes again.

3. Repeat the draining and boiling twice more. Cut peel into slivers ⅛ to ¼ inch thick. Combine the lemon juice and 2 cups sugar and heat to dissolve the sugar.

4. Add cut peel to syrup and boil until rind is glazed and no syrup remains. Remove from heat and let cool. Place on wax paper, sprinkle with sugar and let dry 24 hours. Store in the refrigerator.

Yield: About ¾ pound

Salute to
Spring Weekend

✄

Heavy coats are back in the closet, the broad leaves of the skunk cabbage have unfurled in the swamp and in the city there is new interest in the botanical gardens, the zoo and the miniparks. Celebrate this weekend with a salute to spring and serve shad roe, asparagus soufflé and a rhubarb dessert, a menu featuring three of the few remaining truly seasonal ingredients.

Spring Vegetable Soup°
Broiled Shad Roe°
Asparagus Soufflé°
Boston Lettuce Salad
Rhubarb Cream°

Spring Vegetable Soup

¼ cup olive oil	1 quart chicken
2 onions, thinly	broth or water
sliced	1½ teaspoons basil
2 cloves garlic, finely	½ teaspoon ground
chopped	coriander
1 small eggplant,	1 teaspoon oregano
peeled and cubed	Salt and freshly
(about 1½ cups)	ground black pep-
2 medium-size zuc-	per to taste
chini, sliced	4 ounces small shell
1 green pepper,	macaroni, cooked
seeded and diced	al dente, and
1 can (1 pound 12	drained
ounces) tomatoes	

1. Heat the oil in a heavy kettle and sauté in it the onions and garlic until tender but not browned.

2. Add the eggplant, zucchini and green pepper and cook, stirring, over medium heat until lightly browned, about 8 to 10 minutes.

3. Add remaining ingredients except for macaroni. Bring to a boil, cover and simmer 10 minutes or until vegetables are barely tender.

4. Add macaroni and simmer 4 minutes longer.

Yield: 6 servings

Broiled Shad Roe

2 pair shad roe	Salt and freshly
Lemon juice	ground black pepper
4 strips fatty bacon	to taste

1. Split the pairs of shad roe. Sprinkle with lemon juice, salt and pepper.

2. Wrap each roe in a strip of bacon, using a spiral pattern. Place on a broiler pan.

3. Preheat the broiler and broil 6 inches from the source of heat until the bacon is crisp, turning once, about 3 minutes each side. Do not overcook or the roe will dry out.

Yield: 4 servings

ASPARAGUS SOUFFLÉ

1½ pounds (1 bundle) asparagus	Salt and freshly ground black pepper to taste
Boiling salted water	4 egg yolks
3 tablespoons butter	1 tablespoon grated onion
4 tablespoons flour	5 egg whites
1 cup milk	
⅛ teaspoon grated nutmeg	

1. Remove and reserve 8 asparagus tips for garnish. Wash remainder of asparagus, remove woody portions and cut remainder into 1-inch lengths.

2. Preheat oven to 375 degrees.

3. Place asparagus pieces in a saucepan with boiling salted water barely to cover. Cover and cook until asparagus is crisp-tender.

4. Drain, reserve cooking liquid, and pass asparagus through a food mill or an electric blender, or chop very fine, to make about 1 to 1½ cups of puree or chopped vegetable.

5. Meanwhile, melt the butter in a saucepan, blend in the flour and gradually stir in the milk.

6. Bring to a boil, stirring, until mixture thickens. Season with salt, pepper and nutmeg.

7. Beat the egg yolks lightly. Pour the hot sauce into the egg yolks while beating vigorously. Fold in the onion and the pureed, or finely chopped, asparagus.

8. Beat the egg whites until stiff but not dry and fold into the asparagus mixture.

9. Turn the mixture into a greased 2-quart soufflé dish and bake about 40 minutes, or until well puffed and browned on top.

10. Meanwhile, reheat the reserved cooking liquid and cook the reserved tips in it 3 minutes or until barely tender. Drain. Serve 2 tips on top of each portion of soufflé.

Yield: 4 servings

RHUBARB CREAM

1 pound rhubarb, washed and cut into 1-inch lengths (about 4 cups)	Light brown sugar
	¼ teaspoon cinnamon
	2 eggs, separated
	½ cup heavy cream, whipped
⅓ cup apple juice	

1. Place the rhubarb and apple juice in a saucepan. Bring to a boil, cover and let simmer until tender, about 10 minutes.

2. Pass the mixture through a food mill, or blend until smooth in an electric blender. Return to the saucepan.

3. Beat enough brown sugar (½ to ¾ cup) into the rhubarb to sweeten to taste. Add the cinnamon.

4. Beat the egg yolks with 1 extra tablespoon brown sugar and stir into the fruit mixture. Heat briefly, stirring, until the mixture thickens slightly. Do not allow to boil.

5. Cool and chill the mixture. Beat the egg whites until stiff but not dry and fold into the chilled rhubarb mixture. Fold in the cream.

Yield: 4 servings

Take the Pressure off the Budget Meal

And reduce time spent in the kitchen by using a pressure cooker to fix Lamb Shanks Provençale. About 30 minutes is all it takes. Vegetables are included in the recipe so all that is left to add is rice and a spectacular, but quick, dessert. Those who sit and share the meal will marvel if you are a 9-to-5 worker and it's Friday night at 7. Or, they don't need to know you played 18 holes of golf or did volunteer duty at the hospital all day. Pressure cookers have been on the shelf, instead of the range, for too long. Keep them handy and fix a fricassee or a hearty soup in a fraction of the time it normally takes and expand your repertoire of dishes for the busiest of weekends.

*Lamb Shanks Provençale**
Rice
Endive and Beet Salad
*Reuben's Apple Pancake**

LAMB SHANKS PROVENÇALE

4 *lamb shanks, as close to 1 pound each as possible*
¼ *cup flour*
Salt and freshly ground black pepper
3 *tablespoons oil*
1 *clove garlic, finely chopped*
1 *onion, chopped*
½ *teaspoon thyme*
1 *can (1 pound 3 ounces) plum tomatoes*
2 *medium-size zucchini, cut into 1-inch slices*
1 *small eggplant, peeled and cut into 1-inch cubes*

1. Trim excess fat from the shanks and dredge them in the flour seasoned with salt and pepper to taste.

2. Heat the oil in a pressure cooker and brown the shanks in it on all sides, 2 shanks at a time. Return all meat to the pan and add the garlic, onion, thyme, 2 teaspoons salt and ½ teaspoon pepper and cook 3 minutes.

3. Add the tomatoes and stir to break up. Close the cover (*follow manufacturer's instructions*), place pressure regulator on vent pipe and cook 30 minutes.

4. Let the pressure drop of its own accord. Open pan and add zucchini and eggplant. Close cover securely, replace pressure regulator and cook 1 *minute* only. Let pressure drop of its own accord.

Yield: 4 servings

REUBEN'S APPLE PANCAKE

1 cup flour
¼ cup plus 3 table-
spoons sugar
⅛ teaspoon salt
1 egg
⅔ cup milk, approxi-
mately
¼ teaspoon cinnamon

6 tablespoons clarified
butter (made by
melting ½ cup
butter and pouring
off clear yellow
liquid)
1 large Red Delicious
apple, peeled, cored
and thinly sliced

1. Place the flour, 1 tablespoon of sugar, the salt and egg in a bowl. Gradually beat in the milk until mixture is smooth and the consistency of creamy pancake batter. Let stand at least 30 minutes.

2. Preheat oven to 450 degrees.

3. Mix 2 tablespoons sugar with cinnamon and sprinkle over a heatproof deep 10-inch plate.

4. Slightly warm a heavy, well-seasoned 9-inch omelet pan or flare-sided cast iron skillet with a heatproof handle. Add 3 tablespoons of the clarified butter and the apple slices. Cook, shaking the pan back and forth, until pan is very hot, about 3 minutes.

5. Check the consistency of the batter; it should be fairly thick and creamy. Pour batter on top of apple-butter mixture, shaking pan to distribute evenly.

6. Cook over very high heat until underside is browned. Flip pancake (over the sink is safest) to brown other side, shaking the pan constantly to keep pancake loose in the pan.

7. Sprinkle top of pancake with half the remaining sugar und dribble half the remaining butter over. Flip pancake again. Over the sink is advised because as the sugar caramelizes it splashes when pancake is flipped over. Avoid splashing the skin.

8. Sprinkle second side with remaining sugar and butter. Flip pancake back and forth 3 times more while continuing to cook over very high heat. Care must be taken not to burn the sugar, but it should turn golden brown.

9. Bake in the oven 3 minutes.

10. Slide onto the prepared plate and serve with more cinnamon sugar or sour cream, if desired. Alternately, 2 ounces of warm cognac can be poured over the pancake at the table and flamed.

Yield: 4 servings

Late Supper
After the Show

✖

The weekend everyone stays in town for the concert is the chance to give an after-the-performance supper party. Arrange the room and the buffet table before you go and you will be able to sip champagne with the guests when you return while the the spinach pie is heating in the oven. Here's one occasion when salad and bread are superfluous and only forks are needed.

Champagne
*Torte di Spinaci**
*Lemon Ice Cream**

———————— ✦ ————————

TORTE DI SPINACI

Pastry

3 cups flour
½ teaspoon salt
1 cup butter, cut in
    pieces

1 egg yolk
3 tablespoons cold
    water, approxi-
    mately

Filling

3 tablespoons olive oil

2 large onions, finely chopped

1½–2 pounds fresh spinach leaves or 2 packages (10 ounces each) chopped, frozen spinach

3 smoked pork chops (about 1 pound; each chop 1-inch thick), fat and bones removed and meat diced (1 pound diced country ham can be substituted)

1½ cups freshly grated Parmesan cheese

1 cup (8 ounces) ricotta

Salt and freshly ground black pepper to taste

4 eggs, lightly beaten

1 egg white, lightly beaten

1. To prepare pastry, place the flour, salt and butter in a bowl. Work the butter into the flour until the mixture resembles coarse oatmeal.

2. Mix the egg yolk with 3 tablespoons water and sprinkle over the mixture. Stir with a fork, adding only enough extra water to make a dough that just clings together.

3. Wrap the dough in wax paper and chill briefly.

4. To prepare filling, heat the oil and sauté the onions in it until tender. If fresh spinach is used, remove large stems, wash the spinach leaves well and put into a large kettle. Cover tightly and cook until leaves wilt. Drain well and chop. If frozen spinach is used, cook according to package directions and drain well.

5. Combine drained spinach and sautéed onions and let cool.

6. Add the diced smoked pork, Parmesan cheese, ricotta, salt, pepper and eggs to the cooked spinach mixture.

7. Preheat oven to 425 degrees.

8. Roll out half the pastry and use to line a 10-inch pie plate. Brush the bottom and sides of the pie shell with egg white. Pour in the filling.

9. Roll out remaining pastry and use to cover the filling. Seal and

decorate the edges and make a steam hole. Cut leaves from extra pastry and place around the hole but not over it.

10. Bake 40 minutes, or until pastry is golden and done. Let stand 10 to 15 minutes before cutting.

Yield: 8 servings

Note: The pie can be made early in the day and reheated in a preheated 375-degree oven, about 40 minutes, or until hot through. Cover loosely with aluminum foil to prevent overbrowning. The pie can be frozen after it has cooled and, wrapped well in aluminum foil, stored for up to 2 months. Allow the pie to thaw at room temperature 3 hours and then heat in a 375-degree oven about 1 hour or until heated through.

LEMON ICE CREAM

3 tablespoons lemon juice	1 cup sugar
2 teaspoons grated lemon rind	2 cups light cream
	⅛ teaspoon salt

1. Combine the juice, rind and sugar and blend well.

2. Slowly stir in the cream and salt. Mix well. Pour into a freezing tray and freeze until solid around the outside and mushy in the middle. Stir well with a wooden spoon. Refreeze until solid.

Yield: About 3 cups

Graduation Weekend

✳

Easy-to-eat foods such as hamburgers, hotdogs and pizza are the first choice of most graduating seniors. So, for the beach picnic pack the cooler with buns, two different kinds of burgers and a saucepan of ranchero sauce. But, be prepared for a hungry group to dash in at any time of the day or night that particular weekend. One snack that takes no time to put out is pita, the Middle Eastern flat bread, with a choice of fillings that might include kebabs, falafel or spicy meatballs. The bread can be purchased in most supermarkets but it is not too difficult to make at home if you plan ahead. Have plenty of tomato wedges, shredded lettuce and onion rings for toppings, and tell everyone dessert is in the refrigerator.

BEACH PICNIC

Swedish-Style Hamburgers°
Ranch-Style Hamburgers with Ranchero Sauce°
Watermelon

IN-BETWEEN MEAL AT HOME

Middle Eastern Flat Bread°
Lamb Kebabs°
Falafel°
Spiced Ground Lamb°
Orange Meringue Pie°
Fresh Fruit with Sour Cream Dip°

SWEDISH-STYLE HAMBURGERS

2 pounds ground beef round	3 tablespoons drained capers
2 cups cold, diced, cooked potatoes	2 egg yolks, lightly beaten
1 cup diced cooked beets	¼ cup light cream
1 tablespoon salt	½ cup softened butter
½ teaspoon freshly ground black pepper	2 tablespoons snipped dill weed
⅛ teaspoon allspice	8–10 hamburger buns

1. Combine the beef, potatoes, beets, salt, pepper, allspice, capers, egg yolks and cream and mix lightly. Form into 8 to 10 patties. Broil over charcoal, or under the broiler, to desired degree of doneness, turning once.

2. Combine the butter and dill. Spread on buns, then warm or toast them.

3. Serve burgers in buns.

Yield: 8 to 10 servings

RANCH-STYLE HAMBURGERS WITH RANCHERO SAUCE

2 pounds ground beef round	2 tablespoons canned or fresh hot green chili peppers, seeded and chopped
1½ cups chopped parsley	
1½ cups chopped onions	
2 eggs, lightly beaten	1 teaspoon oregano
2 teaspoons salt	16–20 small, or 8–10 large, tortillas
¼ teaspoon ground cumin	Ranchero sauce (recipe below)

1. Combine all the ingredients except the tortillas and sauce. Mix lightly but well. Shape into 8 to 10 patties. Broil over charcoal, or under the broiler, to desired degree of doneness, turning once.

2. Wrap the tortillas in aluminum foil and heat briefly on a grill or in a warm oven. Serve hamburgers between 2 small tortillas or in 1 large tortilla folded in half. Serve ranchero sauce separately.

Yield: 8 to 10 servings

Ranchero Sauce

2 *tablespoons oil*	2 *tablespoons seeded*
3 *large tomatoes, skin-*	*and chopped chili*
ned, seeded and	*peppers, or to taste*
chopped	1 *tablespoon vinegar*
1 *small onion, minced*	1 *medium-size sweet*
Salt to taste	*green pepper, seeded*
1 *teaspoon sugar*	*and finely diced*

1. Heat the oil in a saucepan, add tomatoes and onion and cook about 25 minutes, until mixture is a thick puree.

2. Add remaining ingredients. Serve warm or cold.

Yield: About 2 cups

MIDDLE EASTERN FLAT BREAD

6 *cups unbleached*	1 *package dry active*
white flour	*yeast*
1 *tablespoon salt*	2½–3 *cups lukewarm*
2 *tablespoons plus* 1	*water*
teaspoon sugar	

1. Place the flour, salt and 2 tablespoons sugar in a large bowl. Set aside.

2. In a small bowl, mix the yeast, remaining sugar and ½ cup water. Set in a warm place until bubbly, about 10 minutes.

3. Stir the yeast mixture and enough warm water into the flour mixture to make a soft dough. The dough should be slightly sticky on the outside.

4. Knead the dough in the bowl until dough is smooth and satiny, at least 10 minutes. It loses the stickiness quickly.

5. Grease the top of the dough with oil, cover the bowl and set in a warm place to rise until doubled in bulk, about 1¼ hours.

6. Punch the dough down, knead briefly and divide into 12 equal pieces. Form each into a smooth ball, cover and let stand 10 minutes.

7. Preheat oven to 450 degrees.

8. Roll out the balls of dough into rounds about 5 inches in diameter. If you are using a gas oven, and have a sense of adventure, slide the rounds of dough directly onto the bottom of the oven. Four will fit in the average oven at one time. Bake 8 minutes or until well puffed and lightly browned.

9. Alternately, the loaves may be placed on ungreased baking sheets and baked 8 to 10 minutes. If tops are pale, place under the broiler briefly. Cool loaves on a board covered with a towel.

Yield: 12 loaves

Note: The loaves puff up in the oven, then collapse as they cool, but retain a pocket for filling. Store in plastic bags in refrigerator or freezer.

LAMB KEBABS

1½ pounds boneless
 leg of lamb, cut
 into 1½-inch cubes
⅓ cup lemon juice
⅓ cup olive oil
1 clove garlic,
 crushed
1 teaspoon salt
¼ teaspoon freshly
 ground black
 pepper
2 tablespoons chopped fresh mint
 leaves, or 1 teaspoon dried

1. Place the lamb pieces in a glass or ceramic bowl. Combine the remaining ingredients and pour over the lamb. Marinate at room temperature 1 hour.

2. Thread the meat onto individual skewers and broil over charcoal, or under the broiler, until browned on the outside and faintly pink in the middle, about 10 minutes. Turn often.

Yield: 4 servings

FALAFEL

2 cups cooked, dried
  chickpeas or 1 can
  (1 pound 4 ounces)
  chickpeas, drained
  and rinsed
⅓ cup water
1 slice firm white
  bread, crusts re-
  moved
½ teaspoon baking
  soda
3 cloves garlic, finely
  chopped
1 egg, lightly beaten
2 tablespoons chopped
  parsley

¾ teaspoon salt
¼ teaspoon freshly
  ground black pepper
¼ teaspoon ground
  cumin
½ teaspoon turmeric
¼ teaspoon basil
¼ teaspoon marjoram
  Cayenne pepper to
  taste
1 tablespoon tahini
  (sesame paste) or
  olive oil
  Flour
  Fat or oil for deep-
  frying

1. Grind the chickpeas through the coarse blade of a meat grinder.

2. Add the water, bread, baking soda, garlic, egg, parsley, seasonings, tahini and 1 tablespoon flour. Mix well. The mixture will be soft.

3. Form the mixture into 1-inch balls, coat with flour and fry, in a basket, 4 or 5 at a time, in the fat or oil heated to 365 degrees. The falafel rise to the surface and are lightly browned when cooked. This takes about 2 minutes. Drain on paper towels.

Yield: About 20 falafel

SPICED GROUND LAMB

1½ pounds ground lean lamb	2 tablespoons tomato sauce
½ pound ground round beef	2 teaspoons paprika
2 slices firm white bread, crusts removed	1½ teaspoons salt Cayenne pepper to taste
½ teaspoon ground cumin	¼ teaspoon finely ground fenugreek seeds
1 teaspoon chili powder	1 egg, lightly beaten
1 large clove garlic, finely chopped	2 tablespoons chopped parsley

1. Grind the lamb, beef and bread together, using the finest blade of the meat grinder.

2. Add remaining ingredients and mix well with the hands. Shape around a spit, or skewer, and broil over charcoal fire until well browned on the outside. Alternately, form into patties or a meatloaf shape and broil over charcoal or under the broiler until well browned on both sides and barely pink in the middle.

Yield: 4 to 6 servings

ORANGE MERINGUE PIE

2 cups sugar	¼ cup plus 2 tablespoons lemon juice
¼ cup plus 2 tablespoons cornstarch	4 eggs, separated
¼ teaspoon salt	3 tablespoons butter
1½ teaspoons grated orange rind	1 baked 9-inch pie shell
3 cups freshly squeezed orange juice	¼ teaspoon cream of tartar

1. In a saucepan, combine 1½ cups sugar, the cornstarch, salt and orange rind. Mix well, then gradually blend in the orange juice and lemon juice.

2. Bring the mixture to a boil, stirring, until mixture is smooth and thick. Cook, stirring, about 3 minutes.

3. Lightly beat the egg yolks. Spoon some of the hot mixture into the yolks, mix well, return to the pan and cook, stirring, until mixture thickens slightly. Stir in the butter. Cool mixture about 10 minutes.

4. Preheat oven to 350 degrees.

5. Pour into the pie shell.

6. Beat the egg whites until they are frothy. Add the cream of tartar and beat at high speed until soft peaks form.

7. Gradually add the remaining sugar while beating at high speed. At this point, the whites should be stiff and shiny.

8. Pile the egg white mixture on top of warm filling, making sure that mixture touches the pastry on all sides. Bake 12 to 15 minutes, or until meringue is lightly browned. Cool on a wire rack.

Yield: 6 servings

Fresh Fruit with Sour Cream Dip

1 cup sour cream	Fresh strawberries
2 tablespoons heavy cream	with stems
	Cubes of fresh pine-
2 tablespoons honey	apple on toothpicks
2 teaspoons grated orange rind	

Combine the sour cream, heavy cream, honey and orange rind and mix well. Refrigerate at least 1 hour before placing in the middle of a platter of fresh fruit dippers.

Yield: 4 servings

Sunday Brunch

✸

Informal entertaining is relaxing for cook and guests, and having a small group stop by for Sunday brunch is one of the easiest ways to entertain. The timing is flexible and doesn't interfere with preparations for the coming week. I've enjoyed brunches set up on a buffet, ones where you order your own omelet when you feel like it, and other successful midday meals served in living rooms and kitchens from the stove or heated cart and balanced on the lap or snack table. Below is a menu that fits all modes of service.

Broccoli Soup✸
Sausage Quiche✸
Boston Lettuce and Cherry Tomato Salad
Poires au Vin✸

———————— ◆•◆•◆ ————————

BROCCOLI SOUP

Stalks from 1 good-
size broccoli bunch
2 tablespoons butter,
margarine or oil
1 small onion, finely
chopped
½ clove garlic, finely
chopped
1 quart chicken broth
or vegetable broth

2 cups water
Salt and freshly
ground black pepper
to taste
2 tablespoons softened
butter mixed with
2 tablespoons flour
(optional)

1. Peel the stalks if they are tough. Slice thinly or dice.
2. Heat the butter, margarine or oil in a heavy saucepan and add the broccoli, onion and garlic. Cook slowly, stirring occasionally, for 10 minutes.
3. Add the broth, water, salt and pepper. Bring to a boil, cover and simmer until the stalks are tender, about 10 minutes. Blend, in three batches, in an electric blender until smooth.
4. Return to the pan, reheat, check the seasoning and, for a thicker soup, whisk in bits of the butter-flour mixture.

Yield: 4 to 6 servings

SAUSAGE QUICHE

1 pound pork sausage meat
1 onion, finely chopped
½ pound Swiss cheese, grated
1 tablespoon flour
1 unbaked 9-inch pie shell
4 eggs, lightly beaten
1½ cups light cream

½ teaspoon salt
¼ teaspoon freshly ground black pepper
¼ teaspoon grated nutmeg
2 tablespoons chopped parsley
½ teaspoon crumbled, dried leaf sage

1. Preheat oven to 375 degrees.
2. Cook the sausage meat in a skillet until brown and crisp, stirring occasionally to break up the lumps. Remove the fat as it accumulates. Remove sausage and drain on paper towels.
3. Heat 2 tablespoons of the sausage drippings in the skillet and sauté in it the onion until tender. Set aside.
4. Place the cheese in a bowl, sprinkle with the flour and toss.
5. Sprinkle the sausage meat over bottom of pie shell, reserving ¼ cup. Sprinkle the onion and the cheese mixture over.
6. Place eggs, cream, salt, pepper, nutmeg, parsley and sage in an electric blender and blend at low speed until mixed. (A rotary beater can also be used.)
7. Pour cream mixture over the meat, onions and cheese and sprinkle with reserved sausage. Bake 35 to 45 minutes, or until a silver knife inserted near the center comes out clean.

Yield: 4 servings

POIRES AU VIN

2 cups sugar
2 cups red Burgundy
  wine
½ teaspoon cinnamon
⅛ teaspoon grated
  nutmeg
1 whole clove

6 Bosc or other firm
  pears (about 2
  pounds)
Boiling water
Unsweetened whip-
  ped cream

1. Combine the sugar, wine, cinnamon, nutmeg and clove in a straight-sided stainless steel, enamel, glass or Teflon-lined pan. Heat, stirring, until the sugar is dissolved.

2. Peel the pears, but leave the stems on. Remove the blossom and cut a small slice off the bottom to allow pears to stand upright.

3. Place pears in wine mixture and add boiling water until pears are almost covered. Cover and cook gently until pears are tender when pierced with a toothpick, about 20 minutes.

4. Arrange the pears on a deep plate. Boil the wine mixture vigorously, uncovered, until it is reduced to 2 cups. Pour around pears.

5. Serve warm or cold, with the whipped cream.

Yield: 6 servings

Old-Fashioned Sunday Morning Breakfast

All week long it's grab a cup of coffee and half a muffin, or wait until you get to the office and nibble on a doughnut. At best, weekday breakfasts are a bowl of enriched cereal and a glass of juice. Sunday is the day to take the time to enjoy a real old-fashioned breakfast and stock up on calories to give strength for all the activities planned and, over lots of steaming coffee and warm blueberry crumb cake, to enjoy conversation with other members of the household or neighbors who drop by. The blueberry cake can be made a day ahead but is best warm from the oven. Be sure to remember the recipe for the next kaffeeklatsch. The cake can be made successfully with frozen berries.

Melon with Lime or Sliced Peaches
Ham or Bacon
Egg and Potato Bake*
Maida's Blueberry Crumb Cake*
Sweet Butter
Hot Coffee

EGG AND POTATO BAKE

2 tablespoons butter
2 tablespoons flour
1 cup milk or butter-
milk
Worcestershire sauce
to taste
Salt and freshly
ground black pepper
to taste

1 cup grated Cheddar
cheese
3 medium-size pota-
toes, cooked and
sliced
3 hard-cooked eggs,
sliced
¼ pound mushrooms,
sliced
Wheat germ

1. Preheat oven to 350 degrees.
2. In a saucepan, melt the butter and blend in the flour. Gradually stir in the milk and bring to a boil, stirring until thickened.
3. Add the worcestershire, salt and pepper. Stir in the cheese until it melts.
4. In an oiled casserole, layer half the potatoes and half the eggs. Top with half the sauce. Repeat the layers, adding the mushrooms to the remainder of the sauce before pouring it over. Sprinkle with wheat germ and bake 20 minutes.

Yield: 4 servings

MAIDA'S BLUEBERRY CRUMB CAKE

2 cups blueberries
2⅓ cups flour
1 teaspoon cinnamon
1¼ cups sugar
½ cup butter
2 teaspoons baking
powder
½ teaspoon salt

1 teaspoon vanilla
1 egg
½ cup milk
Finely grated rind
of 1 lemon
Dry bread crumbs
½ cup finely chopped
walnuts

1. Pick over and wash the berries. Drain in a sieve and turn them in a single layer onto a towel. Pat dry with a second towel and set aside to dry thoroughly.
2. Preheat oven to 375 degrees.

3. In a small bowl, combine ⅓ cup flour, the cinnamon and ½ cup sugar. Cut in ¼ cup of the butter until the mixture resembles coarse crumbs. Set aside.

4. Sift together the remaining flour, the baking powder and salt. Place blueberries in a bowl and sprinkle with 1½ tablespoons of the dry ingredients. Toss gently. Set aside.

5. Cream the remaining ¼ cup butter with the remaining ¾ cup sugar. Beat in the vanilla and the egg very well until the mixture is light and fluffy.

6. Stir in remaining dry ingredients alternately with the milk, starting and ending with the dry. Stir in the rind.

7. Spoon the stiff batter over the blueberries and, with a rubber spatula, fold until just mixed. Turn into a buttered 9-inch square pan that has been dusted with dry bread crumbs. Spread evenly.

8. Sprinkle with the nuts and then the cinnamon topping. Bake 50 minutes or until done. Allow to cool in the pan on a rack for 30 minutes. Loosen with a knife around the sides, place a large sheet of aluminum foil over the cake and invert onto a rack. Place cake plate over bottom and invert again so that the crumb side is up.

Yield: 9 to 12 servings

The Celebration Dinner

The cost of quality veal is high, but a winning lottery ticket, a promotion or any other cause for a celebration can be an excuse to splurge on three- or four-dollar-a-pound slices of veal leg to share with five special friends. Veal, spinach and cheese have a natural affinity for each other, and below is a menu that presents them in an attractive and novel way. The timbales steam while the salad and veal dish are prepared. From beginning to end, the main course takes less than an hour. If there's no extra time, or inclination, to bake, serve imported cheese and fruit for dessert. But, until you've baked the almond torte, and served it with steaming espresso, it is impossible to understand what's been missed.

Roasted Peppers and Anchovies
*Escalopes de Veau**
*Spinach Timbales**
Sliced Tomato Salad with Fresh Basil
Bel Paese and Pears
OR
*Almond Torte**

ESCALOPES DE VEAU

3 tablespoons butter
2 tablespoons chop-
   ped shallots
1 clove garlic, finely
   chopped
¼ pound mushrooms,
   sliced
1 tablespoon chopped
   parsley
   Salt and freshly
   ground black pep-
   per to taste

½ teaspoon oregano
⅓ cup grated carrot
½ cup dry white
   wine
½ cup veal broth or
   chicken broth
1 tablespoon olive
   oil
1½ pounds leg of veal,
   cut in ¼-inch
   slices and pounded
   until thin

1. Heat 1 tablespoon of the butter in a heavy skillet and sauté in it the shallots and garlic until tender.
2. Add mushrooms and cook 3 minutes longer. Add parsley, salt, pepper, oregano, carrot, wine and broth. Bring to a boil and simmer gently 10 minutes.
3. Heat remaining butter with the oil in another heavy skillet.
4. Very quickly sauté in it the pieces of veal so that they are golden brown on both sides. Add meat to the sauce; simmer 2 minutes.

Yield: 6 servings

SPINACH TIMBALES

2 tablespoons butter
2 tablespoons finely
   chopped shallots or
   scallions
1 pound fresh spin-
   ach, well washed
   and finely chopped
4 eggs, lightly beaten
½ cup grated Swiss
   cheese

¾ cup soft bread
   crumbs
1¾ cups milk, scalded
⅛ teaspoon grated
   nutmeg
½ teaspoon salt
¼ teaspoon freshly
   ground black
   pepper

1. Preheat oven to 350 degrees.

2. In a saucepan, melt the butter and sauté the shallots or scallions in it until tender.

3. Add the spinach, cover and cook until tender, about 3 minutes. Drain.

4. Combine the eggs, cheese and bread crumbs. Gradually stir in the milk. Stir in the spinach, nutmeg, salt and pepper. Pour into 6 to 8 greased ramekins or custard cups. Set the cups in a shallow pan and pour boiling water around to reach just over halfway up the cups. Bake 30 minutes or until set.

5. The timbales can be unmolded for serving if desired.

Yield: 6 to 8 servings

ALMOND TORTE

1 cup whole blanched almonds
¾ cup confectioners' sugar
2 egg whites
2 eggs
¾ cup softened butter
1 teaspoon almond extract
3 tablespoons sugar
1½ cups flour
⅓ cup raspberry preserves or currant jelly

1. Grind the almonds in a Mouli grater, Moulinex grinder or through the finest blade of a food chopper.

2. Blend the almonds with the confectioners' sugar, egg whites, 1 egg, ¼ cup of the butter and the almond extract. Chill the mixture.

3. Cream the remaining ½ cup butter with the sugar very well. Beat in the remaining egg. Gradually work in the flour to form a dough. Wrap in wax paper and chill 30 minutes.

4. Preheat oven to 350 degrees.

5. Roll ⅔ of the pastry on a lightly floured board or pastry cloth to an 11-inch circle. Fit the circle into a 9-inch layer pan with a removable bottom, allowing pastry to extend 1 inch up sides.

6. Spread the preserves over the bottom of the pastry shell. Top with the almond mixture.

7. Roll remaining pastry into a 9-inch circle and cut into ½-inch-wide strips. Arrange the strips in a lattice pattern over the almond mixture. Decorate edge of pastry. Bake about 45 minutes, or until done. Cool in the pan. Remove outer ring and leave torte on the pan bottom to serve.

Yield: 6 to 8 servings

Unexpected Guests

Almost everyone is faced at some point with fixing a meal for unexpected guests, and it often seems to happen when the refrigerator is bare except for a dozen eggs and some tired-looking salad greens. However, if you have noodles, or spaghetti, and a few cans of staples in the cupboard, the recipes below can be whipped up in short order even if you are in a rented cottage with a minimum of space and equipment.

Noodles with Anchovy Sauce*
Italian Bread (or Melba toast made from thin slices of bread)
Canned Green and Wax Bean Salad
Meringues* with Ice Cream and Chocolate or Strawberry Sauce

OR

Flan*

NOODLES WITH ANCHOVY SAUCE

⅓ cup olive oil
2 cloves garlic, finely
  chopped
1 small onion, finely
  chopped
1 can (2 ounces) flat
  anchovy fillets,
  drained and
  chopped
1 can (1 pound) Ital-
  ian plum tomatoes
2 tablespoons tomato
  paste
½ teaspoon oregano

Freshly ground
black pepper to
taste
⅓ cup finely chopped
  flat-leaf Italian
  parsley
⅓ cup chopped pitted
  ripe olives
3 tablespoons drained
  capers
Salt (optional)
1 pound narrow
  noodles, cooked al
  dente and drained
  Freshly grated Par-
  mesan cheese

1. Heat the olive oil and sauté in it the garlic and onion until
tender but not browned. Add the anchovies and work them into a
paste with the onion mixture.

2. Add tomatoes, tomato paste, oregano and pepper and bring to
a boil. Simmer, uncovered, 15 minutes.

3. Add the parsley, olives and capers. Taste the sauce and add
salt to taste if necessary. Simmer 5 minutes.

4. Pour the sauce over the noodles and sprinkle liberally with the
cheese.

Yield: 4 servings

MERINGUES

2 egg whites
1½ cups sugar
¼ teaspoon cream of
  tartar

⅓ cup cold water
1 teaspoon vanilla

1. Preheat oven to 275 degrees.
2. Line baking sheet with parchment paper or plain white paper.

3. Combine all ingredients except vanilla in top of a double boiler and mix well for 1 to 2 minutes.

4. Beat over medium heat for 7 minutes or until mixture holds its shape. Remove from heat and add vanilla.

5. Beat 1 minute more with beater at high speed.

6. Drop mixture by rounded serving spoonfuls onto prepared sheet. Bake 45 to 55 minutes or until lightly browned and dry.

Yield: 10 to 15 medium-size meringues

FLAN

1 teaspoon water	*12 egg yolks*
2 tablespoons sugar	*1 teaspoon vanilla*
1⅓ cups plus 2 table-	
spoons sweetened	
condensed milk	

1. Place the water and sugar in a heavy metal 9-inch pie plate and heat gently to melt and then caramelize the sugar to a golden brown. Do not allow to burn.

2. Combine the sweetened condensed milk and egg yolks in a bowl until well blended. Add vanilla and pour over the sugar mixture.

3. Cover with a second pie plate turned upside down and place in a large skillet with enough boiling water to come ¾ the way up the bottom pan. Cook, covered, so that the water barely simmers, for about 30 minutes or until flan is set. Turn out onto a serving plate.

Yield: 6 servings

Progressive Dinner for Twelve

We'll start off at the Waltons' for cocktails and hors d'oeuvre. The main course will be ready to serve yourself at John Avon's studio, and anyone who wants to sample a couple of fabulous desserts should go to the Burtons' new country kitchen. The old-time movie we've rented will start around 11 P.M. if everyone's navigation techniques have been keen.

HOUSE I

Guacamole and Tortilla Chips
John McGuire's Shrimp Muffin Appetizer*
Baked Clams*
Salmon Turnovers*

HOUSE II

Boeuf en Daube*
Homemade Noodles
California Cabernet Sauvignon or Zinfandel
Boston Lettuce and Chicory Salad
Cheese Tray

HOUSE III

Eight-Layer Almond Torte°
Lee's Marlborough Tart°
Espresso
Cognac and Cordials

------ ◆•◆ ------

John McGuire's Shrimp Muffin Appetizer

½ pound uncooked, shelled and deveined shrimp	1 teaspoon soy sauce
	½ teaspoon sugar
	3 English muffins
1 egg, lightly beaten	Corn oil for deep-frying
1 tablespoon cornstarch	Salt (optional)

1. Chop the shrimp finely and set aside. Combine the egg, cornstarch, soy sauce and sugar. Beat to blend. Stir in the shrimp.

2. With a fork, score all around the muffins. Pull apart. Toast only to lightly crisp. Do not brown. Cut each half into 4 pieces.

3. Spread the shrimp mixture on the rough side of the muffin pieces and place, a few at a time, shrimp side down, in the oil, heated to 375 degrees. Fry 1 minute, turn and fry 30 seconds longer. Remove with a slotted spoon and drain on paper towels. Sprinkle with salt if desired.

Yield: 24 pieces

Baked Clams

3 dozen littleneck or cherrystone clams Parmesan-and-oregano-flavored dry bread crumbs	Olive oil
	6 slices bacon, each cut into 6 pieces
	Lemon wedges

1. Preheat oven to 425 degrees.

2. Open the clams, leaving them on the half shell and discarding second half of shell. Sprinkle with crumbs and turn clams. Sprinkle with more crumbs.

3. Place the shells on a pan, or bed of rock salt in a pan, and bake 5 minutes. Sprinkle the top of each with a drop or two of oil and bake a minute or two longer.

4. Top with the bacon pieces and bake until bacon is cooked, about 3 minutes. Serve with lemon wedges.

Yield: 36 baked clams

SALMON TURNOVERS

Pastry

2 cups flour	¼ cup wheat germ
½ teaspoon salt	⅓ cup grated sharp
⅓ cup butter	Cheddar cheese
⅓ cup shortening	Ice water

Filling

1 can (1 pound) salmon, drained, boned, skinned and flaked	¼ teaspoon freshly ground black pepper
2 tablespoons chopped scallions	½ cup mayonnaise
	2 tablespoons lemon juice
½ cup finely shredded carrots	1 tablespoon snipped fresh dill weed
¼ cup finely chopped celery	Milk
	Water
2 hard-cooked eggs, chopped	Flour

1. To prepare pastry, place the flour and salt in a bowl.

2. With the fingertips or a pastry blender, blend in the butter and shortening until mixture resembles coarse oatmeal.

3. Stir in the wheat germ, cheese and enough ice water (about 5 tablespoons) to make a dough. Wrap in wax paper and chill 20 minutes.

4. Preheat oven to 425 degrees.

5. Combine the salmon, scallions, carrots, celery, eggs, pepper, mayonnaise, lemon juice and dill. Mix well and add 2 tablespoons milk to moisten the mixture.

6. Divide dough in half and roll out to a 12-inch square; cut into 8 smaller squares. Place ⅟₁₆ of the salmon mixture over half of each pastry square, leaving ½-inch edge of pastry clear.

7. Moisten edges with water, fold dough over to make triangles and seal edges by pressing with the tines of a fork dipped in flour.

8. Place on an ungreased baking sheet. Brush tops with milk and prick once with a fork. Repeat with the second half of the dough and remaining salmon mixture.

9. Bake about 10 to 15 minutes or until pastry is golden and cooked. Serve hot.

Yield: 16 turnovers

BOEUF EN DAUBE

5 pounds boneless chuck shoulder steak
1 bottle dry red wine (a California Burgundy or a Côtes du Rhône would be an appropriate low-cost choice)
3 sprigs fresh thyme, or 1 teaspoon dried
2 bay leaves
2 sprigs parsley
2 onions, sliced
2 carrots, quartered
2 ribs celery with leaves, quartered

Salt
10 peppercorns, lightly bruised
¼ cup oil
2 cloves garlic, finely chopped
Beef broth
24 small onions, peeled
1 pound mushrooms, sliced
Freshly ground black pepper
½ pound chicken livers
2 tablespoons butter
2 tablespoons flour

1. This recipe should be started 2 days before the daube is to be served.

2. Remove all traces of fat, sinew and gristle from meat and cut into 1-inch cubes. Place in a glass or ceramic bowl. Pour the wine over and add thyme, bay leaves, parsley, sliced onions, the carrots, celery, 2 teaspoons salt and the peppercorns. Stir.

3. Cover and refrigerate overnight. Stir several times.

4. Next day, drain the meat, reserving marinade, and pat dry on paper towels. Heat oil in a large skillet and brown in it the cubes, a few at a time, transferring them to a heavy casserole as they are browned.

5. Add chopped garlic to the skillet. Strain marinade and add the liquid to the skillet. Bring to a boil, stirring to loosen the browned-on particles. Pour over meat. Add broth to cover ¾ of the meat.

6. Bring to a boil, cover and simmer 1½ hours. Add the small onions. Cook 30 minutes and add the mushrooms and salt and pepper to taste. Cook 30 minutes longer.

7. Cool the casserole quickly in ice water. Refrigerate overnight.

8. Before serving, reheat the daube slowly over low heat.

9. Sauté the chicken livers in butter until browned outside but still pink inside. Puree in an electric blender. Add the flour and blend until smooth.

10. Add a little hot broth to liver mixture while blender is on low. Pour into casserole and cook, stirring until sauce thickens slightly.

Yield: 12 to 14 servings

Note: Serve with 3 pounds homemade noodles (see page 153).

EIGHT-LAYER ALMOND TORTE

Cake layers

6 eggs, separated, at room temperature
¾ cup sugar
2 teaspoons almond extract
½ cup flour

1 cup blanched almonds, ground very finely (1⅓–1½ cups ground nuts, see note)
⅛ teaspoon salt

Filling

2 eggs
1½ cups sugar
4 squares (4 ounces) unsweetened chocolate, melted

1 teaspoon vanilla
1½ cups softened butter

Glaze

    ½ *cup sieved apricot*   1 *tablespoon butter*
      preserves   ¼ *cup sliced almonds*
    1 *tablespoon rum*

1. Preheat oven to 375 degrees.
2. To prepare cake layers, beat the egg yolks until stiff. Gradually beat in ½ cup of the sugar until the mixture is light in color and very thick.
3. Beat in the almond extract.
4. Fold in the flour and the ground almonds. Beat the egg whites and salt together until the mixture forms soft peaks. Gradually beat in the remaining ¼ cup sugar and continue beating until meringue mixture is stiff and glossy.
5. Stir ¼ of the egg white mixture into the almond cake batter. Fold in the remaining egg white mixture gently, but completely.
6. Divide the batter between two 15-by-10-inch jellyroll pans that have been lined with wax paper, greased and lightly floured.
7. Bake 12 to 15 minutes or until the cake is golden and done. If only one jellyroll pan is available, hold the second half of the batter to use the same pan again once it has been cooled and relined.
8. Immediately when the cakes come from the oven, turn them upside down onto a kitchen towel, remove the wax paper and cut each layer into 4 equal strips about 3¾ inches wide by 10 inches long. Transfer to a cooling rack.
9. Meanwhile, prepare filling: Mix together the eggs and sugar in a heavy saucepan and heat gradually, while stirring with a wire whisk, until the sugar dissolves and the mixture thickens slightly, about 3 minutes. Do not allow to boil.
10. Remove from the heat and beat in the chocolate and vanilla. Gradually beat in the butter, a tablespoon or two at a time, until butter is absorbed and the mixture is smooth. Refrigerate until it is of spreading consistency.
11. For the glaze, mix the preserves with the rum and set aside. Heat the butter in a small skillet and toast the sliced almonds in it gently until golden. Do not allow to burn. Drain on paper towels.
12. To assemble the torte, place one layer of cake on a serving platter, spread with chocolate filling and continue adding alternate layers of cake and filling, ending with cake.
13. Brush the top layer with the apricot glaze and sprinkle with almonds. Chill several hours before serving.

Yield: 10 to 12 servings
Note: A Mouli grater or a Moulinex grinder is recommended for
grinding the nuts.

LEE'S MARLBOROUGH TART

2 medium-size Mc-Intosh apples, peeled, cored and thinly sliced	½ cup sugar
	⅔ cup heavy cream
	¼ cup sherry or Madeira
1 tablespoon water	3 eggs, well beaten
1 tablespoon light brown sugar	1 unbaked 9-inch pie shell
⅛ teaspoon cinnamon Grated rind and juice of 1 large lemon (about ¼ cup)	3 egg whites
	⅓ cup confectioners' sugar

1. Preheat oven to 400 degrees.
2. Place the apples and water in a small saucepan. Cover and
cook until tender. Add brown sugar and cinnamon and mix well.
Measure ½ cup of this applesauce into a bowl. The remaining applesauce is a snack for a kibitzer.
3. Add the lemon rind and juice, sugar, cream, the sherry and
eggs. Mix well and pour into pie shell. Bake 15 minutes, then reduce oven temperature to 325 degrees and bake 40 minutes longer
or until the filling is set and golden. Cool to room temperature.
4. Preheat oven to 350 degrees.
5. Beat the egg whites until frothy and gradually beat in the
confectioners' sugar until the mixture is thick and glossy. Pile on
top of the pie so that meringue touches the pastry edge at all points.
With the back of a spoon, decorate the surface. Bake 15 minutes or
until lightly browned.
Yield: 6 servings

College Get-Together

※

Sweet Sixteen parties are a thing of the past, but teenagers and college students do like to get together during vacations. Menus do not have to be more elaborate than hamburgers, hot dogs, chili or sloppy Joes, but the bit of extra effort it takes to fix chicken shortcake will be appreciated and the cost will not be much different. Chicken shortcake is a dish that can be kept warm until the teenagers decide to serve themselves.

Chicken Shortcake*
Pear and Pecan Slaw*
Strawberry Layer Cake*

CHICKEN SHORTCAKE

1 stewing chicken
(4½–5 pounds)
1 carrot, quartered
1 rib celery with
leaves, quartered
1 bay leaf
1 onion studded with
2 whole cloves
4 sprigs parsley
12 peppercorns
3½ cups chicken broth
or water
Salt
1 smoked pork butt
(1½–2 pounds)
Cold water

Freshly ground
black pepper
Butter
½ cup flour
12 small white onions
Boiling salted
water
1 pound mushrooms,
sliced
2 tablespoons dry
vermouth or dry
sherry (optional)
½ cup heavy cream
1 egg yolk
1 recipe herbed corn
bread (recipe
below)

1. Wash the chicken and place in a deep, heavy casserole, or Dutch oven, with the neck, gizzard and heart. Add the carrot, celery, bay leaf, onion studded with the cloves, the parsley, peppercorns and chicken broth or water. If water is used, add salt to taste.

2. Bring to a boil, cover and simmer gently for 1 hour or until chicken is tender. Allow to cool in the broth until chicken can be handled.

3. Meanwhile, place the pork butt in a saucepan and cover with cold water. Bring to a boil, cover and simmer 15 minutes to the pound or until the meat is tender. Allow to cool in the broth.

4. Remove the chicken from its broth. Strain the broth back into the cleaned casserole and boil to reduce to about 3 cups. Chill broth for several hours.

5. Remove the chicken in large chunks from the bones, discarding the skin and bones. Season chicken with salt and pepper to taste.

6. Cut the pork butt into 1-inch cubes and mix with chicken. Set aside. The pork broth can be reserved for later use in a bean or pea soup.

7. Remove chicken fat from the top of the chilled chicken broth and make up to ½ cup, adding butter if necessary.

8. Heat the chicken fat/butter in a saucepan, blend in the flour and gradually stir in the defatted broth. Bring to a boil, stirring until mixture thickens. Cook 5 minutes.

9. Melt 2 tablespoons butter in a skillet, add the onions and brown lightly. Transfer onions to a saucepan, add enough boiling salted water to barely cover and cook, covered, until almost tender. Drain.

10. Add the mushrooms to the butter left in the skillet and cook quickly, while stirring, until wilted. Stir the chicken, pork, mushrooms and cooked onions into the sauce. Cook until heated through. Stir in the vermouth or sherry.

11. Mix the cream and egg yolk. Add a little of the hot mixture, return to the bulk of the mixture and reheat, but do not boil. Season to taste with pepper. Serve over squares of hot herbed corn bread.

Yield: 6 to 8 servings

Herbed Corn Bread

1 *cup flour*	1 *cup buttermilk*
1 *tablespoon sugar*	3 *tablespoons melted*
1 *teaspoon salt*	*butter*
½ *teaspoon baking soda*	3 *tablespoons chopped parsley*
1½ *teaspoons baking powder*	1½ *tablespoons chopped fresh sage, or*
¾ *cup yellow cornmeal*	1½ *teaspoons crumbled dried*
2 *eggs, lightly beaten*	*leaf*

1. Preheat oven to 425 degrees.

2. Sift the flour, sugar, salt, baking soda and baking powder into a bowl. Add the cornmeal and mix.

3. Combine the eggs, buttermilk and butter. Stir in the parsley and sage. Stir into the dry ingredients just enough to moisten evenly. Turn into a greased 8-inch square baking pan. Bake 30 minutes or until brown and done.

Yield: 6 to 8 servings

PEAR AND PECAN SLAW

2 cups finely shredded
  green cabbage
1 cup finely shredded
  red cabbage
2 Bartlett or Bosc
  pears, halved, cored
  and diced
½ cup diced pecans
½ cup seeded grapes
½ cup mayonnaise,
  preferably home-
  made

1 tablespoon grated
  lemon rind
2 tablespoons lemon
  juice
2 tablespoons finely
  chopped, drained,
  preserved ginger, or
  crystallized ginger
¼ teaspoon salt

1. In a large bowl, combine the green cabbage, red cabbage, pears, pecans and grapes. Combine the remaining ingredients in a second bowl and pour over the cabbage mixture.

2. Toss lightly to mix. Chill well.

Yield: 6 servings

STRAWBERRY LAYER CAKE

Cake layers

2¼ cups sifted cake
   flour (do not use
   self-rising° flour,
   see note)
1½ cups sugar
3 teaspoons baking
   powder
1 teaspoon salt
½ cup salad oil

6 eggs, separated
1 teaspoon grated
  lemon rind
2 teaspoons lemon
  juice
¾ cup water
½ teaspoon cream of
  tartar

Filling

1 package (10
  ounces) sliced fro-
  zen strawberries,
  thawed

½ envelope unflavored
  gelatin
⅔ cup heavy cream,
  whipped

Frosting

½ cup plus 1 table- 　spoon butter	1½ teaspoons vanilla Red food coloring
1 cup sugar	(optional)
¼ cup light cream	Whole fresh straw-
2 cups confectioners' 　sugar, approxi- 　mately	berries or red rose- buds

1. Preheat oven to 350 degrees.

2. To prepare cake layers, sift together the flour, sugar, baking powder and salt into a mixing bowl. Add the oil, unbeaten egg yolks, lemon rind, juice and water. Beat until smooth.

3. Beat the egg whites and cream of tartar together until very stiff but not dry. Fold the yolk mixture into the whites until just blended. Do not overblend.

4. Pour into 3 ungreased 9-inch layer or heart-shaped layer pans. Bake 35 minutes or until done. To cool, invert pans by resting each on 2 other pans. With help of spatula, remove layers from pans when cool.

5. To prepare filling, remove 2 tablespoons juice from the strawberries and add to the gelatin. Puree remaining strawberries. Heat the soaked gelatin until it dissolves, add to puree and fold in the cream.

6. To prepare frosting, melt the butter and stir in the 1 cup sugar and the cream.

7. Bring the mixture to a boil, while stirring. Cool to room temperature. Meanwhile, stack the cake layers on a plate with the strawberry filling between the layers.

8. Add confectioners' sugar to frosting mixture until frosting is of spreading consistency. Stir in the vanilla and a drop or two of red coloring. Use immediately to cover the sides and top of the cake. Decorate with strawberries or top with rosebuds.

Yield: 10 servings

Note: If cake flour is not available, use 2 cups all-purpose flour.

Granola and other Good Snacks

✱

Making your own granola is one of the most satisfying projects for a wet spring weekend. Small fry can help and discover the feel and taste of the good-for-you ingredients that go into the crunchy stuff. Let the children eat it as a dry snack in a lunch box or while watching TV, with milk for breakfast and as a topping for ice cream and desserts. Before all the granola disappears, rescue two cupfuls to make a batch of lacy cookies. Even preschoolers can mix and shape no-bake almond snowballs, and one batch of apple-wheat germ cookies will make after-school snacks for a week.

Granola *
Lacy Granola Cookies *
No-Bake Chocolate Almond Snowballs *
Apple–Wheat Germ Cookies *

———◆•◆———

GRANOLA

2 cups old-fashioned rolled oats
½ cup chopped almonds
½ cup chopped raw cashews
½ cup unsweetened coconut
¼ cup sesame seeds
½ cup wheat germ
½ cup instant nonfat dry milk solids
½ cup oil
½ cup honey

1. Preheat over to 325 degrees.
2. In a large bowl, combine the oats, almonds, cashews, coconut, sesame seeds, wheat germ and dry milk.
3. Mix together the oil and honey and stir into the dry ingredients. Spread the mixture in a Teflon-lined jellyroll pan and bake about 30 minutes, stirring several times to allow even browning. Cool. Store in tightly covered containers.

Yield: About 8 cups

Note: Leftover granola can be eaten as a snack or cereal and used as a topping on hot desserts. Add raisins, chopped dried apricots and sunflower seeds for more texture and increased food value.

LACY GRANOLA COOKIES

1 *cup butter*	⅛ *teaspoon salt*
¾ *cup sugar*	1 *teaspoon baking*
¾ *cup light brown*	*soda*
sugar	2 *cups homemade*
1 *egg*	*granola (recipe*
1 *teaspoon vanilla*	*above)*
1 *tablespoon grated*	1 *cup raisins*
orange rind	½ *cup chopped*
1½ *cups flour*	*walnuts*

1. Preheat oven to 375 degrees.
2. Cream the butter with the sugars until light and fluffy. Beat in the egg, vanilla and orange rind.
3. Sift together the flour, salt and baking soda and stir into the butter mixture. Stir in the granola, raisins and walnuts.
4. Drop by teaspoonsful, at least 3 inches apart, onto an ungreased cookie sheet and bake 10 minutes or until browned.
5. Allow to rest on the cookie sheet for about 2 minutes, or until cookies become firm enough to remove to a wire rack to cool.

Yield: About 5 dozen 3-inch cookies

Note: To make thicker, less brittle cookies, mix ¼ to ½ cup plain wheat germ into the mixture before dropping onto cookie sheet.

No-Bake Chocolate Almond Snowballs

½ cup butter
4 squares (4 ounces) semisweet chocolate
1 teaspoon vanilla
1 cup finely ground almonds (almonds ground in an electric blender until very fine)
Unsweetened coconut, available in health food stores
1 cup toasted slivered almonds
3 tablespoons honey
⅛ teaspoon salt
½ cup wheat germ

1. Melt the butter and chocolate together over hot water or very low heat. Stir in the vanilla.
2. In a bowl, combine the ground almonds, 1 cup unsweetened coconut, the toasted slivered almonds, honey, salt and wheat germ. Stir in the melted butter mixture. Chill the mixture until it is firm enough to mold into balls.
3. Form the mixture into 1-inch balls and roll in unsweetened coconut. Set on a tray and chill until firm.
Yield: About 30 cookies

Apple–Wheat Germ Cookies

½ cup butter
1 cup light brown sugar
2 eggs
1½ cups flour
¼ cup old-fashioned rolled oats
¼ teaspoon salt
2 teaspoons baking powder
½ teaspoon cinnamon
¾ cup wheat germ
1 cup finely chopped, peeled and cored flavorful apples such as Rome, Macoun or Baldwin

1. Preheat oven to 350 degrees.
2. Cream the butter with the brown sugar until light. Beat in the eggs, one at a time.
3. Combine the remaining ingredients and stir into the creamed mixture. Drop by teaspoonsful onto a greased cookie sheet. Bake 12 to 15 minutes or until lightly browned. Cool on a rack.
Yield: 4 dozen cookies

Weekend Before April 15th

❈

According to nature's calendar, mid-April is a time to welcome spring flowers, the plentiful shad and the first asparagus of the season, but for many the weekend before April 15th is traumatic and frantic. It is the last chance to add up the columns and consult the charts in the income tax sweepstakes. Visions of expensive shad roe vanish as the final figures emerge, and it's smart to get out the pressure cooker and buy cheap cuts of meat. People seem to have forgotten the virtues of the pressure cooker, but it deserves to return to kitchen popularity—especially the new lightweight models. This spring and summer the smart cook will keep cool and save money, time and fuel the pressure-cooker way. The quick cassoulet only takes 30 minutes to prepare.

FRIDAY DINNER

Quick Cassoulet*
Tossed Salad
Broiled Grapefruit

SATURDAY LUNCH

Cottage Cheese Casserole*

SATURDAY DINNER

Chicken Giblet Stew*
Homemade Noodles*
Beet Salad
Raisin Pie*

SUNDAY DINNER

Eggplant and Beef Casserole*
Greek Salad
Fresh Pear Fritters*

QUICK CASSOULET

1 pound navy or pea beans	1 pound sweet Italian sausages, halved
Water	1 large onion, sliced
Salt	1 clove garlic, finely chopped
2 pounds breast of lamb, excess fat removed, and meat cut into bite-size pieces	Freshly ground black pepper to taste
¼ pound salt pork, cut into small dice	1 bay leaf
	4 cups chicken broth or water
	3 sprigs parsley

1. Soak the beans overnight in water to cover with 1 tablespoon salt added.

2. Next day, drain the beans well. Heat the pressure cooker and add the lamb pieces and salt pork and cook, stirring, until meat is browned. Remove meat and reserve. Pour off and discard fat.

3. Add sausages to the pressure cooker and cook until browned. Pour off fat. Return lamb to pan. Add onion, garlic, pepper, bay leaf, broth or water, the parsley, beans and 1 teaspoon salt.

4. *Following manufacturer's directions*, close the cover securely. Place pressure regulator on vent pipe and cook 30 minutes. Allow pressure to drop of its own accord.

Yield: 6 servings

COTTAGE CHEESE CASSEROLE

4 *eggs, separated*	1 *teaspoon lemon*
2 *cups sieved dry, or*	*juice*
pot-style, cottage	1 *tablespoon snipped*
cheese (12 ounces)	*fresh dill weed*
½ *cup mayonnaise*	

1. Preheat oven to 350 degrees.
2. Beat the egg yolks in a large bowl until light and thick. Gradually add the cottage cheese, mayonnaise, lemon juice and dill, beating until smooth.
3. Beat the egg whites until stiff but not dry and fold into the cheese mixture. Pour into a greased 1-quart soufflé dish. Bake 40 to 45 minutes or until a knife inserted halfway between center and edge comes out clean. Serve immediately.

Yield: 4 servings

CHICKEN GIBLET STEW

¾ *pound chicken*	¼ *cup salad or olive*
gizzards	*oil*
¼ *pound chicken*	1 *clove garlic, finely*
hearts	*chopped*
2 *cups chicken broth*	¼ *pound mushrooms,*
or water	*sliced (optional)*
1 *onion, chopped*	1 *cup diced celery*
1 *bay leaf, crumbled*	1 *cup diced carrots*
Salt and freshly	½ *teaspoon basil*
ground black pepper	½ *teaspoon marjoram*
1 *pound chicken*	½ *teaspoon thyme*
livers, cut into bite-	1 *recipe homemade*
size pieces	*noodles (recipe*
¼ *cup flour*	*below), cooked al*
1 *tablespoon butter*	*dente and drained*

1. Wash the gizzards and hearts very well and place in a saucepan with the broth or water, the onion, bay leaf and salt and pepper to taste. Bring to a boil, cover and simmer until tender, about 45 minutes.

2. Remove the gizzards and hearts, chop finely and reserve. Reserve the broth.

3. Coat the liver pieces with the flour seasoned with salt and pepper; reserve any remaining seasoned flour. Heat the butter and 2 tablespoons of the oil in a heavy skillet.

4. Fry the livers in it quickly until browned on all sides. Remove and reserve. Add the remaining oil, the garlic and mushrooms to the skillet and cook 2 minutes. Add celery and carrots and cook 3 minutes, stirring occasionally.

5. Add the reserved broth and chopped gizzards and hearts, bring to a boil, cover and simmer until vegetables are barely tender, about 12 minutes.

6. Add reserved liver pieces, any remaining seasoned flour, the basil, marjoram, thyme and salt and pepper to taste.

7. Heat, stirring, until mixture thickens slightly; cook three minutes longer. Serve over homemade noodles.

Yield: 4 servings

Note: Any combination of gizzards, hearts, wings and necks may be used in the broth, but all bones and skin should be discarded before dicing.

HOMEMADE NOODLES

2¼ cups flour
1 teaspoon salt
1 tablespoon salad or
    olive oil

3 eggs
1 tablespoon water,
    approximately

1. Place the flour and salt on a board and make a well in the center. Add the oil, eggs and 1 tablespoon water to the well.

2. With the fingers, gradually draw the flour into the wet ingredients and combine. Flours vary in their ability to absorb moisture, so it may be necessary to add 1 or 2 more teaspoons of water to make a dough stiff enough to be kneaded.

3. Knead the dough on a lightly floured board until smooth and satiny, about 10 minutes. Cover and let rest 15 minutes.

4. Roll out the dough, using as little extra flour as possible, to a rectangle about 12 by 30 inches long. The dough will be thin and hang over the edge of the board. Set on a towel and let dry, about 20 minutes.

5. Roll from the short side like a jellyroll. For fine soup noodles, cut ⅛-inch slices, or for wider noodles, about ¼-inch slices.

6. Separate the coils of noodles. Spread out and let dry completely, about 1 hour, before using or storing in closed container.

Yield: About ½ pound

Note: To cook, add the noodles to a large kettle of boiling salted water and cook quickly 6 to 8 minutes. Drain. Toss with melted butter.

RAISIN PIE

1¼ cups flour	½ cup golden raisins
¼ teaspoon salt	½ cup chopped, un-
⅔ cup shortening	salted peanuts
2 tablespoons plus ½	2 eggs, well beaten
cup butter	2 teaspoons vinegar
1 egg yolk	¼ teaspoon ground
Ice water	cloves
1 cup sugar	¼ teaspoon grated
½ cup unsweetened	nutmeg
or freshly grated	¼ teaspoon cinnamon
shredded coconut	Whipped cream

1. Place the flour, salt, shortening and 2 tablespoons of the butter in a bowl. Work the fat into the flour until mixture resembles coarse oatmeal.

2. Preheat oven to 350 degrees.

3. Stir into the flour mixture the egg yolk and enough ice water to make a pastry dough. Turn onto a lightly floured board and roll out to fit a 9-inch pie plate. Place in pie plate.

4. Trim and decorate the edge of the pastry. Chill pie shell while making the filling.

5. Heat the remaining ½ cup butter until it melts. Stir in the remaining ingredients except whipped cream and pour into the pie shell. Bake 40 minutes or until filling is puffed and brown. Serve pie warm or cold, topped with whipped cream.

Yield: 6 servings

EGGPLANT AND BEEF CASSEROLE

1 medium-size egg-
  plant
  Salt
  Flour
  Oil
1½ pounds ground
  beef chuck
1 clove garlic, finely
  chopped
1 small onion, finely
  chopped

2 tablespoons chop-
  ped parsley
⅛ teaspoon grated
  nutmeg
½ teaspoon marjoram
  Freshly ground
  black pepper
2 cups drained, can-
  ned Italian plum
  tomatoes, or home-
  made tomato sauce

1. Preheat oven to 375 degrees.
2. Peel and slice the eggplant. Sprinkle with salt and let stand 10 minutes. Rinse slices in cold water. Dip in flour.
3. Heat 2 to 3 tablespoons oil in a skillet, add the slices of eggplant and brown on both sides. Drain.
4. In a bowl, mix together the beef, garlic, onion, parsley, nutmeg, marjoram and salt and pepper to taste.
5. In a greased casserole, alternate layers of eggplant, beef and tomatoes, ending with tomatoes. Bake 40 minutes or until eggplant is tender.
Yield: 4 servings

FRESH PEAR FRITTERS

4 fresh, almost-ripe
  Anjou or Bosc pears
1 cup flour
1 tablespoon plus
  ½ cup sugar
1 teaspoon baking
  powder
¼ teaspoon salt
2 eggs, lightly beaten
½ cup milk
1 tablespoon melted
  butter

¾ teaspoon grated
  lemon rind
  Fat or oil for deep-
  frying
1 tablespoon corn-
  starch
¾ cup water
¼ cup lemon juice
¼ teaspoon grated
  nutmeg

1. Cut each pear into 8 wedges and remove the core. Sift the flour, 1 tablespoon sugar, the baking powder and salt into a mixing bowl.

2. Combine the eggs, milk, butter and ½ teaspoon of the grated lemon rind and pour over the dry ingredients. Mix well.

3. Dip pear wedges into the batter and fry, a few at a time, in the fat or oil heated to 375 degrees, until golden. Drain on paper towels and keep warm until all are fried.

4. Meanwhile, combine the remaining ½ cup sugar and the cornstarch in a saucepan. Stir in the water and bring mixture to a boil, stirring constantly. Cook 2 minutes. Remove from the heat.

5. Stir in the lemon juice, remaining ¼ teaspoon lemon rind and the nutmeg and serve separately with pear fritters.

Yield: 4 servings

Square Dance Buffet

✳

Everybody brings a dish to share when the "swing your partner, do-si-do" sounds of the caller are hushed for a well-earned intermission. The fiddlers continue to play as the square dancers line up at the buffet. This menu doesn't require a kitchen for serving if the hot dishes are carried in heavy casseroles and set over hot plates or in chafing dishes. Let three dancers each make a cheese tart, in disposable pie plates, to cut for appetizers, and two or three can help make a batch of ragout. The more hands there are to shape the elephant ear cookies, the quicker the frying and dusting will go. Two or three per person will not be too many once the first samples have disappeared, especially if there is apple cider or punch to sip.

*Cheese Tart**
*Ragout de Boeuf Jerome**
Pilaf
*Elephant Ear Cookies**

CHEESE TART

Pastry

1½ cups unbleached white flour	½ cup salad oil
1 teaspoon salt	2 tablespoons skim milk powder or
2 tablespoons wheat germ	non-fat dry milk solids

Filling

1–2 tablespoons butter	2 tablespoons flour
2 large onions, sliced	1 teaspoon salt
1½ cups evaporated skim milk	½ teaspoon worcestershire sauce
4 ounces Cheddar cheese, diced	¼ teaspoon freshly ground black pepper
4 ounces Swiss cheese, diced	2 tablespoons freshly grated Parmesan cheese
2 eggs	

1. To prepare pastry, sift the flour and salt into an 8- or 9-inch metal pie plate. Stir in the wheat germ.

2. Measure the oil in a cup, add the milk to the oil and beat with a fork until creamy. Pour into the center of the dry ingredients and mix with a fork to moisten.

3. Press the mixture evenly against the sides of the plate. Cover with clear plastic wrap and refrigerate at least 1 hour.

4. Preheat oven to 400 degrees.

5. In a heavy skillet, heat the butter, add the onions and cook over medium-low heat until they are soft but not brown. Set aside.

6. Place the milk in an electric blender. Add the Cheddar cheese, Swiss cheese, eggs, flour, salt, worcestershire and pepper. Blend until mixture is smooth.

7. Place the onions in the bottom of the chilled pie crust and pour the mixture from the blender over. Sprinkle with Parmesan cheese and bake 20 minutes. Reduce oven heat to 325 degrees and bake 20 minutes longer or until set.

Yield: 6 appetizer servings

Ragout de Boeuf Jerome

2 tablespoons butter	2 tablespoons flour
2 medium-size onions, finely chopped	2 tablespoons dried cèpes (mushrooms imported from France)
3 large cloves garlic, finely chopped	1 tablespoon sweet Hungarian paprika
5 pounds trimmed chicken steak (cut from very tender part of the beef chuck), fat and gristle removed, and meat cut into large cubes	¼ cup tomato paste
	1½ cups dry red wine, approximately
	1 bay leaf
	Salt to taste
	1½ tablespoons mushroom powder

1. Heat the butter in a heavy casserole and sauté in it the onions and garlic until golden. Add the meat, sprinkle with flour and cook, stirring, about 5 minutes or until meat is sealed all around but not browned.

2. Add the remaining ingredients including enough wine to come about ¾ of the way up the meat. Bring to a boil, cover and simmer 1½ hours, or until meat is tender. Remove meat to a warm dish and reduce the gravy by boiling until it is slightly thickened. Pour over the meat.

Yield: 15 servings

Elephant Ear Cookies

3 large eggs	2 cups confectioners' sugar
¼ teaspoon salt	
1 tablespoon plus 2 cups granulated sugar	1 teaspoon powdered cardamom
2 tablespoons plus 4 cups oil	⅔ cup finely ground pistachios (a Mouli grater is best for this)
1 cup milk	
4¼ cups flour, approximately	1 cup water

1. Beat the eggs in the large bowl of an electric mixer. Add the salt, 1 tablespoon granulated sugar, 2 tablespoons oil and the milk and beat to mix.

2. Gradually beat in enough flour to form a soft dough. It will be slightly sticky. Turn onto a floured board and knead for 10 minutes or until smooth and elastic. Cover and let rest 10 minutes.

3. Cut the dough into eighths. Roll out each piece as thinly as possible on a floured board. Lift the dough over the back of the hand and with the fingers of the other hand gradually pull and stretch the dough until it is paper thin, as in making strudel.

4. Cut each dough piece into 12 3½-inch rounds and flute one side of each round to make an approximation of an elephant's ear. Odd-shaped pieces can be left that way rather than rolled again. Fry the cookies, about 4 at a time, in the remaining oil heated to 345 to 350 degrees, until golden; turn to brown the other side. Drain on paper towels.

5. Meanwhile, combine the confectioners' sugar, cardamom and pistachios in a bowl. Place the remaining 2 cups granulated sugar and the water in a small saucepan. Heat, stirring, until sugar dissolves and then simmer 5 minutes.

6. Dip drained cookies in the syrup and then in the pistachio mixture. Set on a rack to cool.

Yield: 96 elephant ear cookies

Dining à Deux

Two for dinner with no leftovers is a challenge, but setting the scene is no problem—a candlelit corner of a city apartment will do and it doesn't have to have a view of the skyline if there are fresh flowers, gleaming crystal, silver and a warm welcome. And to make it a special occasion you don't have to spend most of next week's food budget if you follow the menu below.

Avocado Halves with Vinaigrette Dressing
Chutney Chicken*
Pilaf
Stir-Fried Green Beans
Bibb Lettuce Salad
Strawberry Fluff*

CHUTNEY CHICKEN

1 chicken (2½ pounds), cut into serving pieces
Salt and freshly ground black pepper
3 tablespoons oil
1 tart apple, chopped
1 rib celery, chopped
1 onion, chopped
1 carrot, chopped
2 tablespoons curry powder, or to taste

1 tablespoon flour
½ cup orange juice
2 teaspoons grated orange rind
¾ cup chicken broth
⅓ cup chopped mango chutney
1 bay leaf, crumbled
1 small navel orange, sectioned (optional)

1. Season the chicken pieces with salt and pepper. Heat the oil in a skillet and brown the chicken pieces in it on all sides. Remove chicken and keep warm.
    2. Add the apple, celery, onion and carrot to the oil remaining in the skillet and cook, stirring, 4 minutes.
    3. Sprinkle with the curry powder and flour and cook, stirring, 1 minute longer. Gradually stir in the orange juice and rind, the chicken broth, chutney, bay leaf and salt and pepper to taste.
    4. Bring to a boil, return chicken to the skillet, cover and simmer 30 minutes or until chicken is tender. Garnish with orange segments if desired.

Yield: 2 servings

STRAWBERRY FLUFF

1 cup sliced fresh strawberries	¾ cup vanilla wafer crumbs
⅓ cup sugar	¼ teaspoon grated nutmeg
1½ teaspoons unflavored gelatin	2 tablespoons melted butter
1 tablespoon lemon juice	Strawberry syrup, optional (available in specialty food stores)
1 teaspoon grated lemon rind	
2 egg whites	Whipped cream
Pinch salt	

1. Place the strawberries in an electric blender and blend until smooth, or mash with a fork.
    2. In a small saucepan combine ½ cup of the puree with 3 tablespoons sugar, gelatin, lemon juice and lemon rind. Place over low heat and stir until gelatin dissolves.
    3. Stir in remaining strawberry puree. Cool slightly.
    4. Beat the egg whites with the salt until foamy.
    5. Gradually beat in the remaining sugar and continue beating until stiff peaks are formed. Fold in the berry mixture.
    6. Set the mixture in a bowl of crushed ice and whisk with a wire whisk until mixture holds the imprint of the beater.
    7. Combine the wafer crumbs, nutmeg and butter and mix well.

8. Spoon ⅓ of the strawberry mixture into a serving dish. Sprinkle with half the crumbs. Spoon another third of the berry mixture over the crumbs and top with remaining strawberry mixture.

9. Chill several hours or overnight. Serve with strawberry syrup if desired and whipped cream.

Yield: 2 servings

Vegetarian Dinner

✖

Pack an extra punch of nutrition into meals the weekend everyone decides to turn vegetarian. When the food is made to taste good, it could become a once-a-week habit and it could help the budget. This particular combination is fancy enough to offer as brunch, lunch or dinner to the most fastidious tastemakers if you pour a chilled Moselle or a Tavel Rose.

*Mushroom Chowder**
*Tiens**
*Cauliflower with Pumpkin Seed Sauce**
*Pearl Gordon's High Protein Muffins**
*Brown Rice Apple Betty**

———————— ◆•◆ ————————

MUSHROOM CHOWDER

¼ pound butter
1 cup finely chopped onion
1 cup diced celery
1 cup diced carrot
¼ cup diced white turnip
¾ pound mushrooms, sliced
1 cup skinned, seeded and chopped ripe tomatoes

1 cup diced potatoes
4 cups boiling vegetable-flavored broth or chicken broth
½ teaspoon thyme
1 tablespoon chopped parsley
Salt and freshly ground black pepper to taste

1. Melt the butter in a heavy kettle and sauté the onion in it until tender but not browned. Add the celery, carrot and turnip and cook 5 minutes. Add the mushrooms and cook 3 minutes longer.

2. Add the remaining ingredients. Simmer, covered, until the vegetables are tender but not mushy, about 10 minutes.

Yield: 6 servings

TIENS

2 tablespoons un-salted butter

3 tablespoons olive oil

2 pounds fresh spin-ach, roughly chopped

2 pounds Swiss chard, roughly chopped

3 medium-size onions, chopped

3 cloves garlic, finely chopped

6 small zucchini, finely diced

1 small green pepper, seeded and finely diced

1 cup chopped fresh basil leaves

½ cup finely chop-ped parsley

1½ teaspoons salt

¼ teaspoon freshly ground black pepper

8 eggs, beaten

¾ cup freshly grated Romano cheese

¾ cup freshly grated Jarlsberg or Swiss cheese

½ cup fresh bread crumbs

1. Place the butter and oil in a large heavy kettle. Add the spin-ach and chard and cook, covered, until leaves wilt.

2. Preheat oven to 375 degrees.

3. Remove the greens to a fine strainer and press out all the liquid. Return the greens to the kettle and reserve the liquid for soup or stew. Add the onions, garlic, zucchini and green pepper to the kettle and cook, covered, until vegetables are barely tender, stirring occasionally.

4. Transfer vegetables to a strainer and press out every vestige of liquid. Combine the vegetables with the basil, parsley, salt and

pepper and divide between 2 well-buttered 9-inch or 10-inch scalloped earthenware quiche pans or pie plates.

5. Pour half the eggs over each pie. Sprinkle half of each cheese and half the bread crumbs over each pie. Bake 25 to 30 minutes. Serve warm or chilled.

Yield: 6 servings

CAULIFLOWER WITH PUMPKIN SEED SAUCE

1 *medium-size cauli-flower*
Boiling salted water
½ *cup shelled pump-kin seeds (available in health food stores)*
¼ *cup blanched al-monds*
¼ *teaspoon cumin seeds*

1 *clove garlic, finely chopped*
3 *canned hot green chilies, seeded and chopped*
¼ *cup chopped parsley*
¾ *cup vegetable-fla-vored broth or chicken broth*
½ *cup grated sharp Cheddar cheese (optional)*

1. Break the cauliflower into flowerets. Pour boiling water into a saucepan to a depth of 1 inch. Place the flowerets in the pan stem down in the water. Cover and cook quickly until barely tender, about 10 minutes.

2. Meanwhile, place the pumpkin seeds, almonds and cumin seeds in a skillet over medium heat. Toss frequently until lightly browned.

3. Place the browned seeds and nuts in an electric blender and blend 30 seconds.

4. Add the garlic, chilies and parsley and blend until smooth.

5. Turn into a saucepan. Gradually stir in the broth, bring to a boil and simmer 3 minutes.

6. Drain the cauliflower and arrange in a baking dish. Pour the sauce over and serve immediately. Or, sprinkle with the grated cheese and place under a preheated broiler until cheese melts.

Yield: 6 servings

PEARL GORDON'S HIGH PROTEIN MUFFINS

2 cups soy flour
1 cup nonfat dry
milk solids
1 teaspoon salt
1 teaspoon baking
powder
1 cup pitted, chopped
dates

1 cup chopped nuts
3 eggs
3 tablespoons oil or
melted butter
Grated rind of 1
orange
¾ cup orange juice
3 tablespoons honey

1. Preheat oven to 325 degrees.

2. Sift the soy flour, milk solids, salt and baking powder into a bowl. Add the dates and nuts and rub flour mixture through them with the fingers.

3. Combine the remaining ingredients in an electric blender and blend well. Stir into the dry ingredients until just moistened. Spoon into greased, medium-size muffin tins. Bake 25 minutes or until done. Cool on a rack.

Yield: About 18 muffins

BROWN RICE APPLE BETTY

1 cup raw brown rice
Water
¼ teaspoon salt
4 medium-size apples
(preferably McIn-
tosh), cored and
sliced

1 teaspoon cinnamon
½ cup chopped wal-
nuts
¼ cup lemon juice
½ cup honey
¼ cup unsweetened
shredded coconut

1. Place the rice, 2½ cups water and the salt in a heavy saucepan. Bring to a boil, cover and simmer very gently, without stirring, about 40 minutes or until rice is barely tender. Add more water if necessary.

2. Preheat oven to 350 degrees.

3. Mix the apples, cinnamon, walnuts and lemon juice together. Oil a deep 9-inch or 10-inch pie plate.

4. Spread half the cooked rice in the bottom of the plate. Top with half the apple mixture and cover with remaining rice and then remaining apple mixture. Drizzle the honey over all. Sprinkle with coconut. Bake 30 minutes or until apples are tender.

Yield: 6 servings

Ulla's Friday Night Supper

✕

Ulla Anobile entertains friends according to the traditions of her native Finland. And, she is a superb cook. An invitation to "come at eight Friday evening" promises interesting people, good conversation, beer and, later, an unusual supper. Guests fill their own rye cakes with the rice and egg mixture to eat with their fingers. Cucumber caviar and liver pâté are spread on toast triangles.

Sultsinat (Old Carelian Rye Cakes)*
Kerkkukaviaari (Cucumber Caviar)*
Maksatahna (Liver Paste)*

———◆•◆———

SULTSINAT (Old Carelian Rye Cakes)

Cakes

Rye flour	1 cup water
1 cup unbleached white flour	4 tablespoons softened butter
1 teaspoon salt	

Filling

6 tablespoons softened butter	½ teaspoon salt, or to taste
2 cups hot, cooked rice	2 hard-cooked eggs, chopped

1. To prepare cakes, place 2 cups rye flour, the white flour and salt in a bowl. Pour in the water and work with the hands to make a dough. Add more water if necessary.

2. Sprinkle a board with rye flour and shape dough on it into a roll about 2 inches in diameter. Cut the roll into 20 equal-size pieces.

3. Sprinkle each piece of dough with rye flour and roll out into a very thin round cake, about 8 inches in diameter.

4. Heat a heavy 6- to 8-inch skillet until very hot. Do not grease the pan. Fry the cakes quickly in the skillet until dark brown spots appear on the underside of each cake and the top is blistered.

5. Spread with butter, stack on an ovenproof plate, cover with a slightly damp towel or napkin and keep warm while cooking remainder of cakes. The pan should be brushed out with a dry towel between cakes.

6. To prepare filling, mix all the ingredients together. Set the napkin-covered stack of cakes by a bowl of filling for guests to fill their own cakes, roll them up and eat them with their fingers.

Yield: 6 to 8 servings

KERKKUKAVIAARI (Cucumber Caviar)

2 medium-size barrel dill pickles, finely chopped

½ European-style un-peeled cucumber or 2 small regular cucumbers, peeled, halved and seeded

2 hard-cooked eggs, chopped

1 small onion, grated

2 tablespoons soft bread crumbs

2 tablespoons Dijon or Düsseldorf mustard, or to taste

1 teaspoon sugar

½ teaspoon freshly ground white pepper, or to taste

¼ cup heavy cream, whipped

Thin toast squares

1. Chop the pickles and cucumber very finely. Place in a sieve and squeeze out as much of the liquid as possible.

2. Place drained mixture in a bowl and add the eggs, onion, bread crumbs, mustard, sugar and pepper. Mix well. Fold in the

cream. Pour into a serving bowl and chill. Serve with thin toast squares.

Yield: 6 to 8 servings

Maksatahna (Liver Paste)

10 tablespoons soft- ened butter	¼ teaspoon caraway seeds, ground in a
1½ pounds chicken livers	mortar with a pestle
2 tablespoons cognac	Salt and freshly
1 cup finely grated Swiss cheese	ground black pep- per to taste
½ cup finely grated Romano or Parme- san cheese	Toast squares

1. Heat 2 tablespoons of the butter in a heavy skillet, add the chicken livers and cook quickly over high heat until browned on all sides. Remove livers and chop finely.

2. Add the cognac to the skillet and stir to loosen all the browned-on particles.

3. Beat the remaining butter until light and creamy. Add the livers, cheeses, cognac mixture, caraway seeds, salt and pepper. Mash and beat well with a wooden spoon. Turn into a buttered bowl or crock. Chill at least 2 hours.

4. Unmold onto a serving plate or serve from a crock, with toast squares.

Yield: 6 to 8 servings

SUMMER

Summer Picnic

Incredibly elegant fitted hampers toted aboard a yacht or a Piper Cub or in an Alfa Romeo, should provide more than a peanut butter sandwich and a banana. A weekend jaunt to a private island or a visit to the annual sports-car rally calls for a carefully chosen assortment of luncheon dishes to share with other outdoor enthusiasts. Marinated shrimp and rice salad will look appetizing, and taste delectable, with tiny sandwiches plucked from a hollowed-out loaf carrier. Transport cherries and strawberries in plastic containers for dessert, and lager beer in a cooler. No fitted hamper? When you are hungry, this picnic food will taste the same from paper plates and brown paper bags stowed in the back of a station wagon.

*Shrimp Sausalito**
*California-Style Rice Salad**
*Sandwiches-in-a-Loaf**
Cherries
Strawberries

SHRIMP SAUSALITO

¾ cup oil
⅓ cup lemon juice
½ cup brandy
¼ cup chopped scal-
  lions
¼ cup chopped parsley
1 tablespoon chopped
  fresh tarragon, or 1
  teaspoon dried

Salt and freshly
ground black pepper
to taste
3 pounds large
  shrimp, cooked,
  shelled and de-
  veined

1. In a bowl, combine all ingredients but the shrimp.
2. Add the shrimp, toss to coat them all and marinate overnight, stirring several times. Transport in an insulated cooler with ice packs.
   Yield: 8 to 10 servings

CALIFORNIA-STYLE RICE SALAD

4 cups cooked long-
  grain rice, chilled
1 bunch scallions,
  finely chopped
2 tomatoes, skinned
  and cut into wedges
1 avocado
  Lemon juice
1 package frozen arti-
  choke hearts, cooked
  according to pack-
  age directions and
  cooled
1 green pepper, diced
1 sweet red pepper,
  diced
1 cucumber, peeled
  and diced
1 cup diced celery

1 can (1¾ ounces)
  flat anchovies,
  chopped
1 can (9½ ounces)
  solid white tuna,
  broken into chunks
1 can (6 ounces) pit-
  ted black olives,
  drained
4 hard-cooked eggs
  Salt and freshly
  ground black pepper
  to taste
½ cup olive oil
3 tablespoons wine
  vinegar
1 teaspoon Düsseldorf
  mustard
  Watercress

1. Place the rice in a large bowl and add the scallions and tomatoes.

2. Peel and cube the avocado, toss in lemon juice to coat, drain and add to the rice mixture. Toss the artichoke hearts in lemon juice, drain and add to the bowl.

3. Add the green and red peppers, cucumber, celery, anchovies and tuna. Reserve 8 to 10 olives for garnish and add remaining olives to rice mixture. Chop 2 eggs roughly and add. Add salt and black pepper. Toss to mix.

4. Combine the oil, vinegar and mustard, mix well and pour over the rice salad. Toss, cover and chill well.

5. Slice or quarter the remaining eggs and use with watercress and the reserved olives to garnish the salad. Transport in an insulated container with ice packs.

Yield: 8 servings

SANDWICHES-IN-A-LOAF

1 large round loaf
(about 1–2 pounds)
rye, potato or
cottage-style white
bread
1 loaf pumpernickel,
thinly sliced

11 ounces softened
cream cheese
Celery salt to taste
1 bunch watercress

1. Cut a slice off the top of the round loaf and set aside. With the fingers, scoop out the bread from the center of the loaf, leaving a shell ¼ to ½ inch thick. The bread can be used in a stuffing or bread pudding or dried for crumbs.

2. Trim the pumpernickel slices to make neat stacks of slices. Spread one side of each slice with cream cheese seasoned with celery salt. Arrange watercress on half the slices and cover with remaining slices.

3. Place sandwiches in the hollowed-out loaf, cover with reserved top slice and wrap in clear plastic. The sandwiches will stay fresh for hours if the loaf is in a fairly cool place.

Yield: 8 servings

Kebab Beach Party

Informal, cook-your-own barbecue parties that involve more than just hamburgers and hot dogs can be a disaster. The one exception is the kebab barbecue where individual skewers have been threaded with a variety of well-marinated tidbits that will cook in five minutes or less. Plates are optional unless you plan to serve bowls of rice with the kebabs. Small hibachis wedged into the rocks on the beach, or set on the wall around a patio, work better than a large grill. And, don't forget the asbestos mittens to prevent scorched fingers. An insulated rice cooker or a wide-mouthed Thermos will keep rice warm enough to serve without reheating. Top off the party with homemade ice cream brought to the scene in the ice cream maker packed with a freezing mixture, or, for even more fun, ask guests to crank an old, hand-turned machine and make their own.

Vegetable, Lamb, Beef,
Chicken, and Shrimp and Scallop Kebabs*
Fruit Ice Cream*

VEGETABLE KEBABS

1 small eggplant, unpeeled and cubed

2 small zucchini, cut into 1-inch slices

2 small yellow squash, cut into 1-inch slices

1 pint cherry tomatoes

½ pound mushroom caps

1 large green pepper, cubed

1. Steam the eggplant, zucchini and yellow squash separately over boiling water for 6 to 8 minutes, but do not let them go limp.

2. Alternating light and dark colors, thread all vegetables onto individual bamboo skewers that have been soaked in water. Brush with some of the marinade from the meat or fish that the vegetables are to be eaten with and cook over hot coals until done, turning often.

Yield: 10 to 12 skewers

LAMB KEBABS

½ cup olive oil
2 tablespoons lemon juice
2 cloves garlic, finely chopped
½ bay leaf, crumbled
1 tablespoon chopped fresh mint

1 teaspoon salt
½ teaspoon freshly ground black pepper
1½ pounds boned leg of lamb, cut into 1-inch cubes

1. Combine all the ingredients except the lamb in a glass or ceramic bowl. Mix well. Add the lamb, toss and refrigerate 2 to 4 hours. Stir occasionally.

2. Thread lamb cubes onto individual bamboo skewers that have been soaked in water. Cook over hot coals about 8 minutes or until done to desired degree.

Yield: 8 skewers

BEEF KEBABS

⅔ cup oil
¼ cup wine vinegar
1 onion, sliced
1 bay leaf
½ teaspoon thyme
1 teaspoon salt
½ teaspoon freshly ground black pepper

½ teaspoon crushed dried red pepper (optional)
1 pound well-trimmed top round, cut into 1-inch cubes

1. In a ceramic or glass bowl, combine all the ingredients except the beef. Mix well. Add the beef cubes, toss and marinate in the refrigerator 2 to 4 hours. Stir occasionally.

2. Thread beef cubes onto individual bamboo skewers that have been soaked in water. Cook over hot coals about 8 minutes or until meat is browned but still pink in the middle.

Yield: 4 to 6 skewers

CHICKEN KEBABS

¼ cup soy sauce
1 tablespoon dry sherry
1 scallion, finely chopped
1 tablespoon finely chopped fresh ginger

¼ teaspoon sugar
2 whole chicken breasts, skinned, boned and cut into 1-inch cubes

1. In a glass or ceramic bowl, combine the soy sauce, sherry, scallion, ginger and sugar. Add the chicken pieces, toss to coat and let stand at room temperature 30 to 60 minutes.

2. Thread chicken cubes onto individual bamboo skewers that have been soaked in water. Grill over hot coals about 10 minutes or until done, turning frequently.

Yield: 4 to 6 servings

SHRIMP AND SCALLOP KEBABS

1 cup oil
¼ cup lemon juice
Salt and freshly ground black pepper to taste
1 clove garlic, finely chopped
1 tablespoon snipped fresh dill weed

3 shallots, finely chopped
1 tablespoon chopped parsley
1 pound raw shrimp, shelled and de-veined
1 pound sea scallops

1. In a glass or ceramic bowl, combine the oil, lemon juice, salt and pepper. Divide mixture in half and add garlic and dill to one and shallots and parsley to the other.

2. Add the shrimp to the garlic marinade and the scallops to the shallot mixture. Cover bowls and marinate about 20 minutes, stirring occasionally.

3. Thread shrimp and scallops onto individual bamboo skewers that have been soaked in water. Cook over hot coals about 6 minutes or until shrimp are pink and scallops opaque, turning several times.

Yield: 8 to 12 skewers

FRUIT ICE CREAM

3 cups milk
3 cups sugar
1½ cups heavy cream
1 can (13½ ounces)
  evaporated milk
  Electric or hand-
  cranked ice cream
  maker
  Boiling water
  Crushed ice
  Rock salt

1 teaspoon grated
  lemon rind
¾ cup lemon juice
2 teaspoons grated
  orange rind
1½ cups orange juice
3 ripe bananas,
  mashed
1½ cups undrained,
  crushed pineapple

1. Heat the milk and sugar together, stirring until the sugar dissolves. Add the cream and evaporated milk, cool and chill.

2. Prepare ice cream container and dasher according to manufacturer's instructions. This usually includes washing and rinsing.

3. Fill the container with boiling water. Pour water off and allow to cool.

4. Place the dasher in position and pour in the chilled milk and cream mixture. The container should not be more than ¾ full to allow for expansion.

5. Set the container in the bucket and fit lid and crank or motor in place. Measure about 8 quarts crushed ice and 3 cups rock salt. Pack a 2-inch layer of ice around the container, sprinkle with 3 or 4 tablespoons rock salt and continue layers until bucket is full.

6. Set machine going or start cranking and freeze for about 30

minutes or until mixture is partly frozen. Replace layers of ice and salt as needed. Check the drain hole in the bucket frequently to make sure drain hole is open at all times.

7. Add the remaining ingredients to the container and continue to freeze until machine slows or stops. Take care that no salt or ice gets into the hole in top of the container.

8. Pack the ice cream into containers and freeze, or remove the dasher, cover can and set in empty bucket. Pack with 4 parts crushed ice to 1 part rock salt and season 1 to 2 hours.

Yield: 1 gallon

Sixteen for Dinner Without Going Bankrupt

Or wearing yourself to a frazzle.

Arroz con pollo is the answer, and if the number of guests doubles before you get to the market, the recipe can be doubled. Then there are all those different drink orders to worry about. Have you remembered the tonic water, limes, new bottle of Canadian Club and Triple Sec for the Margaritas? Forget them for once and fix pitchers of fruit-filled sangria and you won't have to make dessert unless the budget and time allow. Two easy-to-make flans will serve 16. Set up a buffet on the porch or terrace and guests can help themselves and no one is stuck in a corner.

Bob Medina's Arroz con Pollo*
Sangria*
Flan*

BOB MEDINA'S ARROZ CON POLLO

½ cup Goya brand
or imported Spanish
olive oil
3 medium-size onions,
roughly chopped
3 broiler-fryer chick-
ens, excluding necks
and livers, cut up
3 tablespoons salt
6 cloves garlic, finely
chopped
Cold water
3 carrots, sliced
½ green pepper, diced
1 can (1 pound) Goya
brand canned, dried
peas, drained

1 can (8 ounces)
tomato sauce
1 jar (4¾ ounces)
Goya brand or im-
ported stuffed green
olives, undrained
2 tablespoons vino
seco, a salted and
seasoned dry white
cooking wine
½ teaspoon bijol, a
yellow coloring
(optional)
3 cups raw long-
grain rice
4 pimentos, cut into
triangles

1. Heat the oil in a heavy kettle or large casserole. Add the onions and chicken pieces and let cook very slowly without browning.
2. In a mortar, mash the salt and garlic together with a pestle
until they form a paste. Add to the chicken. Add about 1 quart cold
water or enough so the chicken pieces are almost covered.
3. Add the carrots, green pepper, peas, tomato sauce, olives, vino
seco and bijol. Bring the mixture to a boil, stirring occasionally.
4. Add the rice, return to the boil, cover and simmer gently about
40 minutes, or until the liquid has been absorbed and the chicken is
tender. If the dish is to be reheated for serving later, cook only 30
minutes. Garnish with pimento pieces.
Yield: 12 to 16 servings
Note: Unusual ingredients for this dish can be purchased at most
Spanish grocery stores.

SANGRIA

1 navel orange, un-
  peeled, center core
  discarded and re-
  mainder diced
1 cup canned or fresh
  pineapple chunks
  with juice
¼ grapefruit, center
  core discarded and
  remainder diced
½ lime, diced
½ lemon, diced
1 cup seedless or
  seeded grapes, stems
  removed

1 red-skinned apple,
  cored and diced
1 cup small canta-
  loupe balls
½ cup sugar
1 cup orange juice
¼ cup lemon juice
½ cup Spanish brandy
1 bottle red Rioja
  wine
Ice cubes
Club soda (optional)

Combine the fruit, sugar, orange juice, lemon juice, brandy and wine in a large pitcher. Stir well and add ice cubes to cool the mixture before serving. If desired, club soda can be added to taste.

Yield: 4 servings

Note: Make 4 pitchers to serve 16.

FLAN

1½ cups sugar
1½ cups milk
1½ cups heavy cream
1 piece (2 inches)
  vanilla bean
4 eggs, lightly beaten
3 egg yolks

¼ teaspoon grated
  lemon rind
¼ cup orange juice
½ teaspoon salt
2 teaspoons dark rum
1 teaspoon almond
  extract

1. Preheat oven to 350 degrees.

2. Place ¾ cup sugar in a small, heavy skillet and heat gently, stirring constantly with a wooden spoon, until sugar melts, is free from lumps and turns a pale golden brown. Pour immediately into a warm, lightly greased, 1-quart ring mold and rotate to coat the mold.

3. Put milk, cream and vanilla bean in the top of a double boiler and heat gently over hot water.

4. Beat eggs, egg yolks, lemon rind and orange juice together. Add remaining sugar and the salt. Mix well.

5. Add ½ cup hot milk mixture to egg mixture. Return to bulk of milk mixture in top of double boiler. Cook 2 minutes over hot, but not boiling, water.

6. Stir in rum and almond extract. Remove vanilla bean. Pour custard mixture over caramel. Set mold in pan of hot water, ¾ inch deep. Bake until custard is set, about 30 minutes.

7. Cool custard and chill several hours or overnight.

8. To unmold, run a knife around the edge of the pan to loosen. Place serving dish over mold and quickly turn upside down.

Yield: 8 servings

Note: Make two to serve 16.

Group Friday Night Supper

❧

Sharing a summer place on Fire Island or at Malibu is a dream come true. Everyone pitches in to share the chores, and there's time for tennis, relaxing and a party or two every weekend. When it is your turn to take the Friday night supper, make it a box-affair with tangy lemon-lime chicken and cold steak and garden salads. They travel well and can be made on Thursday evening after work. Pick up the wine, bread, fruit and paper plates on Friday noon and arrive with a meal that can wait for latecomers. And, there are no pans to wash.

Lemon-Lime Chicken*
Cold Steak Salad*
Garden Salad*
French Bread
Fresh Fruit
Jug of Red Wine

———————◆•◆———————

LEMON-LIME CHICKEN

2 broiling chickens
(2½ pounds each),
quartered
2 lemons
2 limes
Salt and freshly
ground black pepper
to taste
1 teaspoon ground
ginger
½ teaspoon garlic
powder

3 tablespoons chopped
parsley
1 tablespoon chopped
fresh tarragon, or 1
teaspoon dried
3 tablespoons snipped
fresh dill weed
Sweet paprika to
taste
¼ pound butter,
melted

1. Preheat oven to 375 degrees.
2. Butter a roasting pan, line with aluminum foil and butter
again. Place chicken quarters skin side up in pan. Sprinkle with
juice of ½ lemon and ½ lime.
3. In the order listed, sprinkle salt, pepper, ginger, garlic powder,
parsley, tarragon, dill and paprika over chicken. Dribble melted
butter over all.
4. Cover loosely with foil and bake 30 minutes. Remove foil;
bake 20 minutes longer or until done. Let cool.
5. Squeeze juice of ½ lemon and ½ lime over cooled chicken.
Chill. Slice remaining lemon and lime for garnish.
Yield: 4 servings

COLD STEAK SALAD

2 pounds boneless
sirloin, cut into ½-
inch cubes
½ cup butter
¾ pound mushrooms,
sliced
1 package (9 ounces)
frozen artichoke
hearts, cooked and
cooled
1 cup finely diced
celery

1 pint small cherry
tomatoes
2 tablespoons chopped
chives
2 tablespoons chopped
parsley
2 cups salad dressing
(see page 188)
2 teaspoons Dijon
mustard

1. In a large skillet over high heat, sauté the meat cubes, a few at a time, in the butter until browned on all sides. Transfer to a large bowl and cool.

2. Quickly sauté the mushrooms in butter remaining in skillet and add with artichoke hearts, celery, tomatoes, chives and parsley to bowl. Mix lightly. Mix the dressing and mustard and pour over all. Toss, cover and marinate overnight.

Yield: 6 servings

GARDEN SALAD

1 pound green beans, cut into 1½-inch lengths
Boiling salted water
1 pound wax beans, cut into 1½-inch lengths, or 2 cans (1 pound each) wax beans drained
1 can (1 pound) kidney beans, drained
3 oranges, peeled, cut into thin slices and quartered, or 2 cans (11 ounces each) mandarin oranges, drained
½ red onion, sliced thinly
1 bunch scallions, chopped
Whites of 2 hard-cooked eggs, chopped
1 cup salad dressing (recipe below)

1. Cook the green beans in boiling salted water until barely tender, about 8 minutes; drain.

2. If fresh wax beans are used, cook as the green beans above. Combine green, wax and kidney beans, orange slices or mandarin oranges, the onion and scallions.

3. Add egg white to dressing and pour over beans. Toss and chill before serving.

Yield: About 6 servings

Salad Dressing

2¼ cups oil
 ¾ cup wine vinegar
 6 shallots, finely
     chopped
 ⅓ cup chopped
     parsley

⅓ cup snipped fresh
    dill weed
    Salt and freshly
    ground black pep-
    per to taste
⅛ teaspoon Tabasco

Combine all ingredients in a glass jar and shake.
Yield: About 3 cups

"A Small Reception at Home Following the Ceremony"

Something more than canapés and cake is needed for guests who may have come a distance to attend the ceremony. The pièce de résistance should be sophisticated and elegant and in the refrigerator ready to whisk into place on the flower-decked buffet table. The colorful lobster platters and the raspberry mousse can be made at least a day ahead, the cake ordered from the French patisserie weeks in advance and, with hired help to serve and clean up, the mother of the bride can be as serene and misty-eyed as any romantic movie might portray. Champagne is served before and during the affair and for the traditional toasts.

Champagne
Homard en Bellevue à la Parisienne*
Pumpernickel and Watercress Sandwiches
Raspberry Mousse*
Wedding Cake

HOMARD EN BELLEVUE À LA PARISIENNE

1 bottle dry white wine	2 live lobsters (3–4 pounds each)
4 quarts water	3–4 pounds lobster tails
1 onion, sliced	Truffle or pimento
2 carrots, quartered	8 cups fish aspic (recipe below)
2 ribs celery, quartered	4 cups herbed mayonnaise (recipe below)
2 sprigs parsley	
2 teaspoons black peppercorns	12 cups macédoine of vegetables (recipe page 192)
2 bay leaves	16 stuffed hard-cooked egg halves
1 lemon, halved	
2 sprigs fresh tarragon or thyme	

1. Combine the wine, water, onion, carrots, celery, parsley, peppercorns, bay leaves, lemon and tarragon or thyme in a fish poacher or large kettle. Bring to a boil, cover and simmer 20 minutes.

2. Plunge the lobsters, one at a time, into the boiling mixture; cover and cook 18 to 20 minutes. Drain. Cook the tails 5 minutes. Chill lobsters.

3. Using scissors, cut along either side of the underside of each lobster's tail and remove the meat in one piece. Remove meat from tails and cut all the tail meat into medallions or slices about ½ inch thick. Place on a rack over paper. Decorate with truffle or pimento slices. Spoon some of the aspic over the medallions and chill.

4. Stir ¾ cup slightly thickened aspic into the mayonnaise and stir enough into the macédoine to moisten.

5. Remove the small claws and spongy body from the lobsters. Pick out the meat, tomalley and coral and add to the vegetable salad. Set each lobster on a platter and pile the macédoine into the cavities. Decorate each with the medallions. Using an ice cream scoop, alternate mounds of salad with stuffed egg halves around the lobsters. Top salad with remaining medallions. Some of the aspic may be spooned over the filled and decorated lobsters.

Yield: 16 to 20 servings

Note: The large claws are used for garnish in a formal presentation, but for friends and family one might prefer to extract the claw meat and add it to the salad. In that case, the stomach sac behind the eyes should be removed before the cavity is filled.

Fish Aspic

3–4 pounds fish heads
and bones
2 quarts water
2 cups dry white
wine
2 small onions
2 sprigs parsley
2 bay leaves
2 teaspoons salt

1 teaspoon pepper-
corns
5 tablespoons unflav-
ored gelatin
½ cup cold water
6 egg whites, lightly
beaten
6 crushed egg shells

1. Place the fish heads and bones in a saucepan with 2 quarts water, the wine, onions, parsley, bay leaves, salt and peppercorns. Bring to a boil, cover and simmer 20 minutes.

2. Strain and return to the saucepan. Soak the gelatin in the cold water and stir in with the egg whites and shells. Bring to a simmer slowly, stirring gently.

3. Allow to boil gently without stirring until stock clears, about 8 minutes. Strain through wet flannel set in a strainer. Cool and chill until aspic starts to thicken.

Yield: About 8 cups

Herbed Mayonnaise

4 egg yolks
2 tablespoons Dijon
mustard
1 teaspoon salt
¼ teaspoon freshly
ground white
pepper
Pinch of cayenne

2 cups olive oil
2 cups salad oil
½ cup lemon juice
2 tablespoons chopped
parsley
2 tablespoons chopped
chives

Place the egg yolks, mustard, salt, white pepper and cayenne in a bowl and beat until thick. Mix the oils and add gradually, drop by drop, beating all the time. The last ½ cup of oil can be added in a thin stream. Beat in the remaining ingredients.

Yield: About 2 cups

Note: Extra mayonnaise should be used in the hard-cooked egg stuffings.

Macédoine of Vegetables

5 cups cooked, finely diced carrots	4 cups cooked tiny peas
5 cups finely diced knob celery (celeriac) or celery	2 cups peeled, diced tart apples

Mix vegetables and apples together.
Yield: 16 cups

RASPBERRY MOUSSE

4 envelopes unflavored gelatin	½ teaspoon almond extract
1½ cups cold water	¼ teaspoon salt
4 packages (10 ounces each) frozen raspberries, thawed	8 egg whites
	2 cups heavy cream, whipped
¾ cup sugar	⅔ cup crumbled amaretti (hard Italian macaroons)
2 tablespoons lemon juice	

1. Soak the gelatin in the water. Sieve the raspberries and discard the seeds.

2. Combine softened gelatin, raspberry puree, ¼ cup of the sugar and the lemon juice in a small saucepan. Heat, stirring to dissolve gelatin. Add the almond extract. Cool the mixture until it is the consistency of unbeaten egg white.

3. Beat the salt and egg whites together until they form soft peaks. Gradually beat in the remaining ½ cup sugar and continue beating until very stiff.

4. Fold egg whites, cream and crumbled macaroons into the raspberry mixture.

5. Turn the mixture into two 1½-quart soufflé dishes, each fitted on the outside with a double strip of oiled aluminum foil extending about 3 inches above the top of the dish. Secure each collar with an elastic band. Chill several hours. Remove foil collars to serve.
Yield: 16 to 20 servings

Cook Innovatively this Weekend

Charles De Carlo, who is president of Sarah Lawrence College in Bronxville, New York, attacks cooking the same way the school of about 600 women and 200 men approaches education—with a flair for the experimental. The results of Mr. De Carlo's kitchen experiments are frequently shared with students who visit the president's home for Sunday concerts, meetings of the student senate and Friday night rap sessions. Below is the menu for one of Mr. De Carlo's peasant-style buffets with Italian accents, a buffet that won acclaim from this guest for its originality and good taste. Students at the buffet were offered a choice of chilled Soave or Bardolino wines.

*Marinated Cod and Shrimp**
*Spinach Sauce with Fettucine**
*Chicken and Sausage**
Fresh Fruit Compote with Ricotta Sauce
Soave and Bardolino

MARINATED COD AND SHRIMP

1 cup chicken broth
1 cup milk
1½ pounds codfish fillets
12 large shrimp, shelled, deveined and split lengthwise
½ cup finely chopped onion
½ cup finely chopped parsley
¼ cup drained capers
½ teaspoon fennel powder
½ teaspoon celery powder
¼ teaspoon Tabasco
½ cup olive oil
½ cup rice vinegar or white vinegar
Salt and freshly ground black pepper to taste

1. Place the broth and milk in a large skillet and bring to a boil. Add codfish and shrimp, cover and simmer very gently 4 to 6 minutes, or until fish is cooked.

2. Remove cod to a serving platter. Remove shrimp and discard cooking liquid. Cut shrimp into ½-inch pieces and combine with onion, parsley, capers, fennel powder, celery powder, Tabasco, oil, vinegar, salt and pepper. Spread over the cod, adding more vinegar and oil if necessary. Chill several hours.

Yield: 6 servings

SPINACH SAUCE WITH FETTUCINE

½ cup olive oil
3 cloves garlic, finely minced
2 packages (10 ounces each) frozen chopped spinach, thawed
1 cup chicken broth
8 anchovy fillets, mashed
1 tablespoon chopped fresh basil or 1 teaspoon dried
½ cup chopped parsley
1 cup grated pecorino or Parmesan cheese
1½ cups ricotta
Salt and freshly ground black pepper to taste
3 pounds fettucine, cooked al dente, drained and tossed with melted butter, two beaten eggs and pepper to taste

1. Heat half the oil, add garlic and cook briefly. Add the spinach and half the broth. Cook, stirring, 5 minutes.

2. Combine the anchovies, basil, parsley, grated cheese, ricotta and remaining oil and broth. Beat until smooth. Fold into the spinach and heat.

3. Season the mixture with salt and pepper and pour over the fettucine in a deep platter or bowl. Serve with extra grated cheese.

Yield: 8 servings

Chicken and Sausage

6 *whole chicken breasts, boned, skinned and cut into ½-inch strips*
1 *cup olive oil*
1 *tablespoon leaf sage*
2 *cloves garlic, minced*
 Juice of 2 lemons
½ *teaspoon salt*
½ *teaspoon crumbled dried red pepper*
6 *sweet, fennel-flavored Italian sausages, sliced*

½ *cup butter*
2 *cups sliced mushrooms*
3 *large onions, chopped*
½ *cup dry red wine*
1 *large can (2 pounds 3 ounces) Italian plum tomatoes*
 Freshly grated Parmesan cheese to taste

1. Place the chicken breast strips in a ceramic, glass or stainless bowl. Combine the oil, sage, garlic, lemon juice, salt and red pepper and pour over chicken; toss lightly. Allow to marinate in the refrigerator 4 to 6 hours.

2. Fry the sausage slices in a skillet until browned and transfer to a casserole. Discard fat.

3. Add the butter to the skillet. Drain the chicken pieces from the marinade, reserving marinade, and sauté in the butter until opaque and lightly browned. Add to casserole.

4. Sauté the mushrooms in the butter remaining in the skillet and add to the casserole. Sauté the onions in the skillet until soft.

5. Add reserved marinade, the wine and tomatoes. Cook sauce, uncovered, about 25 minutes or until slightly thickened. Pour over chicken and sausage. Reheat. Serve sprinkled with cheese.

Yield: 8 servings

Quick and Easy for Two

꧁

Fifteen minutes is all it takes to fix this menu, and there are many Sunday evenings when that is all the time there is between working in the garden and the beginning of an important TV special. This menu is also just right after an exhausting day in the sailing regatta; when you get back to the rented cottage as the sun is setting it's more important to sit with a cool drink on the porch watching the sky than to juggle pans on the tiny stove. This menu is a boon, too, for the office worker on a Friday night when one special guest is expected.

Chicken Livers with Cognac and Sherry
Broccoli
Cucumbers in Yogurt
*Crème au Chocolat**

CHICKEN LIVERS WITH COGNAC AND SHERRY

¼ pound bacon slices,
diced
1 cup finely diced
leeks or onions
1 pound chicken liv-
ers, halved
2 tablespoons warm
cognac
¼ pound mushrooms,
sliced
1½ tablespoons flour
½ teaspoon thyme

½ teaspoon marjoram
¼ teaspoon summer
savory
1 cup chicken broth
Salt and freshly
ground black pep-
per to taste
⅓ cup dry sherry
2 cups (about 4
ounces) thin noo-
dles, cooked al
dente and drained

1. Fry the bacon in a skillet until crisp. Remove and reserve.
2. In the fat remaining in the skillet, sauté the leeks or onions until tender but not browned. Add the livers and brown quickly on all sides.
3. Add the cognac and ignite. When the flames die down, add the mushrooms and cook 3 minutes longer. Sprinkle with the flour and cook, stirring, 1 minute.
4. Add the thyme, marjoram, summer savory and broth and bring to a boil, stirring. Simmer 3 minutes or until livers are cooked but still pink in the middle. Season with salt and pepper and stir in the sherry.
5. The noodles can be stirred into the liver mixture or used as a bed for them. Sprinkle with reserved bacon bits.
Yield: 2 servings

CRÈME AU CHOCOLAT

2 squares (2 ounces)
unsweetened choco-
late
1 tablespoon water

1 large egg, separated
2 tablespoons dark rum
2 tablespoons coffee
liqueur

1. In the top of a double boiler, melt the chocolate with the water, stirring constantly.
2. Stir in the egg yolk, rum and liqueur. Remove from the heat. Beat the egg white until stiff but not dry and fold into the chocolate mixture. Spoon into demitasse cups or small dishes and chill 1 hour or longer.
Yield: 2 servings

Independence Day Weekend

✖

This important American celebration deserves a special menu using traditional ingredients and recipes. In New England those would include poached salmon, the first new potatoes and fresh garden peas. An all-fish menu is appropriate, and the curried scallop appetizers can be prepared in shells or ramekins early in the day and baked at the last minute. Set the blueberry torte on a red and white napkin alongside a platter of watermelon wedges for a patriotic look.

Curried Scallop Appetizer*
Charles Chevillot's Poached Salmon*
New Potatoes
Fresh Peas
Bibb Lettuce Salad
Fresh Blueberry Torte*
Watermelon Wedges

CURRIED SCALLOP APPETIZER

1 *pound bay scallops, or quartered sea scallops*	1 *teaspoon curry powder, or to taste*
1 *cup dry white wine*	3 *tablespoons flour*
⅛ *teaspoon thyme*	*Salt to taste*
3 *tablespoons butter*	3 *tablespoons heavy cream, approximately*
½ *tart apple, peeled, cored and finely chopped*	¼ *cup buttered soft bread crumbs*
¼ *cup finely chopped celery*	2 *tablespoons freshly grated Parmesan cheese*

1. Place the scallops, wine and thyme in a saucepan. Cover, bring to a boil and simmer 5 minutes. Drain scallops, reserving liquid. Arrange scallops in 4 to 6 buttered shells or ramekins.

2. Melt the butter in a skillet and sauté in it the apple and celery until tender. Sprinkle with the curry powder and flour and cook 2 minutes.

3. Gradually stir in 1½ cups reserved liquid. Bring to a boil, stirring, and cook 2 minutes.

4. Add salt and cream to make a rich creamy sauce. Spoon over the scallops.

5. Sprinkle with crumbs and cheese. Glaze briefly under the broiler, or heat in an oven preheated to 375 degrees, until bubbly and browned, about 8 minutes.

Yield: 4 to 6 servings

CHARLES CHEVILLOT'S POACHED SALMON

Court bouillon

6 quarts cold water
1 fifth dry white wine
1 large onion, sliced
2 ribs celery, each cut
  into 3 pieces
2 carrots, thinly sliced
1 tablespoon whole
  white peppercorns
4 sprigs parsley, tied
  together

3 lemons, quartered
6 bay leaves
3 sprigs fresh tarragon,
  or 1 teaspoon dried
1 tablespoon whole
  cloves
1 fresh salmon (6
  pounds) with head
  and tail on, cleaned
  and scaled

Sauce Chevillot

1 cup lightly salted
  butter, very cold,
  cut in small pieces
3 tablespoons French
  red wine vinegar

7 medium-size shallots,
  finely chopped
Salt and freshly
  ground black pepper
  to taste

1. To prepare court bouillon, place the water, wine, onion, celery, carrots, peppercorns, parsley, lemons, bay leaves, tarragon and cloves in a large fish poacher. Bring to a boil, cover and simmer 20 minutes.

2. Place the salmon on the poacher rack, or wrap in double layer of muslin, and lower into the court bouillon. Cover and simmer, but do not allow to boil, 20 minutes. Let salmon rest 20 minutes longer before removing, and then drain over the poacher by placing two pieces of wood crosswise over the top of the pan for support.

3. Keep the fish warm while preparing the sauce.

4. Place the butter in a heavy saucepan, add the vinegar, shallots, salt and pepper and place over medium heat. Whisk vigorously with a wire whisk until butter is melted, sauce is very frothy and mixture is almost to the boiling point.

5. Carve the fish into 6 portions, removing the skin and brown part beneath, and serve with sauce spooned over each portion.

Yield: 6 servings

FRESH BLUEBERRY TORTE

Pastry shell

1¼ cups flour	3 tablespoons butter
⅛ teaspoon salt	2 tablespoons short-
¼ teaspoon grated	ening
nutmeg	2 egg yolks
2 tablespoons sugar	Ice water

Filling

4 cups fresh blue-	½ cup sugar
berries (about 1½	3 tablespoons quick-
pints)	cooking tapioca or
Grated rind of 2	instant flour
lemons	½ teaspoon cinnamon
2 tablespoons lemon	
juice	

Meringue

3 egg whites, at	⅓ cup confectioners'
room temperature	sugar
⅛ teaspoon cream of	
tartar	

1. To prepare pastry shell, sift the flour, salt and nutmeg into a bowl. Add the sugar, butter and shortening. With the fingertips, or pastry blender, work the butter and shortening into the dry mixture until it resembles coarse oatmeal.

2. Stir in the egg yolks and just enough ice water to make a dough that can be gathered into a ball. Transfer the dough to a board and knead 2 strokes. Roll immediately to fit a 9-inch pie plate, or metal tart pan, or wrap in wax paper and chill 30 to 60 minutes before rolling. Fit in plate or pan and trim edges of pastry.

3. Chill the lined plate or pan 20 minutes or longer.

4. Preheat oven to 400 degrees.

5. Line the chilled pastry shell with aluminum foil and fill with raw rice or dried beans. Bake 8 to 9 minutes or until pastry is set. Remove foil and rice or beans. Bake 2 to 3 minutes longer or until pastry is dry but not browned. Remove shell and reduce oven heat to 375 degrees.

6. Wash, drain and dry the blueberries. Toss with the lemon rind

and juice. Add the sugar, tapioca and cinnamon and toss again to evenly coat the berries.

7. Pour the berry mixture into the pastry shell. Use the same piece of foil to make a loose tent over the berries.

8. Bake 35 to 40 minutes. Remove torte and reduce oven heat to 325 degrees. Remove foil.

9. Beat the egg whites with the cream of tartar until frothy. Add the confectioners' sugar and beat until the meringue is stiff and glossy. Pile the meringue onto the hot pie, making sure that meringue touches all edges of the pastry to avoid shrinkage. Leave the surface rough or swirl a pattern with the back of a spoon. Bake 10 to 15 minutes or until lightly browned. Serve warm.

Yield: 6 to 8 servings

Soups with a Shiver

Chilled soups that can be made in a hurry are a boon on a hot summer weekend when no one really feels like eating. Cooks who care will have some crunchy corn melba tucked away in an airtight container to offer with the cold soups. The consistency of the soups may vary slightly according to the yogurt used—homemade or commercial, skim or whole milk—but this will not change the appetizing and cooling flavor of strawberry or cucumber.

Chilled Strawberry Soup*
Tom's Chilled Cucumber Soup*
Maida's Corn Melba*

CHILLED STRAWBERRY SOUP

1 *quart strawberries, rinsed, dried, hulled and sliced*	¼ *cup confectioners' sugar, or to taste*
2 *tablespoons dry white wine*	2 *cups plain yogurt*

1. Place the strawberries and wine in the container of an electric blender and blend until smooth. Force the mixture through a sieve to strain out the seeds.

2. Return the puree to the blender, add the sugar and yogurt and blend until mixed. Chill briefly before serving in chilled soup bowls.

Yield: 4 servings

Tom's Chilled Cucumber Soup

2 cucumbers, peeled,
  seeded and roughly
  chopped
1–2 cloves garlic,
  crushed
⅔ cup sour cream
1 cup plain yogurt
2 tablespoons plus

2 teaspoons snipped
  fresh dill weed
Salt and freshly
  ground black pepper
5 tablespoons chopped
  walnuts
4 small sprigs dill
  weed

1. Place the cucumbers, garlic, sour cream and yogurt in the container of an electric blender and blend until smooth.
2. Add 2 tablespoons dill and salt and pepper to taste. Mix and chill briefly. Place 1 tablespoon walnuts in each of 4 chilled bowls, pour in the soup and garnish with remaining walnuts and dill.

Yield: 4 servings

Maida's Corn Melba

¼ pound softened
  butter
2 tablespoons sugar
2 eggs, lightly beaten
2 cups flour
2 teaspoons baking
  powder

½ teaspoon salt
1 cup milk
1 cup water
½ cup stone-ground or
  regular yellow corn-
  meal

1. Preheat oven to 375 degrees.
2. Beat the butter and sugar together until light. Beat in the eggs. Sift together the flour, baking powder and salt and stir into the batter alternately with the milk and water.
3. Add the cornmeal and mix until smooth.
4. Pour about 1¼ cups (⅓ of the batter) into a buttered 10-by-15-inch jellyroll pan. Tip to cover the bottom of the pan with a very thin layer. Repeat with two other pans and remaining batter.
5. Bake 15 minutes or until set. Cut into small squares or oblongs and return to the oven. Bake 10 minutes or until first pieces are dry and lightly browned. Remove them to a rack. Continue to bake and remove pieces until all are done. Cool on a rack and store in a tightly covered tin.

Yield: 60 to 80 pieces, depending on the size

Lunch Afloat in
a No-Galley Boat

꒰

Being invited for a spin in a power boat is a treat for any landlubber. Sea breezes can whip up hearty appetites, so offer to take a picnic lunch. Most cockpits or decks have a corner to stow a styrofoam ice chest that, with ice packs, will keep eggs and salads cool. An insulated jug of fruit-filled sangria can be beverage and dessert if you have a container of cookies along.

Jackie's Scotch Eggs*
Caraway Potato Salad*
Sweet and Sour Bean Salad*
Pickles and Cherry Tomatoes
Sangria
William Greenberg's Sand Tarts*

———— •••• ————

JACKIE'S SCOTCH EGGS

1 *pound spicy, lean sausage meat*	*Seasoned dry bread crumbs*
6 *hard-cooked eggs, shelled*	*Fat or oil for deep-frying*
1 *egg, lightly beaten*	

1. Divide the sausage meat into 6 pieces and mold one piece around each hard-cooked egg to give an even coating.

2. Dip into beaten egg and then into bread crumbs, repeating twice if necessary.

3. Heat fat or oil to 370 degrees and fry the eggs, in a basket, two or three at a time, until well browned. Drain on paper towels. Cool and refrigerate until ready to serve. Cut in half before serving.

Yield: 6 servings

Note: Eggs for hard-cooking should be fresh for easy peeling. Make a minute pinhole in the shell at the wide end, place in a pan with cold water and heat slowly to simmering, or have the eggs at room temperature and use warm water. Drain off hot water and place under cold running water. When cool enough to handle, crackle the shell all over by gently rolling the egg back and forth and peel starting at the wide end.

CARAWAY POTATO SALAD

6 *medium-size potatoes*	1 *onion, finely chopped*
Boiling salted water	½ *cucumber, thinly sliced*
¼ *cup oil*	
¼ *cup wine vinegar*	2 *tablespoons chopped parsley*
2 *teaspoons salt*	
½ *teaspoon ground savory*	1 *tablespoon caraway seeds*
¼ *teaspoon marjoram*	½ *cup mayonnaise*
¼ *teaspoon freshly ground black pepper*	2 *tablespoons Dijon mustard*

1. Scrub potatoes and place in boiling salted water to cover. Simmer until tender.

2. Drain potatoes, pare and slice into a bowl. Combine the oil, vinegar, salt, savory, marjoram and pepper in a small jar. Shake and pour over hot potatoes. Stir, cover and marinate 30 minutes.

3. Add onion, cucumber, parsley and caraway seeds. Combine mayonnaise and mustard and add to potato mixture. Toss and chill.

Yield: 6 servings

Sweet and Sour Bean Salad

1 can (16 ounces) diagonal-cut green beans	1 can (8 ounces) diagonal-cut wax beans, drained
½ cup wine or cider vinegar	1 medium-size onion, sliced and separated into rings
½ cup sugar	
1 teaspoon celery seeds	1 tablespoon chopped green pepper
¼ teaspoon dry mustard	1 tablespoon chopped sweet red pepper
	Boston lettuce cups

1. Drain the green beans and place liquid in a saucepan. Add vinegar, sugar, celery seeds and mustard to the pan. Bring to a boil.

2. Put the green beans, wax beans, onion rings, green pepper and red pepper in a 2-quart bowl or container and pour boiling vinegar mixture over.

3. Cover and chill. Drain. Serve in Boston lettuce cups.

Yield: About 6 servings

William Greenberg's Sand Tarts

1 pound lightly salted butter	1½ teaspoons vanilla
Sugar	6 ounces (1½ cups) pecans
1 egg	4½ cups flour

1. Cream the butter and 1 cup sugar together until very light and fluffy. Beat in the egg and vanilla.

2. Grate the pecans, using a Mouli grater, or pass through the fine grinder of a meat grinder. There should be about 2½ cups fluffy ground pecans. Do not use an electric blender.

3. Fold the nuts into the batter. Fold in the flour. Divide dough in half. Wrap in wax paper and chill until the mixture can be rolled, about 1 hour.

4. Preheat oven to 325 degrees.

5. Roll out half the dough to a thickness of ⅓ inch and cut into 1-inch rounds. Place on ungreased baking sheets. Bake 20 to 25 minutes or until the bottoms are lightly browned. Tops will remain pale. Cool on a wire rack. Repeat with second half of dough.

6. Roll the cooled cookies in sugar and store in a closed container.

Yield: About 10 dozen cookies

Guests for the Weekend

And you don't want to spend all day in the kitchen. Judicious planning, and the menus below, can give you time to join in all the activities, including swimming, water skiing, tennis and sunbathing, that are lined up for the weekend. Weeks, or days, before, make the strawberry ice cream and stash it away in the freezer. Market on Thursday for all basic supplies and the perishables you'll need Friday night and Saturday morning. Thursday evening grind the spices for the curry and store them in a tightly stoppered jar; make the lemon fluff for Saturday lunch and chill the fluff in individual soufflé dishes. Pickle the beans, hard-cook the eggs and cook the beets for the main-dish salad. Follow the suggestions for preparing ahead that appear with the menus and the weekend will be spent with friends, not in the kitchen.

FRIDAY NIGHT
(poach salmon for Saturday lunch)

*Alan Hooker's Curried Shrimp**
Rice   Chutney   Cashews   Coconut
Melon

SATURDAY BREAKFAST
(make fruited rum custard for dinner parfait
and shop for rest of perishables)

Sliced Nectarines
Ham and Eggs
OR
*Cornmeal Soufflé**
Broiled Tomatoes
*Apricot–Whole Wheat Muffins**

SATURDAY LUNCH
(marinate lamb)

*Salad Alaska**
*Lemon Fluff**

SATURDAY DINNER

*Lamb Shish Kebab**
Pilaf with Pine Nuts
Tossed Green Salad
*Blueberry Parfait**

SUNDAY BRUNCH

Fresh Fruit
*Frittata**
Hot Rolls
Coffee

SUNDAY DINNER

*Chicken with Fresh Corn and Lima Beans**
*Potato Casserole**
*Sliced Tomato Salad**
*Strawberry Ice Cream**

Alan Hooker's Curried Shrimp

1 tablespoon mustard seeds
4 whole cloves
¾ teaspoon poppy seeds
½ teaspoon whole black peppercorns, or to taste
1½ teaspoons ground cardamom
¾ teaspoon turmeric
2½ onions
2 tablespoons butter
2 cloves garlic, finely chopped

½ cup coconut milk
2½ pounds shrimp, shelled and deveined
¼ cup water
3 ribs celery, sliced
1 green pepper, diced
½ cup buttermilk, at room temperature
½ cup sour cream, at room temperature
Salt to taste

1. In an electric blender, or with mortar and pestle, grind mustard seeds, cloves, poppy seeds, peppercorns, cardamom and turmeric until fine. This is the curry mixture called massala.

2. Finely chop the half onion. Heat the butter and sauté in it the half onion and the garlic until tender. Add spice mixture and cook, stirring, until thick.

3. Add the coconut milk and bring to a boil. Add the shrimp and cook until they turn pink, about 10 minutes.

4. Meanwhile, chop remaining onions coarsely and place in a saucepan with the water, celery and green pepper. Cover and simmer until crisp-tender. Add to the shrimp mixture.

5. Stir in the buttermilk, sour cream and salt and keep warm for 10 to 15 minutes to allow flavors to blend, but do not allow to boil.

Yield: 6 to 8 servings

CORNMEAL SOUFFLÉ

2 cups milk	1 cup ground cooked
1 tablespoon butter	ham or chicken
⅓ cup yellow corn-	⅛ teaspoon grated
meal	nutmeg
1½ cups grated Ched-	Salt and freshly
dar cheese	ground black pep-
3 eggs, separated	per to taste

1. Preheat oven to 325 degrees.
2. Heat the milk and butter together to boiling. Gradually stir in the cornmeal and cook, stirring, until mixture is very thick.
3. Remove the saucepan from the heat and add the cheese. Stir until the cheese melts. Lightly beat the egg yolks and stir in along with the ham or chicken, the nutmeg, salt and pepper.
4. Beat the egg whites until stiff but not dry and fold into the cornmeal mixture. Turn into a 2-quart casserole or soufflé dish and bake 45 to 60 minutes or until puffed and set.

Yield: 4 servings

APRICOT–WHOLE WHEAT MUFFINS

1 cup stone-ground	½ teaspoon grated
whole wheat flour	nutmeg
1 cup flour	1 cup milk
⅓ cup sugar	¼ cup oil
3 teaspoons baking	1 egg, lightly beaten
powder	1 cup snipped dried
1 teaspoon salt	apricots

1. Preheat oven to 425 degrees.
2. Place the whole wheat flour, flour, sugar, baking powder, salt and nutmeg in a bowl. Stir to blend.
3. Combine the milk, oil and egg and stir into the dry ingredients, mixing just enough to moisten.
4. Add the apricots and stir to blend in.
5. Fill paper-lined or greased muffin pans about ⅔ full. Bake 20 to 25 minutes. Serve warm.

Yield: 1 dozen muffins

SALAD ALASKA

8–10 cups salad greens,
preferably a mixture
of romaine, Boston
and Bibb lettuce,
washed, dried,
crisped and torn
into bite-size pieces
1 bunch scallions,
finely chopped
1 large green pepper,
seeded and diced
1 large sweet red
pepper, seeded and
diced
1 cup sliced, cooked
and chilled arti-
choke hearts
2 cans (7¾ ounces
each) red salmon,
skinned and boned,
or 3 cups flaked,
poached fresh sal-
mon, chilled

1 recipe Ruth's
pickled beans (rec-
ipe below)
1 bunch tiny beets,
cooked, peeled and
chilled
6 hard-cooked eggs,
halved
12 anchovy fillets
(optional)
4–6 small, cooked,
red-skinned pota-
toes, skinned and
sliced
3 medium-size toma-
toes, skinned and
cut into small
wedges
6–12 black olives
1 recipe salad dress-
ing (recipe below)

1. Place the greens, scallions, green pepper, red pepper and arti-choke hearts in a deep spaghetti dish or shallow salad bowl. Toss lightly.

2. Place the salmon in a mound in the middle of the greens. Drain the beans, reserving 1 tablespoon marinade, and arrange in piles at 12, 3, 6 and 9 o'clock positions.

3. Arrange the beets in one quadrant and place hard-cooked egg halves, topped with anchovy fillets, in another. Toss the potato slices with the reserved bean marinade and arrange in the third quadrant.

4. The tomato wedges go in the last section and the black olives can be ringed around the salmon or the outer edge of the salad.

5. Toss the salad with the dressing at the table after guests have seen the composition.

Yield: 6 servings

Ruth's Pickled Beans

1 pound tender young green beans	½ cup snipped fresh dill weed
Boiling salted water	¾ teaspoon oregano
Ice water	3 cloves garlic, finely chopped
1¼ cups cider vinegar	6 whole black pep- percorns, roughly crushed
1½ cups water	
⅓ cup oil	
4 teaspoons dry mus- tard	1 tablespoon sugar
1¾ teaspoons salt	1 dried hot red pep- per, seeded and chopped

1. Trim the beans and wash them. Line them up and cut to an even length of about 4½ inches. The trimmings can be used in soup.

2. Tie the beans in 2 bundles and cook in boiling salted water for 8 minutes or until crisp-tender. Drain and cover with ice water. Let stand 5 minutes. Drain. Untie the beans.

3. In a saucepan, mix together all remaining ingredients. Bring to a boil; simmer 4 minutes. Pour over beans and refrigerate 12 to 48 hours.

Yield: 6 servings

Salad Dressing

3 tablespoons Dijon or Düsseldorf mus- tard	1 tablespoon lemon juice
½ cup olive oil	1 teaspoon sugar
½ teaspoon salt	1 small clove garlic, finely chopped
¼ teaspoon freshly ground black pepper	1 tablespoon drained capers
3 tablespoons wine vinegar	

With a wire whisk, beat the mustard while adding the oil drop by drop until a thick sauce is formed. Gradually blend in the remaining ingredients.

Yield: About ⅔ cup

LEMON FLUFF

4 extra-large eggs,
    separated
1 cup sugar
¼ cup lemon juice
1 tablespoon grated
    lemon rind
1½ teaspoons unfla-
    vored gelatin
⅓ cup water

2 teaspoons butter
⅛ teaspoon salt
½ cup heavy cream,
    whipped
¼ cup flaked coconut
2 tablespoons orange
    juice
1 tablespoon grated
    orange rind

1. In the top of a double boiler, beat the egg yolks very well. Gradually beat in ½ cup of the sugar. Stir in the lemon juice and lemon rind. Heat over simmering water, stirring constantly, until mixture thickens and coats the back of the spoon.

2. Meanwhile, soak the gelatin in the water and heat gently to dissolve. Add the butter, salt and dissolved gelatin to the lemon mixture. Cool until mixture starts to thicken.

3. Beat the egg whites until frothy. Gradually beat in the remaining sugar until mixture is stiff. Fold into egg yolk mixture and turn into individual soufflé dishes. Chill several hours or overnight.

4. Decorate with the whipped cream. Mix the coconut with the orange juice and orange rind and sprinkle over.

Yield: 4 to 6 servings

LAMB SHISH KEBAB

Marinade

⅓ cup fresh lemon juice	¼ teaspoon freshly ground black pepper
⅓ cup water	
1½ teaspoons salt	2 teaspoons worcestershire sauce
¼ teaspoon thyme	
½ teaspoon rosemary, crushed	2 small cloves garlic, crushed
½ teaspoon grated lemon rind	

Kebabs

1½ pounds boneless leg of lamb, cut into 1-inch cubes	12 firm cherry tomatoes
2 green peppers, cut into 12 wedges	6 white onions, partly cooked
	2 tablespoons oil

1. Combine all the ingredients for the marinade. Pour over the lamb and let stand refrigerated for at least 2 hours.

2. Remove meat, pat dry and thread on skewers alternately with the green peppers, tomatoes and onions.

3. Brush the meat with oil. Broil over charcoal fire *or* place on a cold broiler pan and broil in a preheated broiler for about 5 minutes. Turn and broil 6 minutes longer or until the meat is the desired degree of doneness.

Yield: 6 servings

BLUEBERRY PARFAIT

½ cup sugar	2 tablespoons butter
2 tablespoons cornstarch	2 tablespoons dark rum
⅛ teaspoon salt	¼ cup chopped mixed candied fruits
1 cup milk	
1½ cups heavy cream	2 cups blueberries, rinsed and drained
4 egg yolks, well beaten	

1. In the top of a double boiler, mix the sugar, cornstarch and salt together. Stir in the milk and 1 cup of the cream. Bring to a boil, stirring. Cover and set over hot water for 10 minutes, stirring occasionally.

2. Beat in the yolks and butter and cook, while stirring, until mixture thickens slightly. Cool to lukewarm. Stir in the rum and candied fruits. Beat remaining cream until stiff and fold in. Chill.

3. Spoon alternate layers of fruited rum custard and blueberries into parfait glasses.

Yield: 6 servings

FRITTATA

3 tablespoons oil	½ green pepper,
1 medium-size zuc-	seeded and diced
chini, thinly sliced	Salt to taste
1 large tomato,	4 eggs, lightly beaten
skinned and	¼ cup milk
chopped	¼ cup chopped
4 scallions, chopped	parsley

1. Heat the oil in a skillet. Add the zucchini and cook 4 minutes. Add tomato, scallions and green pepper and cook, stirring, about 4 minutes or until zucchini is crisp-tender. Season with salt.

2. Combine the eggs, milk and parsley and pour over the vegetables. Cook, stirring with a fork, until bottom is set. Cook a minute or two longer without stirring until bottom is browned and top set. Fold over to make an omelet shape and slide onto a warm platter.

Yield: 2 servings

Note: Make 3 (to order) to serve 6.

CHICKEN WITH FRESH CORN AND LIMA BEANS

1 frying chicken (3½ pounds), cut into serving pieces
⅓ cup flour
Salt and freshly ground black pepper to taste
¼ cup oil
½ cup chopped onion
1 can (29 ounces) tomatoes

1 tablespoon worcestershire sauce
1 teaspoon sugar
⅛ teaspoon cayenne pepper
2 cups fresh lima beans, about 1 pound
2 cups corn kernels cut from cobs, about 4 ears

1. Coat the chicken pieces with the flour seasoned with salt and pepper. Heat the oil in a heavy skillet or casserole, add the chicken pieces and brown on all sides.

2. Add the onion and cook until transparent and lightly browned.

3. Add tomatoes, worcestershire, sugar, cayenne and salt to taste. Bring to a boil, cover and simmer 20 minutes or until chicken is almost tender.

4. Add the lima beans and cook, covered, 5 minutes. Add the corn and cook 5 to 8 minutes longer or until vegetables are crisp-tender.

5. Remove chicken pieces; bone and skin and return chicken meat to the vegetable mixture. Reheat.

Yield: 4 to 6 servings

POTATO CASSEROLE

6 medium-size potatoes, cooked and sliced
2 cups creamed cottage cheese
2 tablespoons melted butter
2 tablespoons flour
1 teaspoon salt
2 tablespoons chopped chives

¼ teaspoon freshly ground black pepper
½ teaspoon thyme
⅓ cup milk
½ cup buttered soft bread crumbs
2 tablespoons freshly grated Parmesan cheese
Butter

1. Preheat oven to 350 degrees.

2. Place a layer of the potatoes in the bottom of a greased 1½-quart casserole. Beat the cottage cheese and melted butter together and spread a layer over the potatoes.

3. Combine the flour, salt, chives, pepper and thyme, and sprinkle some of the mixture over the cottage cheese.

4. Repeat the layers, ending with potatoes. Pour milk over all.

5. Combine the crumbs and Parmesan cheese and sprinkle over the casserole. Dot with butter and bake 30 minutes.

Yield: 6 servings

SLICED TOMATO SALAD

6 large beefsteak
    tomatoes, skinned
    and thickly sliced
Salt
Freshly ground
    black pepper
¼ cup finely chopped
    scallions

2 tablespoons chopped
    fresh basil leaves,
    or 2 teaspoons dried
¼ cup wine vinegar
¾ cup olive oil
1 clove garlic, finely
    chopped
1 teaspoon worces-
    tershire sauce
½ teaspoon sugar

1. Arrange layers of the tomato slices in a serving dish, sprinkling each layer with salt and pepper to taste, scallions and basil.

2. Combine the vinegar, oil, garlic, worcestershire, sugar, 2 teaspoons salt and ½ teaspoon pepper by beating or shaking in a jar. Pour over the tomatoes and chill well.

Yield: 8 servings

STRAWBERRY ICE CREAM

1½ pints fresh straw-
    berries
¾ cup superfine sugar

Juice of 1 lemon
½ cup heavy cream

1. Wash and hull the berries. Push through a food mill and then sieve to remove the seeds. Stir the sugar into the strawberry juice and stir to dissolve. Let stand 30 minutes; stir again. Add lemon juice and chill thoroughly.

2. Stir in the cream and freeze in an ice cream maker according to manufacturer's directions.

Yield: About 1 quart

Stay for a Bite After We Finish Playing

An invitation to come over for bridge or backgammon and stay for something to eat could mean lunch, brunch or a light supper, and the same menu would work for all. There are many dishes that can be made ahead and are easy to serve, tasty and unusual. Anita's artichoke pie would qualify on all counts. Make and bake the pie early on the day and reheat in a 375-degree oven until warmed through. Make sure not to overheat or the pie will become rubbery. The peach sherbet will keep for weeks in the freezer so make a batch when the fruit is ripe and the sherbet will be ready for this affair and spur-of-the-moment snack-desserts.

Minted Melon Balls
*Anita's Artichoke Pie**
Chicory and Leaf Lettuce Salad
*Fresh Peach Sherbet**

Anita's Artichoke Pie

- *3 tablespoons olive oil*
- *2 medium-size onions, finely chopped*
- *2 packages (8 ounces each) frozen artichoke hearts*
- *Boiling salted water*
- *8 eggs*
- *1½ cups freshly grated Parmesan cheese*
- *Freshly ground black pepper to taste*
- *1 cup ricotta*
- *Pastry for a double-crust 10-inch pie*

1. Heat the oil in a small, heavy skillet and sauté the onions in it until translucent but not browned. Cook the artichoke hearts in boiling salted water in a covered saucepan until they are crisp-tender. Drain and cut into bite-size pieces.

2. Preheat oven to 450 degrees.

3. Beat 4 of the eggs lightly. Combine the onions, artichoke pieces, Parmesan cheese, pepper, ricotta and the beaten eggs. Mix well.

4. Line a 10-inch pie plate with half the pastry and fill with the artichoke mixture.

5. Make 4 depressions in the artichoke mixture and break the remaining eggs into them. Roll out the remaining pastry and cover the pie. Seal the edges and decorate. Make steam holes in the crust.

6. Bake the pie 10 minutes, reduce oven heat to 400 degrees and bake about 30 minutes longer or until the pastry is done. Allow the pie to stand 10 minutes before cutting.

Yield: 6 to 8 servings

FRESH PEACH SHERBET

5 large, ripe peaches	1 can sweetened con-
1 tablespoon plus ¼	densed milk
cup lemon juice	4 eggs, separated
1 cup confectioners'	
sugar	

1. Dip the peaches into a saucepan of boiling water for about 30 seconds. Peel, pit and dice. Mix with 1 tablespoon of the lemon juice and the confectioners' sugar.

2. In a bowl, combine the remaining lemon juice, the sweetened condensed milk and egg yolks. Blend well.

3. Stir in the peaches. Beat the egg whites until stiff but not dry and fold into peach mixture. Pour into a 9-by-13-by-2-inch baking pan. Cover and freeze for about 2 hours, or until mixture is solid around the edges.

4. Turn into a chilled bowl. Break into pieces and beat until all the ice crystals are broken up, but do not allow to melt completely. Return to the pan and freeze until just firm, about 2 hours.

Yield: About 2 quarts

Sharing-the-Chores Weekend

"On Saturday we'll go for a cruise around the lake and maybe catch our lunch, but there will be a picnic hamper in the galley just in case the trout aren't biting. Might be fun to visit the County Fair on Sunday; we haven't been in years and there are all kinds of new exhibits planned.

"See you at the cottage Friday night—I'll bring dinner with me; Susan will bring something for Saturday; and we're counting on you to come up with a meal for Sunday. Nothing elaborate and do bring all the ingredients you need; the nearest store is ten miles away and it's closed on Sunday. Breakfasts will be on a get-what-you-want basis.

"P.S. Do bring the children, too."

FRIDAY NIGHT SUPPER

Noodles Alfredo
Calamari*
Caesar Salad
Cheesecake or Cantaloupe

SATURDAY PICNIC AFLOAT

*Cold Fruited Meatloaf**
Horseradish
*Cold Chicken Breasts with Cucumber Salad**
Cherry Tomatoes
Crusty Rolls
Wine
Watermelon

SATURDAY DINNER

Sliced Tomatoes with Fresh Basil
*Spareribs with Sauerkraut**
Blueberries and Cream

SUNDAY DINNER

*Cold Zucchini Soup**
*Turkey Breast Cordon Bleu**
Risotto
Fresh Corn
Honeydew Melon

CALAMARI

1–1½ pounds fresh or
 thawed frozen cala-
 mari (squid)
Salt
Juice of 1 lemon
3 tablespoons olive
 oil
2 onions, chopped
2 cloves garlic, finely
 chopped

3 large ripe tomatoes,
 peeled and chopped
½ cup dry red wine
1 tablespoon tomato
 paste
½ teaspoon oregano
 Freshly ground
 black pepper
1 tablespoon pine nuts
 (optional)

1. Hold the squid under running water; remove the insides and the transparent shell or spine bone from the pocketlike part. Pull off the speckled purple membrane.

2. Remove the ink sacs from sides of the head. Take out the eyes and the hard beak-like object in the center of the tentacles.

3. Cut the pocket into ¼-inch rings and the tentacles into strips. Sprinkle with salt and lemon juice.

4. In a skillet, heat the olive oil and sauté the onions in it until golden and tender. Add the garlic and squid and cook quickly for 2 minutes.

5. Meanwhile, heat the tomatoes, wine, tomato paste, oregano and salt and pepper to taste in a small saucepan and simmer 10 minutes. Pour over the squid mixture.

6. Simmer for 5 to 8 minutes or until squid is tender. Do not overcook or the squid will toughen. Add the pine nuts if desired.

Yield: 4 to 6 servings

COLD FRUITED MEATLOAF

2 pounds ground lean beef, or 1½ pounds ground lean beef and ½ pound ground lean pork	1 onion, finely grated
	1 cup fine dry bread crumbs
	3 eggs, lightly beaten
	1½ teaspoons salt
1 cup finely chopped peeled and cored tart apples	¼ teaspoon freshly ground black pepper
1 cup finely chopped peeled and cored Bosc pears	½ teaspoon sage
	¼ teaspoon grated nutmeg
	½ teaspoon allspice

1. Preheat oven to 350 degrees.

2. Place all ingredients in a large bowl and mix gently, but thoroughly, with the hands. Pack into a 9-by-5-by-3-inch loaf pan and bake 1¼ hours. Cool. Chill.

Yield: 6 servings

Cold Chicken Breasts with Cucumber Salad

3 whole chicken
breasts, halved
1 carrot, sliced
1 rib celery, sliced
1 onion, sliced
1 bay leaf
Salt
Freshly ground
black pepper
Cold water or
chicken broth
2 egg yolks
1 teaspoon Dijon mustard
Pinch cayenne
pepper

2 tablespoons wine
vinegar
½ cup olive oil
½ cup vegetable oil
1 tablespoon unflavored gelatin
¼ cup cold water
2 tablespoons heavy
cream
3 cucumbers, peeled
and thinly sliced
½ teaspoon sugar
2 tablespoons white
vinegar
1 tablespoon snipped
fresh dill weed

1. Place chicken breasts in a skillet. Add the carrot, celery, onion, bay leaf, salt and black pepper to taste and enough water or broth to barely cover. Bring to a boil, cover and simmer 15 minutes or until tender.

2. Drain and cool chicken. Remove skin and bones and place chicken on a rack over wax paper or a platter.

3. Meanwhile, make mayonnaise by placing the egg yolks, mustard, cayenne, ½ teaspoon salt and 1 tablespoon wine vinegar in a bowl. Beat until thick.

4. Mix the oils and add drop by drop to the yolk mixture until mixture is heavy and thick. Soak the gelatin in ¼ cup cold water and heat to dissolve.

5. Stir the remaining wine vinegar, the gelatin mixture and the cream into the mayonnaise. Spoon over the breasts. Chill well.

6. Sprinkle the cucumbers with salt, let stand 10 minutes, rinse with water and drain well. Combine them with sugar, white vinegar and dill. Chill 20 minutes.

7. Arrange cucumbers on a platter and set chilled chicken breasts on top.

Yield: 6 servings

SPARERIBS WITH SAUERKRAUT

4 pounds meaty
    spareribs, cut into
    pieces
1½ quarts fresh or
    canned sauerkraut
1 large onion, thinly
    sliced
1 large carrot, sliced
2 teaspoons caraway
    seeds
1 clove garlic, finely
    chopped

2 tablespoons chop-
    ped parsley
1 bay leaf, crumbled
    Salt and freshly
    ground black
    pepper to taste
1½ cups dry white
    wine, approxi-
    mately
2 tart apples, peeled
    and thickly sliced
8 smoked pork chops

1. Preheat oven to 350 degrees.

2. Brown the ribs, a few at a time, in a heavy Dutch oven or casserole until they are mahogany colored. Set aside.

3. In the fat remaining in the Dutch oven or casserole, sauté the sauerkraut and onion for 8 minutes, stirring often. Add the carrot, caraway seeds, garlic, parsley, bay leaf, salt and pepper.

4. Bury the ribs in the sauerkraut mixture.

5. Pour in wine until it comes about halfway up the mixture. Cover and bake 1½ hours. Add the apples and smoked pork chops and bake 1½ hours longer. Check the level of liquid several times during the cooking and if mixture becomes dry, add more wine.

Yield: 8 servings

COLD ZUCCHINI SOUP

2 pounds zucchini,
    washed and sliced
1 quart richly flavored
    chicken broth (pref-
    erably homemade)
1 teaspoon oregano
2 tablespoons butter
2 tablespoons flour

3 cups half-and-half,
    milk or mixture of
    cream and milk
    Salt and freshly
    ground black pepper
    to taste
2 tablespoons chopped
    parsley

1. Combine the zucchini and broth in a saucepan and simmer

until the vegetable is tender. Puree the mixture in an electric blender. Add the oregano.

2. Melt the butter. Remove from the heat and blend in the flour. Gradually stir in the half-and-half, milk or cream and milk and cook, stirring with a wire whisk, until mixture comes to a boil and thickens slightly.

3. Add the pureed zucchini, salt and pepper. Chill. Serve in chilled bowls, garnished with parsley.

Yield: 8 servings

TURKEY BREAST CORDON BLEU

1 frozen turkey breast on the bone (3–4 pounds), thawed
¼ cup flour
Salt and freshly ground black pepper to taste
3 tablespoons butter

3 tablespoons oil
6–8 slices cooked ham
6–8 thin slices Gruyère cheese
3 tablespoons dry white wine
1 tablespoon chopped parsley

1. Remove the 2 supremes or halves of breast meat from the bone and discard the skin. Cut each breast half into 3 or 4 thin slices. Place the slices between wax paper and pound with a mallet until they are as thin as veal cutlets.

2. Dredge the pieces of breast meat in the flour seasoned with salt and pepper.

3. In a large heavy skillet or 2 medium-size skillets, heat the butter and oil, add the pieces of turkey and cook slowly until lightly browned and tender.

4. Top each cutlet with a slice of ham and one of cheese. Add the wine. Cover and cook 10 minutes longer.

5. Sprinkle with parsley and serve immediately.

Yield: 6 to 8 servings

After the Wine Tasting

Wine tastings continue to be a popular way to entertain six people or a couple of dozen people, and the tastings run the gamut from sampling great vintage wines to comparing the latest finds in inexpensive jug wines. Late summer is a good time for setting out a couple of jugs of California white wine along with imports from Spain and Chile. French bread and a couple of mild cheeses are the only foods you really need. However, for those who linger to enjoy their No. 1 choice, be prepared to serve a light supper such as the menu below. Fresh basil from the garden, or the nearest Italian market, goes into the pesto which can be stored in the refrigerator for several days; and it only takes eight minutes, once the kettle of water is boiling, to cook the tagliarini—less time if the noodles are homemade. Add a big tossed green salad and offer a basket of fresh fruit or filbert brûlée and almond tarts.

Tagliarini with Pesto*
Tossed Green Salad
Filbert Brûlée*
Almond Tarts*

TAGLIARINI WITH PESTO

2 cups fresh basil
leaves, washed (see
note)
½ teaspoon salt
2 cloves garlic
⅓ cup pine nuts

½ cup freshly grated
Sardo or Parmesan
cheese
⅓ cup olive oil
1 pound tagliarini or
fine noodles, cooked
al dente and
drained

1. Place the washed leaves, salt and garlic in an electric blender and blend until well mixed. Add the nuts and blend again.

2. Add the cheese and blend until smooth and then gradually add the olive oil while blending on low speed.

3. Pour the pesto over the hot drained noodles and toss.

Yield: 4 servings

Note: Fresh basil is available at most Italian markets. This is one dish where dried basil will not work.

FILBERT BRÛLÉE

½ cup shelled and
sliced, or diced,
filberts
2 cups heavy cream
Light brown sugar

⅛ teaspoon salt
7 egg yolks, lightly
beaten
2 tablespoons dry
sherry

1. Preheat oven to 400 degrees.

2. Spread the filberts on a shallow pan and toast for 10 minutes in the oven, stirring occasionally. Set aside.

3. Place the cream, ⅓ cup brown sugar and the salt in the top of a double boiler and bring to just below a boil.

4. Add a little of the hot cream mixture to the yolks, mix well and return to the bulk of the mixture. Heat, stirring over hot water until the mixture is the consistency of a medium-thick cream sauce. Do not allow to boil. Stir in the sherry.

5. Pour the mixture into 1 large, or 6 individual, ovenproof dishes and chill overnight. Two hours before serving, sprinkle the tops of

the custards with filberts and then with an even, ¼-inch layer of brown sugar.

6. Place dishes or dish under a preheated broiler and broil 2 to 3 minutes or until sugar melts and begins to turn darker. Watch carefully so that it doesn't burn. Chill.

Yield: 6 servings

ALMOND TARTS

Pastry

1½ cups flour	Cold water
½ cup butter	

Filling

8 ounces almond paste (see note)	1 cup confectioners' sugar
½ cup sugar	¼ teaspoon almond extract
3 egg whites, lightly beaten	

1. To prepare pastry, place the flour in a bowl and, with a pastry blender, 2 knives or the fingertips, blend the butter in.

2. Add a tablespoon or two of water and stir to form a dough. Refrigerate until firm enough to roll, about 1 hour.

3. Meanwhile, work the almond paste together with the other filling ingredients. At the beginning the easiest thing to use is the hands, and later a wooden spoon.

4. Preheat oven to 350 degrees.

5. Roll out the pastry on a lightly floured board or pastry cloth as thin as possible. Cut into 2-inch rounds and fit into small (2-bite size) muffin tins.

6. Place a tablespoon of the filling in each. Roll out scraps of pastry and cut into ¼-inch strips and use to form crosses on the top of the filling.

7. Bake 30 to 40 minutes or until golden brown. Remove from the tins and cool on a rack.

Yield: 18 small tarts

Note: Almond paste is available in cans in most specialty food stores.

Family Reunion

Set out under the big oak tree, on a red and white checkered table-cloth, this old-fashioned picnic is planned for the annual get-together of several generations and lots of assorted cousins, nieces and nephews. It could also be held in a Brooklyn backyard or in someone's garage if the weather is uncooperative. The important thing is that no one has to be in a hot kitchen during the festivities. Everything except the turkey and corn is made ahead and lends itself to daughters-in-law and aunts bringing a dish, or a jar of pickles, to share. The turkey on the spit will have plenty of cooks, and they don't have to be experts. A special thrill for the small fry would be to get the old hand-cranked ice cream maker down from the attic and let them make a batch of sherbet or custard ice cream. Most of the recipes serve twelve, but when there are many dishes to sample, the size of portions is greatly reduced. This spread would be ample for thirty or more, and even the most finicky youngster will find a couple of things, at least, to his liking.

Barbecued Turkey*
Grilled Corn on the Cob
Bryanna's Savory Loaf*
Fish and Macaroni Salad*
Emma Amaral's Chilled Fried Fish*
Polish Salad*
Chicken Wings and Rice Salad*
Potato Salad Supreme*
Carrot Pickles*
Quick Cucumber Pickles*
Herbed Vegetable Cold Plate*
Cornell Bread*

Pistachio Almond Dessert°
Butter Cookies°
Peach Preserve Cake°
Cantaloupe and Ginger Sherbet°
Jean Fraser's Fruit Fool°

————————— •◦• —————————

BARBECUED TURKEY

1 turkey (6–10 pounds), thawed if bought frozen	¼ cup light brown sugar
Salt and freshly ground black pepper	2 teaspoons Düsseldorf mustard
2 onions	⅛ teaspoon cayenne pepper
2 cloves garlic, crushed	1 tablespoon lemon juice
¼ cup wine vinegar	2 tablespoons oil
½ cup chicken broth or dry white wine	½ cup ketchup
	2 tablespoons worcestershire sauce

1. Wash and pat dry the bird inside and out. Sprinkle inside cavity with salt and pepper. Place 1 whole onion and 1 garlic clove in the cavity and truss the bird very tightly, flattening the wings over the breast and tying securely.

2. Insert rotisserie spit rod in front of tail; run diagonally through breast bone. Fasten tightly with spit forks at both ends and tie legs together securely with twine. Test rod until it balances.

3. Insert a meat thermometer in the thickest part of inside thigh, making sure thermometer doesn't touch bone or spit and clears coals as it turns.

4. When 5 pounds of coals are ash gray, knock off ash and push to back of firebox. Add more coals to edges as needed to keep heat even during cooking.

5. Place a drip pan of heavy-duty aluminum foil directly under turkey in front of coals.

6. Attach spit and start rotisserie. A 6- to 8-pound bird takes about 2½ to 3 hours, and an 8- to 10-pound bird takes 3 to 4½ hours.

Times vary according to weather conditions and differences in equipment.

7. Meanwhile, chop the remaining onion and crushed garlic clove. Combine the onion, garlic and remaining ingredients in a small saucepan. Bring to a boil, stirring. Simmer, uncovered, 20 minutes and use to baste the turkey during the last 30 minutes of cooking time. Turkey is done when thermometer registers 180 to 185 degrees, or when the thickest part of the drumstick feels soft.

Yield: 12 to 16 servings

BRYANNA'S SAVORY LOAF

1 pound beef liver, cut into chunks	½ teaspoon freshly ground black pepper
1 egg	
2 tablespoons tomato sauce	1 pound lean sausage meat
1 small onion, sliced	½ cup wheat germ or quick-cooking oats
1 clove garlic	
1½ teaspoons salt	

1. Preheat oven to 325 degrees.

2. Liquefy the liver in an electric blender, adding a small amount at a time.

3. Add the egg, tomato sauce, onion, garlic, salt and pepper to the blender with the liver and blend until smooth.

4. In a bowl, mash the sausage meat together with the wheat germ or oats. Gradually beat in the liver mixture.

5. Pour into an 8½-by-4½-by-2½-inch loaf pan and bake 1 hour or until set and browned on top. Pour off any accumulated fat.

6. Unmold and serve hot with homemade tomato sauce, or allow to cool in the pan, unmold, chill and serve cold as an appetizer, cold meat course or sandwich filling.

Yield: 12 slices

FISH AND MACARONI SALAD

8 ounces elbow maca-
roni, cooked al
dente, drained and
cooled
2 pounds flaked fresh
or drained canned
crab meat; or flaked
canned tuna; or
shelled and de-
veined cooked
shrimp
2 small green peppers,
diced

2 small sweet red
peppers, diced
1 cup diced celery
2 cups sour cream
½ cup light cream
¼ cup lemon juice
2 teaspoons sugar
Salt and freshly
ground black pepper
to taste
2 tablespoons snipped
fresh dill weed
1 teaspoon dry mus-
tard

1. Combine the macaroni, crab meat, tuna or shrimp, the green peppers, red peppers and celery. Toss lightly.
2. Combine the remaining ingredients and pour over the macaroni mixture. Mix lightly and chill before serving.

Yield: 12 servings

EMMA AMARAL'S CHILLED FRIED FISH

3 pounds cod, had-
dock or flounder
fillets
½ cup flour
Salt and freshly
ground black
pepper

Olive oil
1½ cups cider vinegar
1½ bay leaves
¼ teaspoon whole
saffron
¾ cup finely chopped
onion

1. Cut the fish into serving pieces and roll in the flour seasoned with salt and pepper.
2. Pour olive oil into a heavy skillet to a depth of ⅛ inch. Heat the oil and fry the fish in it quickly, a few pieces at a time, until fish is lightly browned on both sides and cooked through. Drain on paper towels. Place on a deep platter.

3. Cover the fish and refrigerate for about 30 minutes. Combine the remaining ingredients and pour over the chilled fish. Serve immediately or refrigerate for an hour or so.

Yield: 12 servings

POLISH SALAD

6 potatoes, cooked and diced	6 hard-cooked eggs, diced
3 cups sliced cooked carrots	Homemade mayonnaise
3 cups cooked green peas	Salt and freshly ground black pepper to taste
6 large sour pickles, diced	

Combine potatoes, carrots, peas, pickles and eggs in a bowl. Moisten with mayonnaise and season with salt and pepper.

Yield: 12 to 14 servings

Note: One-half of the mayonnaise recipe on page 191, omitting the parsley and chives, will provide enough mayonnaise for this salad, or use any standard mayonnaise recipe that will yield approximately 1 cup of dressing.

CHICKEN WINGS AND RICE SALAD

3 *pounds chicken wings (about 16)*
¼ *cup imported soy sauce*
5 *tablespoons wine vinegar*
¼ *cup light brown sugar*
½ *cup oil*
1 *tablespoon chopped fresh ginger, or ½ teaspoon ground*
1 *clove garlic, finely chopped*
2 *cups cooked, cold rice*
½ *cup thinly sliced water chestnuts*
4 *small scallions, finely chopped*

⅓ *cup roasted, blanched almonds, sliced or chopped*
2 *navel oranges, peeled and cut into segments, and halved or quartered if large*
Freshly ground black pepper to taste
1 *tablespoon finely chopped parsley*
⅛ *teaspoon dry mustard*
¼ *teaspoon sugar*
Boston lettuce leaves

1. Remove wing tips and discard, or use for soup. Cut wings in half.

2. In a large bowl, combine 3 tablespoons of the soy sauce, 3 tablespoons of the vinegar, the brown sugar, ¼ cup oil, the ginger and garlic. Mix well. Add the wing pieces and toss to mix.

3. Allow wings to marinate in the refrigerator at least 4 hours, or overnight.

4. Preheat oven to 400 degrees.

5. Place the wings and marinade in a baking dish and bake until tender, about 30 minutes, turning several times and basting with the marinade.

6. Cool and chill the wings.

7. Combine the rice, water chestnuts, scallions, almonds and orange slices. In a small bowl, beat together the remaining soy sauce, vinegar and oil with the pepper, parsley, mustard and sugar. Pour over rice mixture and toss.

8. Serve the rice salad in lettuce cups and arrange wings around them.

Yield: 10 servings

POTATO SALAD SUPREME

1 pound mushrooms, wiped, stems removed
1 cup wine vinegar
1 cup olive oil
½ cup lemon juice
2 teaspoons salt
1 teaspoon freshly ground black pepper
12 cups sliced, cooked potatoes (5 pounds approximately)
2 teaspoons oregano
½ cup finely chopped flat-leaf Italian parsley
12 cooked, chilled artichoke hearts, halved
1 cup chopped celery
1 cup finely chopped scallions
2 green peppers, cut into thin strips

1. Slice the mushrooms into a bowl. Combine ¼ cup wine vinegar, the oil, lemon juice, 1 teaspoon salt and ½ teaspoon pepper and pour over the mushrooms. Allow to marinate 30 minutes.

2. Place the potatoes in a salad bowl. Add remaining vinegar, salt and pepper and the oregano. Toss. Add the mushrooms and remaining ingredients. Toss again and serve.

Yield: 12 to 14 servings

CARROT PICKLES

3 bunches carrots, washed, scraped and cut into ¼-inch sticks to fit pint canning jars
4 teaspoons mustard seeds
1 tablespoon mixed pickling spices
1½ cups sugar
1½ cups white vinegar
1½ cups water
1 teaspoon salt

1. Steam the carrot sticks over rapidly boiling water for 3 minutes. Immediately plunge into ice water. Drain.

2. Pack the sticks into 3 or 4 pint canning jars. Add 1 teaspoon mustard seeds to each jar.

3. Tie the pickling spices in a muslin bag and place in a saucepan with the remaining ingredients. Bring to a boil and boil 5 minutes. Remove the spice bag.

4. Pour the boiling liquid over the carrot sticks, leaving ¼-inch headspace. Adjust caps and process 25 minutes in a boiling water bath. Cool and test seal.

Yield: 3 to 4 pints

QUICK CUCUMBER PICKLES

4 pints thinly sliced, unpeeled, unwaxed cucumbers (about 6 medium-size cucumbers; see note)
1½ cups thinly sliced onions
⅓ cup salt

2 cloves garlic
2 quarts crushed ice
1 quart sugar
1½ teaspoons turmeric
1½ teaspoons celery seeds
2 tablespoons mustard seeds
3 cups white vinegar

1. Combine the cucumbers, onions, salt and garlic in a glass or ceramic crock or bowl. Cover with the ice and let stand at room temperature for 3 hours. The ice removes the bitterness from the cucumbers.

2. Drain the mixture well in a colander and discard the liquid.

3. In a large kettle, combine the sugar, turmeric, celery seeds, mustard seeds and vinegar. Bring the mixture to a boil and stir until all the sugar is dissolved.

4. Add the drained cucumber mixture, bring to a boil and cook 5 minutes.

5. Pack the hot pickles into hot, sterilized jars to within ½ inch of the jar tops. Adjust the caps and rings and make sure each jar is firmly sealed.

6. Process the jars in a boiling water bath for 5 minutes. The boiling water should extend at least 1 inch above the jars. Remove the jars, adjust seals and allow to cool.

7. When the jars are cool, remove the rings and test the caps for a tight seal. Store in a cool, dry place. These pickles should be used within a month or two for maximum crispness.

Yield: 6 pints

Note: Many commercially produced cucumbers have been coated with wax to preserve freshness. Unwaxed cucumbers are usually available at suburban or country farm vegetable stands.

Herbed Vegetable Cold Plate

1 *pound asparagus,*
steamed until crisp-
tender
1 *pound string beans,*
steamed until crisp-
tender
1 *celery root, cut into*
julienne strips
½ *pound mushrooms,*
sliced
3 *tablespoons salad*
oil (optional)

1 *red onion, thinly*
sliced into rings
½ *cup olive or salad*
oil
½ *cup wine vinegar*
½ *teaspoon thyme*
½ *teaspoon rosemary*
¼ *teaspoon oregano*
2 *tablespoons snipped*
fresh dill weed
Salt to taste
¼ *cup chopped parsley*
1 *clove garlic, crushed*
Juice of 1 lemon

1. Arrange the cooked asparagus and beans and celery root in an attractive design on a platter.

2. Sauté the mushrooms in 3 tablespoons oil for 3 minutes, or use mushrooms raw, if desired. Scatter mushrooms and onion rings over vegetables.

3. Combine the olive oil with remaining ingredients. Mix well and pour over the vegetables. Refrigerate for at least 3 hours before serving.

Yield: 12 servings

Cornell Bread

3 cups lukewarm water	¾ cup nonfat dry milk solids
2 packages dry active yeast	3 tablespoons wheat germ
2 tablespoons honey	4 teaspoons salt
6 cups unbleached white flour, approximately	2 tablespoons oil
½ cup full-fat soy flour	Melted butter (optional)

1. Place the water, yeast and honey in a large bowl. Stir to mix and let stand in a warm place 5 minutes.

2. Sift together 6 cups flour, the soy flour and dry milk solids. Stir in the wheat germ.

3. Add the salt and about ½ to ¾ of the flour mixture to the yeast mixture so that the batter has a consistency that can be beaten. Beat for 2 minutes in an electric mixer, or 75 strokes by hand.

4. Add the oil and work in the remainder of the flour mixture, adding extra flour if needed to form a dough. Turn the dough onto a floured board and knead 10 minutes or until the dough is smooth and elastic.

5. Place in a greased bowl, grease the top of the dough lightly, cover and let rise in a warm place until almost doubled in bulk, about 45 minutes.

6. Punch the dough down, fold over the edges and turn upside down in the bowl. Cover and let rise 20 minutes longer.

7. Turn onto a board; divide into 3 parts. Form into balls, cover and let stand 10 minutes.

8. Roll out one ball into a rectangle twice as big as an 8½-by-4½-by-2½-inch loaf pan. Fold the long sides into the center. Fold short sides to the center. Pinch to seal layers and fit into a greased loaf pan. Repeat with the other two balls.

9. Cover pans and let dough rise in a warm place until doubled in bulk, about 45 minutes.

10. Preheat oven to 350 degrees.

11. Bake loaves 50 to 60 minutes. Cover with aluminum foil if tops begin to overbrown. Bread is done when it sounds hollow

when tapped on the bottom. Brush tops with melted butter for a soft crust. Cool on a rack.

Yield: 3 loaves

PISTACHIO ALMOND DESSERT

2 cups heavy cream, whipped	¼ cup slivered blanched almonds
⅓ cup honey	¼ cup chopped pistachio nuts
Few drops almond extract	Pinch salt

1. Place whipped cream in a bowl and gradually fold in the honey and almond extract. Fold in the nuts and salt.
2. Pour into a mold, soufflé dish or bowl and freeze until solid. Remove from the freezer a short while before serving and unmold onto a plate.

Yield: 10 servings

BUTTER COOKIES

1 cup butter	1 teaspoon cream of tartar
1½ cups confectioners' sugar	¼ teaspoon salt
1 egg	1 egg white, lightly beaten
1 teaspoon vanilla	Sugar
2½ cups flour	Finely chopped pecans or walnuts
1 teaspoon baking soda	

1. Cream the butter and gradually beat in the confectioners' sugar until the mixture is light and fluffy. Beat in the egg and vanilla.
2. Sift together the flour, baking soda, cream of tartar and salt and gradually work into the butter mixture. Divide in half. Wrap each half in wax paper and chill until dough can be handled.
3. Preheat oven to 400 degrees.
4. Roll half the dough on a lightly floured board to a thickness of ⅛ inch. With floured cookie cutters, cut into desired shapes. Transfer to a baking sheet. Brush lightly with egg white and sprinkle with sugar.

5. Bake 6 to 8 minutes or until lightly browned at edges.

6. Cool on a rack.

7. Form the remaining half of the dough into rolls 1½ inches in diameter. Wrap in wax paper and chill several hours or overnight. Cut into ⅛-inch slices. Brush with egg white and sprinkle with nuts. Transfer to a baking sheet and bake 6 to 8 minutes. Cool on a rack.

Yield: About 6 dozen cookies

PEACH PRESERVE CAKE

Cake layers

¾ cup butter
1 cup sugar
3 eggs, separated
2 cups flour
⅛ teaspoon salt
½ cup buttermilk

1 teaspoon baking soda
1 cup (12-ounce jar) peach or apricot preserves

Filling and frosting

2 cups sugar
1 cup milk
1–1½ cups shredded coconut
1 small orange, ground and drained of extra juice

1 cup chopped walnuts or pecans
1 cup crushed pineapple, drained

1. Preheat oven to 350 degrees.

2. To prepare cake layers, cream the butter and sugar together until very light and fluffy. Beat in the egg yolks, one at a time.

3. Sift together the flour and salt. Stir the buttermilk with the baking soda. Beginning and ending with flour mixture, stir flour mixture into the batter alternately with buttermilk mixture.

4. Fold in the preserves.

5. Beat the egg whites until stiff but not dry and fold into the batter. Spoon into two greased 9-inch layer pans lined on the bottom with wax paper.

6. Bake 35 to 45 minutes or until cake layers test done. Cool on a rack.

7. To prepare frosting, put the sugar and milk in a heavy saucepan and bring to a boil, stirring until the sugar is dissolved.

8. Boil, stirring to prevent sticking, only until mixture reaches 260 degrees on a candy thermometer. Cool slightly and then beat until creamy.

9. As mixture thickens, quickly stir in 1 cup coconut, the orange, nuts and pineapple. Use to fill and frost the cooled cake layers. Sprinkle top and sides with extra coconut.

Yield: 10 servings

CANTALOUPE AND GINGER SHERBET

6 cups cantaloupe
puree (the pulp
from 3 large canta-
loupes, put through
an electric blender,
sieve or food mill)
1½ cups sugar
Grated rind of 3
limes

2 tablespoons lime
juice
¼ teaspoon salt
2 envelopes unfla-
vored gelatin
½ cup water
¼ cup finely chopped
crystallized ginger

1. Combine the cantaloupe puree, sugar, rind, juice and salt and stir to dissolve the sugar.

2. Soften the gelatin in the water for 5 minutes, then heat to dissolve the gelatin. Stir along with ginger into the cantaloupe mixture. Turn the mixture into the can of an ice cream freezer so that it is only ¾ full. Freeze according to manufacturer's instructions until cranking becomes difficult or motor slows.

3. Remove the dasher, replace cover with cork in the hole or transfer the sherbet to plastic containers, cover and ripen for 1 to 2 hours or until serving time by placing in a mixture of 4 parts crushed ice to 1 part rock salt. Or, the containers may be placed in the home freezer, from which they should be removed for a while before serving.

Yield: About 6 cups

JEAN FRASER'S FRUIT FOOL

2 pints blueberries,
picked over and
washed
¼ cup water, approxi-
mately
2 teaspoons lemon
juice
Superfine sugar to
taste

2 eggs, lightly beaten
¼ cup sugar
1¼ cups milk, scalded
¼ teaspoon vanilla
1 cup heavy cream,
whipped

1. Place the blueberries in a saucepan with barely enough water to cover the bottom of the pan. Bring to a simmer, cover and cook slowly until tender.

2. Force the fruit through a fine sieve to make a puree. Add lemon juice and sweeten to taste with superfine sugar. Cool.

3. Combine the eggs and sugar in a saucepan and gradually whisk in the milk. Heat, stirring, until mixture thickens. Do not allow to boil. Cool slightly. Add vanilla. Combine custard with fruit puree and cool to room temperature.

4. Fold in half the cream, transfer to a serving bowl and chill. Decorate with remaining cream before serving.

Yield: 8 to 12 servings

FALL

Treats for Halloween

An hour or two spent in the kitchen with youngsters during the weekend before the witches ride on their broomsticks can be fun. It can also produce homemade goodies to wrap and parcel out to the hobgoblins and clowns that come knocking at the door. How much nicer to munch on caramel popcorn or let a bright-red cinnamon candy melt in the mouth than open up the same old gum and candy bars. Halloween costume parties at school or home will be remembered for the tiny jewellike cookies that were served with juice or hot cocoa as well as for the bags of candies carried away. Children four years old and up can help with some part of the preparation.

*Veronica's Jewel Cookies**
*Wrede Smith's Caramel Popcorn**
*Red Cinnamon Candy**
*Soft Coconut Candy**
*Mrs. Neeling's Chocolate Rounds**

VERONICA'S JEWEL COOKIES

1 *cup butter*	5½ *cups flour*
1 *cup shortening*	1 *teaspoon salt*
1¼ *cups sugar*	1 *teaspoon baking*
1 *egg*	*powder*
1 *tablespoon vanilla*	*Chopped candied*
¼ *teaspoon lemon*	*cherries or citron*
extract	*peel, for garnish*

1. Preheat oven to 350 degrees.

2. Cream the butter, shortening and sugar together until fluffy. Beat in the egg, vanilla and lemon extract.

3. Sift together the flour, salt and baking powder and add to the creamed mixture. Stir with a spoon or with the hand to incorporate the flour.

4. The dough can be rolled out immediately or chilled for a short period and then rolled.

5. Roll out ⅙ of the dough at a time on a lightly floured board to a thickness of ¼ inch. Cut with small, fancy cookie cutters and place on a lightly greased baking sheet. Decorate each cookie with a piece of cherry or citron peel.

6. Bake 10 minutes or until lightly browned. Cool on a rack and store in an airtight tin or jar. The cookies will keep a week to 10 days.

Yield: About 350 ½- to 1-inch cookies

Note: If the cutting becomes too tedious, after the dough is rolled sprinkle it with sugar and cinnamon (¼ cup sugar to 1 tablespoon cinnamon) and cut with a pastry wheel or knife into diamond shapes.

WREDE SMITH'S CARAMEL POPCORN

3 tablespoons corn oil	¼ cup light corn syrup
½ cup yellow hullless popcorn	½ teaspoon salt
½ cup butter	½ teaspoon vanilla
1 cup firmly packed light brown sugar	¼ teaspoon baking soda

1. Preheat oven to 250 degrees.

2. Pour corn oil into a 4- to 5-quart heavy, deep skillet or kettle. Place over medium-high heat and add a kernel of popcorn. When the kernel pops, remove it and add the ½ cup popcorn. Place cover on kettle, leaving a small air space at the edge of the cover. Shake pot frequently until popping stops. Remove pot from heat.

3. Measure 2½ quarts of the popcorn (the remainder can be eaten plain) and place in a large roasting pan or metal bowl. Place in oven and keep warm.

4. Melt butter in a 2-quart saucepan. Stir in sugar, syrup and

salt. Bring mixture to a boil and boil 5 minutes. Remove from heat and stir in vanilla and baking soda. Pour over the warm popcorn, mixing well to coat each piece of popcorn.

5. Separate pieces of popcorn and place 1 layer only on 2 large baking sheets. Bake in 250-degree oven 1 hour. Cool completely (it crisps on standing). Store in airtight container.

Yield: 2½ quarts

RED CINNAMON CANDY

3 cups sugar
⅓ cup light corn
    syrup
3 tablespoons vinegar
1 cup boiling water

1 teaspoon red food
    coloring
½ teaspoon oil of cin-
    namon, or to taste
    (see note)

1. Place the sugar, corn syrup, vinegar and boiling water in a heavy 2-quart saucepan. Bring to a boil, stirring only until the sugar dissolves.

2. Wrap a piece of muslin around the end of a spoon handle and secure with a rubber band. Dip in cold water and use to wash down any sugar crystals around the sides of the pan.

3. Boil, without stirring, until the mixture registers 310 degrees on a candy thermometer or a drop of the syrup dropped in a bowl of cold water crackles and hardens.

4. Turn off the heat and add the red food coloring and oil of cinnamon. With the pan at arm's length, gently shake the pan to distribute the oil and color. Pour immediately into a large, buttered, ironstone or heatproof platter to form an ⅛-inch layer. Use 2 platters if necessary.

5. Allow the platters to stand until the outside of the candy can be handled; it will be firm but still very pliable. With buttered scissors (and buttered fingers), cut off strips of candy from the outside edges, then cut strips crosswise into ½-inch pieces. Set on buttered paper to dry out.

6. Continue to work into the center, cutting strips all around the rectangle of candy until all is used.

7. Store in an airtight jar or a tin with tight-fitting cover. Separate layers with parchment paper.

Yield: About 1 pound
Note: Oil of cinnamon is available in some pharmacies.
This candy should be made on a day with low humidity for best results.

SOFT COCONUT CANDY

2 cups light brown
    sugar
2 cups granulated
    sugar
1 cup coconut milk,
    drained from fresh
    coconut

½ cup water
2 cups finely grated
    fresh coconut
2 teaspoons vanilla

1. Place the sugars, coconut milk, water and coconut in a heavy saucepan. Bring to a boil, stirring until the sugar has dissolved. With a brush dipped in water, wash down the sugar crystals around the sides of the pan.

2. Boil the mixture, stirring occasionally, until the mixture registers 238 degrees on a candy thermometer. Remove from the heat and set aside without further stirring until the mixture registers 120 degrees on the thermometer. Add the vanilla.

3. With a wooden spoon, beat the mixture until it thickens and becomes opaque. Just before the mixture becomes too thick to beat, pour into a buttered 8-inch-square pan. When set, cut into squares. Once the candy has set in the pan sufficiently to handle, the squares can be formed into balls and rolled in finely grated fresh coconut. Or, the candy may be left in squares, if preferred.

Yield: 25 pieces

Mrs. Neeling's Chocolate Rounds

2½ cups coarsely crushed vanilla wafers
1 cup confectioners' sugar
1 cup coarsely chopped pecans
¾ cup Marmot

Chocolat Suisse (or other chocolate-flavored liqueur) approximately
Cocoa or unsweetened shredded coconut

1. Combine the wafer crumbs, sugar and pecans and mix well. Add ¾ cup chocolate liqueur and stir to moisten all ingredients. Add more liqueur if necessary.

2. Form mixture into 1- to 1½-inch balls and roll in cocoa or coconut. The cocoa may be placed in a small bag and a few balls at a time shaken in it to coat. Store in a paper-lined box. The candies improve if kept a day or two.

Yield: 25 pieces

Note: Set these aside for Halloween chaperones.

Thanksgiving Weekend

Although Thursday is not officially part of any weekend, many families arrange to be together for four days at the end of November and others wait until the Saturday or Sunday to share a Thanksgiving feast. Oysters, turkey and cranberries are traditional parts of our family's meal, but the stuffing, vegetables and desserts change as we do not have a particular affinity for creamed onions, sweet potatoes and pumpkin pie. And, although the snow may not fall on the way to grandmother's house, here is a menu she would be proud to serve.

*Oyster Bisque**
*Roast Turkey**
*Mike's Festive Dressing**
*Crane House Carrot Pudding**
*Broccoli and Corn Casserole**
*Corn and Pepper Relish**
*Pickled Peppers**
*Cranberry Salad Mold**
*Crane House Pumpkin Bread**
*Fruited Peanut Pie**

Oyster Bisque

1 *quart shucked oysters*	½ *bay leaf, crumbled* *Salt and freshly*
2 *cups chicken broth*	*ground black pep-*
1½ *cups stale bread crumbs, crusts removed*	*per to taste*
	2 *tablespoons butter*
	2 *tablespoons flour*
1 *small onion, sliced*	1 *quart scalded milk*
2 *ribs celery, diced*	*or mixture of milk*
Sprig parsley	*and cream*

1. Drain the liquor from the oysters and place in a kettle with the broth, bread crumbs, onion, celery, parsley, bay leaf, salt and pepper. Bring to a boil and simmer gently about 15 minutes.

2. Separate the tougher parts of the oysters and grind through a food mill. Add to the simmering mixture. With scissors, dice the soft parts of the oysters; reserve.

3. When the oyster pieces in the bread mixture are very tender, after cooking about 15 minutes, pass through a food mill twice—first with the coarse blade and then with the fine one. An electric blender can be used.

4. Reheat the soup. Add the reserved oysters and cook 2 minutes. Mix together the butter and flour to make a smooth paste. Gradually whisk a little at a time into the simmering soup.

5. Add the milk or milk and cream and check the seasoning.
Yield: 8 servings

How to Thaw and Roast a Thanksgiving Turkey

To thaw a frozen turkey, place the bird on a tray in the refrigerator in the original wrap, which has been punctured, for 2 to 4 days or about 24 hours for each 5 pounds of turkey.

Alternately, the bird may be thawed in the unopened plastic bag submerged in cool water for 4 to 10 hours. Changing the water often will hasten thawing.

A relatively quick way of thawing a turkey is to leave it in the original wrap, place it in a very heavy-duty brown bag or wrap several thicknesses of newspaper around it, and leave it at room temperature. A bird under 12 pounds will take 6 to 12 hours; over 12 pounds, 12 to 18 hours.

Check the bird frequently during the last hours of thawing and refrigerate immediately if completely thawed.

Never stuff a bird until ready to cook it, and do not thaw commercially stuffed frozen birds—cook them frozen.

To prepare the turkey for the oven, rinse well with cold water, drain, pat dry, season and stuff if desired. Push drumsticks under the band of skin at tail, or truss.

Place the stuffed bird on a rack in a shallow roasting pan, breast side up. If a roasting thermometer is to be used, insert it so that the bulb is in the center of the inside of the thigh muscle; do not let bulb touch the bone.

Brush the skin with melted fat or butter and roast in a preheated 325-degree oven. Do not cover or add water. Roast according to the accompanying chart, basting occasionally.

When the turkey is two-thirds cooked, cut the cord or band of skin at the drumsticks and place a tent of aluminum foil over the bird to prevent excessive browning. When the bird is done, the thermometer should register 180 to 185 degrees, and the thickest part of the drumstick should feel soft.

For a more moist breast, the turkey can be roasted breast side down for half the cooking time, following the same chart.

Timetable for Cooking Turkey
(at 325 degrees)

Weight	Stuffing	Roasting
6 to 8 pounds	1 to 1½ quarts	3 to 3½ hours
8 to 12	1½ to 2¼	3½ to 4½
12 to 16	2¼ to 3	4½ to 5½
16 to 20	3 to 3¾	5½ to 6½
20 to 24	3¾ to 4½	6½ to 7

MIKE'S FESTIVE DRESSING

8 tablespoons butter
1 pound ground beef round
1 cup chopped onions
⅓ cup chopped green pepper
⅓ cup chopped celery
¼ cup chopped parsley
2 tablespoons sugar
1 tablespoon salt
2 teaspoons freshly ground black pepper

½ teaspoon cinnamon
1 cup cooked, peeled chestnuts (see note)
½ pound pine nuts, or blanched almonds, slivered
½ cup golden raisins or chopped apricots
3 cups hot cooked rice

1. In a large skillet, heat 2 tablespoons of the butter and sauté the beef in it until browned on all sides. Add the onions, green pepper and celery and cook until vegetables are transparent.

2. Melt the remaining butter and stir in to the beef mixture with the parsley, sugar, salt, black pepper, cinnamon, chestnuts, the pine nuts or almonds and the raisins or apricots.

3. Add the rice, stir and use to stuff a 12-pound turkey. Or, the dressing can be spooned into a casserole and heated in a 350-degree oven to serve as a side dish with pork, ham or fowl.

Yield: 2 quarts stuffing

Note: The dressing can be used to stuff 2 ducks if the amount of butter used is reduced to the 2 tablespoons used in step 1.

A 10-ounce can of chestnuts packed in water, drained, can be used, or 1½ cups (about 12 ounces) fresh chestnuts in the shell will yield 1 cup cooked and peeled.

CRANE HOUSE CARROT PUDDING

1½ tablespoons cornstarch
1 cup milk
3 eggs, separated
¼ cup sugar
3 cups mashed, cooked carrots (2 large bunches carrots)

1 cup stale bread crumbs
3 tablespoons melted butter
1 teaspoon salt
1 cup light cream
¼ cup sherry
¾ teaspoon freshly grated nutmeg

1. Preheat oven to 300 degrees.
2. Mix the cornstarch with a little of the milk. Heat remaining milk and stir some of hot milk into cornstarch mixture.
3. Return to the pan and cook, stirring, until mixture thickens.
4. Beat the egg yolks with the sugar and gradually stir in some of the hot cornstarch mixture. Return to the pan and cook, stirring, until mixture thickens slightly.
5. Remove from the heat and add the carrots, bread crumbs, butter and salt. Mix well. Stir in the cream, sherry and nutmeg.
6. Beat the egg whites until stiff but not dry and fold into the carrot mixture. Pour into a greased 2-quart pudding mold or deep ring mold. Set in a pan of hot water and bake 30 minutes.
7. Increase oven heat to 350 degrees and bake 50 minutes longer or until the pudding is puffed, golden and set.

Yield: 8 to 10 servings

BROCCOLI AND CORN CASSEROLE

2 eggs, lightly beaten
¼ cup light cream or milk
1 tablespoon grated onion
1 cup soft bread crumbs
2 tablespoons melted butter
2 cans (16–17 ounces each) cream-style corn

Salt and freshly ground black pepper to taste
2 cups broccoli flowerets (about half a bunch), cooked 5 minutes in boiling salted water and drained
3 slices bacon, cooked until crisp, and crumbled
1–2 pimentos, diced

1. Preheat oven to 350 degrees.
2. Mix the eggs with the cream and onion. Soak the crumbs in the mixture. Add the butter and corn and mix well.
3. Season with salt and pepper. Arrange the broccoli in a buttered baking dish or casserole. Pour the corn mixture over and toss lightly. Sprinkle with the bacon bits and pimento pieces. Bake 30 minutes or until heated through and set.

Yield: 6 to 8 servings

CORN AND PEPPER RELISH

9 ears fresh corn,
  shucked
½ small head fresh
  cabbage, cored and
  finely shredded
4 small white onions,
  chopped
2 sweet red peppers,
  washed, cored,
  seeded and diced
2 sweet green pep-
  pers, washed, cored,
  seeded and diced

2 teaspoons crushed,
  dried, hot pepper
  pods
1 teaspoon celery
  seeds
2 teaspoons mustard
  seeds
3 cups white vinegar
1 cup water
2 tablespoons salt
1 cup sugar

1. Scrape the kernels from the ears of corn and place in a kettle along with corn milk scraped from the cobs.

2. Add remaining ingredients, bring to a boil and simmer 20 minutes. Pack into hot, sterilized jars, leaving ¼-inch headspace. Process 10 minutes in a boiling water bath. Cool and test the seals. Store in a cool, dark, dry place.

Yield: About 5 pints

PICKLED PEPPERS

2 quarts large, firm,
  sweet red peppers,
  washed, seeds and
  membranes removed
  and cut into strips
  to fit pint-size
  canning jars

4 teaspoons salt
4 teaspoons mustard
  seeds
3 cups white vinegar
3 cups water

1. Pack the pepper strips into 4 pint-size canning jars. Add 1 teaspoon salt and 1 teaspoon mustard seeds to each jar.

2. Combine the vinegar and water in a saucepan. Bring to a boil and pour over the pepper strips, leaving ¼-inch headspace. Adjust

the caps and process in a boiling water bath 10 minutes. Cool and test the seals. Store in a cool, dark, dry place.

Yield: 4 pints

CRANBERRY SALAD MOLD

4 cups (1 pound) fresh cranberries
1 cup plus 1 table-spoon sugar
1 envelope unflavored gelatin
½ cup orange juice
1 cup chopped celery
1 cup chopped, peeled apple
1 cup chopped pecans or walnuts
2 cucumbers, peeled and thinly sliced
Salt
½ cup white vinegar
2 tablespoons water
1 tablespoon snipped fresh dill weed
⅛ teaspoon freshly ground white pepper
Salad greens, washed and crisped

1. Pick over and wash the cranberries. Drain and put through a food grinder, using the coarse blade. Stir in the cup of sugar and let stand 15 minutes. Stir occasionally.

2. Sprinkle the gelatin over the orange juice and let soften. Heat while stirring until gelatin dissolves.

3. Add gelatin mixture, celery, apple and nuts to the cranberries. Mix well and turn into a rinsed 5- to 6-cup ring mold and chill until firm.

4. Place the cucumber slices in a glass or ceramic bowl. Sprinkle with salt and weight down with a heavy plate. Let stand 2 hours.

5. Rinse the slices in cold water, drain well and return to the bowl. Combine the vinegar, 1 tablespoon sugar, water, dill and pepper and pour over the cucumber slices. Cover and chill at least 2 hours.

6. Unmold the cranberry ring onto a serving plate ringed with salad greens and fill the center with cucumber slices.

Yield: 8 to 10 servings

CRANE HOUSE PUMPKIN BREAD

1 cup corn oil
4 eggs, beaten
⅔ cup water
2 cups canned
  pumpkin
3⅓ cups flour
1½ teaspoons salt

1 teaspoon grated
  nutmeg
1 teaspoon cinnamon
2 teaspoons baking
  soda
3 cups sugar
½ cup golden raisins
½ cup chopped nuts

1. Preheat oven to 350 degrees.
2. Combine the oil, eggs, water and pumpkin and mix well.
3. Sift together the flour, salt, nutmeg, cinnamon and baking soda and stir into the pumpkin mixture. Stir in the sugar and then the raisins and nuts.
4. Turn the mixture into 2 greased loaf pans, either 12 by 3⅓ by 2½ inches, or 9 by 5 by 3 inches. Bake 1 hour or until done. Cool in the pans 15 minutes, turn out and finish cooling on a rack.

Yield: 2 loaves

FRUITED PEANUT PIE

1¼ cups flour
⅛ teaspoon salt
⅓ cup shortening
¼ cup very finely
  ground roasted,
  unsalted peanuts
  (a Mouli grater
  does the best job)
  Ice water
½ cup butter
1 cup sugar
½ cup chopped, un-
  salted raw peanuts
  or unsalted roasted
  peanuts (see note)

¼ cup mixed candied
  fruits, chopped
1 teaspoon grated
  lemon rind
1 tablespoon lemon
  juice
½ cup raisins
½ cup flaked coconut
3 eggs, lightly beaten
¼ teaspoon grated
  nutmeg
¼ teaspoon cinnamon
  Whipped cream
  Roasted peanut
  halves

1. Place the flour and salt in a bowl and blend in the shortening until the mixture resembles coarse oatmeal.

2. Add the finely ground nuts and stir in enough water to make a dough. Roll out on a lightly floured board and use to line a 9-inch pie plate.

3. Decorate the edge and chill while making the filling.

4. Preheat oven to 350 degrees.

5. Melt the butter and combine with remaining ingredients except the cream and peanut halves. Pour into the pie shell and bake 40 minutes or until set and lightly browned.

6. Cool to room temperature. Decorate with whipped cream and peanut halves before serving.

Yield: 6 to 8 servings

Note: Raw unsalted peanuts give the pie a more subtle flavor than do roasted ones. Raw unsalted peanuts can be bought shelled and skinned in Chinatown markets or in the shell at most nut stores. Eight to 10 ounces of nuts in the shell yield 1 cup of nutmeats.

Sunday After Thanksgiving

✖

An invitation to come over for supper the Sunday after Thanksgiving is especially welcome for friends who have been away for the long weekend and arrive home to an empty refrigerator. With a little ingenuity, and the menu below, the hostess can reduce an inventory of leftovers, from turkey to a pumpkin centerpiece, and not shortchange the most fastidious guest. Set the dishes on the stove or hot plate in the kitchen to keep warm and as people arrive let them help themselves to soup and a sandwich or a taste of everything.

*Croque-Monsieur**
*Country Soup in a Pumpkin**
OR
*Turkey Vegetable Soup**
*Tortière de Famille**
*Cranberry Fouler**

◆ ◆◆ ◆

CROQUE-MONSIEUR

½ cup butter, clarified
8 slices firm sandwich
 bread
4 thin slices baked
 ham
4 thin slices roasted
 turkey breast

4 slices mozzarella
 cheese
Freshly ground
 black pepper to
 taste
Pinch allspice

1. Lightly butter one side of each slice of bread. Place a slice of ham, one of turkey and one of mozzarella on the buttered side of 4 slices of bread.

2. Season with pepper and allspice. Top with remaining bread, buttered side down. Heat enough of the remaining butter to cover the bottom of a heavy, heated skillet. Sauté the sandwiches in it slowly, turn and brown the second side, making sure that the cheese has melted. Cut into quarters and serve as an appetizer with drinks or to those who want only soup and a sandwich.

Yield: 8 appetizer or 4 main-course servings

COUNTRY SOUP IN A PUMPKIN

1½ cups fresh bread crumbs made from leftover rolls or firm bread
1 unblemished pumpkin with a good stem (6–7 pounds)
Salt
6 tablespoons butter
2 cups finely chopped onions
Freshly grated nutmeg to taste
Freshly ground black pepper to taste

1 cup (4 ounces) coarsely grated Swiss cheese
¼ cup freshly grated Parmesan cheese
6 cups turkey stock made from the carcass and giblets, approximately
1 bay leaf
½ cup heavy cream
Chopped flat-leaf Italian parsley

1. Preheat oven to 300 degrees.

2. Spread the bread crumbs in a shallow roasting pan and dry in the oven for about 15 minutes, stirring occasionally. Remove pan.

3. Increase oven heat to 400 degrees.

4. With a sharp knife, cut a cover 4 inches in diameter out of the top of the pumpkin. With a long-handled spoon, scrape out the seeds and stringy material from the inside. Sprinkle the inside lightly with salt.

5. Heat the butter in a heavy skillet and cook the onions in it until tender and translucent. Stir in the crumbs and cook 2 minutes,

or until the butter has been absorbed. Stir in 1 teaspoon salt, the nutmeg and pepper.

6. Remove from the heat and stir in the cheeses. Spoon the mixture into the pumpkin. Pour in the turkey stock until it reaches to within 1 inch of the rim. Place bay leaf on top and replace pumpkin cover.

7. Put the pumpkin in a buttered baking dish and bake 1½ hours, or until the pumpkin begins to soften and the soup is bubbling. Reduce oven heat to 350 degrees and bake 30 minutes longer. Pumpkin should be tender but hold its shape. If pumpkin starts to brown, cover with aluminum foil.

8. Just before serving, remove the cover and stir in cream and chopped parsley. Serve the soup with a scraping of pumpkin.

Yield: 8 servings

TURKEY VEGETABLE SOUP

1 turkey carcass with most of meat removed, broken up	½ teaspoon thyme Cold water
2 whole cloves	1 package (10 ounces) frozen baby lima beans
3 onions	
4 ribs celery	1 package (10 ounces) frozen peas
8 carrots	
1 leek	1 cup uncooked narrow noodles
3 parsley sprigs	
1 bay leaf Salt and freshly ground black pepper to taste	2 cups diced cooked turkey meat
	¼ cup chopped parsley

1. Place the turkey carcass in a large kettle. Stick a clove into each of 2 onions and add to kettle.

2. Cut 2 celery ribs into quarters and 4 carrots into thirds. Add to kettle along with the leek, parsley sprigs, bay leaf, salt, pepper, thyme and enough cold water to barely cover the bones.

3. Bring to a boil, cover and simmer 3 hours or until all meat has dropped from the bones. Strain the broth into a clean saucepan and boil, uncovered, to reduce to 2 quarts if necessary. Chop remaining onion, celery and carrots and add. Simmer, covered, 8 minutes.

4. Add the lima beans and peas and return mixture to the boil. Add the noodles and cook 8 minutes or until tender. Add the turkey meat, correct the seasoning if needed and reheat. Sprinkle with chopped parsley.

Yield: 6 servings

TORTIÈRE DE FAMILLE

Pastry

1⅔ cups flour	1 egg yolk
Pinch salt	1 tablespoon oil
½ cup cold butter	¼ cup ice water

Filling

6 tablespoons clarified butter or oil	3 cups bite-size cooked turkey pieces
½ cup coarsely chopped carrots	1 cup diced baked ham
½ cup coarsely chopped celery	Steamed or leftover white onions, peas, asparagus, carrots or other firm-texture vegetables
2 scallions, sliced	
3 tablespoons finely diced baked ham	
¼ cup flour	
3 cups rich stock made from turkey carcass	1 egg
¼ teaspoon curry powder	1 tablespoon water
Salt and freshly ground black pepper to taste	

1. To prepare pastry, place the flour and salt in a bowl. Work in the butter until the mixture is the consistency of coarse oatmeal.

2. Beat the egg yolk with the oil and water, and stir into the flour, using a fork, until it forms a dough. Wrap in wax paper and chill for 20 minutes.

3. To prepare filling, heat the clarified butter in a heavy skillet and cook in it the carrots, celery, scallions and 3 tablespoons ham

for 10 minutes. Sprinkle with the flour, stir to blend and continue to cook, while stirring, until flour turns a golden brown.

4. Blend in the stock gradually. Season with curry powder, salt and pepper. Simmer, stirring occasionally, for 30 minutes. Add the turkey, 1 cup ham and the cooked vegetables and transfer to a shallow baking dish, about 8 by 13 inches.

5. Preheat oven to 375 degrees.

6. Roll out the chilled pastry to a size 1 inch larger than the dish. Place over the filling, turn under the extra pastry for a double edge and decorate. Brush with egg mixed with water. Make a steam hole and bake the pie 45 minutes or until browned and done.

Yield: 8 servings

CRANBERRY FOULER

1 pound cranberries
1 cup sugar
Juice of 1 orange
Grated rind of 2 oranges
¼ cup butter
¾ cup old-fashioned rolled oats
⅓ cup dark brown sugar
⅓ cup flour
1 cup heavy cream, whipped
Vanilla bean
1 tablespoon confectioners' sugar

1. Preheat oven to 375 degrees.

2. Wash cranberries, drain well and shake off excess water.

3. Place the berries, sugar, orange juice and rind in a 6-cup porcelain soufflé dish. Mix.

4. With the fingers, mix together the butter, oats, brown sugar and flour. Sprinkle mixture evenly over the berries. Bake 40 minutes. Cool to lukewarm.

5. Whip the cream with the scrapings from a 2-inch section of the vanilla bean and the confectioners' sugar and serve with the warm dessert.

Yield: 8 servings

Holiday Preparations

Preparations for Christmas start early in December in our house with the making of plum puddings and fruitcakes. There will never be a compromise as far as the pudding recipe is concerned, and big bowls of fruit-filled batter must be stirred by every member of the family to bring good luck. The steamed puddings will keep for months. Over the years our holiday cakes have become lighter, with less fruit and nuts, and this particular recipe makes a poundcake-style loaf with just enough candied fruit and raisins to make the loaf festive. Wrap the cooled cake in a rum-soaked cheesecloth and store in a tin, in a secret place, until Christmas.

Helene Borey's Plum Pudding with Hard Sauce*
Light Fruitcake*

HELENE BOREY'S PLUM PUDDING WITH HARD SAUCE

½ pound currants
2 tablespoons plus ¼
   cup brandy
   Hot water
¼ pound glacéed
   orange peel
¼ pound glacéed
   lemon peel
¼ pound glacéed
   citron peel
½ pound soft, dark,
   bulk-pack raisins
½ pound shelled wal-
   nuts, finely ground
1 cup flour

1 teaspoon baking
   soda
1 teaspoon salt
1 teaspoon cinnamon
¼ teaspoon grated
   nutmeg
¼ teaspoon mace
½ pound ground suet
3 slices thinly sliced
   firm bread
   Apple juice
1 cup dark brown
   sugar
3 eggs, lightly beaten
⅓ cup black currant
   preserves

1. Place the currants in a bowl. Sprinkle with 2 tablespoons of the brandy and add enough hot water to barely cover the fruit. Set aside while finely chopping the orange, lemon and citron peel.

2. Place the raisins, chopped peel and the walnuts in a large bowl. Sift together the flour, baking soda, salt, cinnamon, nutmeg and mace and add to the bowl.

3. Stir in the soaked currants and the suet. Tear the bread slices into a small bowl and dampen with apple juice. Add to the fruit mixture.

4. Stir in the brown sugar, eggs and preserves and beat well. Turn into a well-oiled 2-quart pudding mold (preferably one that has a cover). Secure the metal cover with string or use wax paper and then a final covering of aluminum foil. Set on a rack with boiling water coming at least halfway up the mold or steam in the top of a steamer for 6 hours.

5. Uncover and pour remaining brandy over. Place a fresh piece of wax paper next to the pudding and cover with lid or foil. Store in a cool place to ripen (about 3 weeks). Steam 3 more hours before serving.

6. The second steaming can be done ahead and the pudding un-molded, wrapped in foil and reheated in a 300-degree oven for an hour.

7. Serve with hard sauce (recipe below).

Yield: 10 to 15 servings

Note: To serve the pudding, warm ½ cup bourbon with 1 teaspoon sugar, then put a match to mixture before pouring over the pudding.

Hard Sauce

½ *pound whipped unsalted butter, softened*	2 *cups sifted confectioners' sugar*
⅛ *teaspoon salt*	1 *egg yolk*
	¼ *cup heavy cream*
	¼ *cup cognac*

Place half the ingredients in an electric blender and blend at medium speed until smooth. Add remaining ingredients and continue blending until smooth and creamy. Refrigerate, but remove at least 1 hour before serving.

Yield: About 4 cups

LIGHT FRUITCAKE

3 *cups plus 2 tablespoons cake flour*	1 *cup plus 2 tablespoons sugar*
1 *cup softened unsalted butter*	¼ *teaspoon salt*
1 *teaspoon baking powder*	¼ *cup light corn syrup*
1 *teaspoon vanilla*	⅓ *cup milk*
4 *eggs*	1¼ *cup raisins*
	1¼ *cups diced candied fruits*
	¾ *cup chopped walnuts*

1. Preheat oven to 350 degrees.

2. Place 3 cups flour, the butter, baking powder and vanilla in a mixing bowl and with an electric mixer at low speed or with a wooden spoon beat until mixture is creamed together.

3. Beat the eggs, sugar and salt together until light and thick.

4. Stir the egg mixture gradually into the creamed butter and flour gently but firmly until smooth.

5. Mix together the syrup and milk and stir into the batter.

6. In a bowl, mix together the raisins, candied fruit and nuts. Toss with the remaining flour and stir into the batter. Turn into a greased 9-by-5-by-3-inch loaf pan and bake 1½ hours or until cake is done.

Yield: 1 loaf

Make-Ahead Dinner for Six

꙲

There is no gelatin in the oeufs en gelée appetizer that Behri Knauth of Stonington, Connecticut whips up as part of an easy-on-the-hostess dinner for six. Using the packaged product was cheating she found out during the year and a half she spent as a private pupil of Simone Beck, co-author with Julia Child of the two-volume *Mastering the Art of French Cooking*. But the sour cream sauce for the celery root accompaniment to the molded appetizer was Mrs. Knauth's original idea. Blending the classic with innovative twists is an art and a science and the results from preparing Mrs. Knauth's menu below can be the reward.

*Oeufs en Gelée**
*Celery Root with Sour Cream**
*Mushroom Salad**
*Chicken in Red Wine**
Potatoes Anna
Spinach
Fresh Fruit Compote with Grand Marnier
(made a day ahead to allow the flavors to blend)

OEUFS EN GELÉE

Necks, wings and
gizzards from 6–8
chickens
Cold water
2 carrots, sliced
1 large onion, sliced
¼ white turnip, diced
½ cup diced celery
with leaves
2 whole cloves
1 bay leaf
1 teaspoon thyme
Salt and freshly
ground black pepper
to taste
1 tablespoon Madeira

1 tablespoon chopped
fresh basil or dill
weed
2 ounces thin-sliced,
cooked, smoked
ham, diced
6 fresh or pickled
tarragon leaves or
thin radish slices
6 eggs mollet (eggs
poached 3 minutes
and plunged into
cold water)
Salad greens or
parsley and dill

1. One or two days ahead, place the necks, wings and gizzards in a soup kettle. Cover with water and bring to a boil. Skim off all the scum while the mixture boils vigorously for 10 minutes.

2. Add the carrots, onion, turnip, celery, cloves, bay leaf, thyme, salt and pepper. Reduce heat, cover tightly and simmer slowly 12 to 24 hours, adding more water as necessary.

3. Strain the broth into a clean saucepan. There should be about 3 to 4 cups. (Mrs. Knauth does not clear her broth.) Add the Madeira and the basil or dill and check for seasoning. The broth should be slightly oversalted.

4. If there is any doubt, check the jelling consistency by chilling the mixture overnight. Next day heat to melt and cool slightly.

5. In egg-shaped molds or custard cups, arrange the ham and the tarragon leaves or radish slices in a pattern. Spoon in a layer of broth and chill. Set the eggs on chilled layer and add remaining broth. Chill well.

6. Unmold onto salad greens or garnish with parsley and dill.

Yield: 6 servings

CELERY ROOT WITH SOUR CREAM

1 egg, beaten until light and thick	2 teaspoons grated onion
1 teaspoon salt	1 tablespoon imported prepared mustard, or to taste
⅛ teaspoon freshly ground black pepper	
⅛ teaspoon sugar	1½ cups sour cream
1 tablespoon lemon juice	1 medium-size celery root, peeled and grated finely

1. Combine the egg with the remaining ingredients except the celery root.

2. Use enough of the sour cream sauce to moisten the celery root well. Chill.

Yield: 6 servings

MUSHROOM SALAD

1 tablespoon Dijon mustard	⅛ teaspoon sugar
½ cup olive oil, approximately	¾ pound mushrooms Salt and freshly ground black pepper to taste
1½ tablespoons wine vinegar	
1 tablespoon finely chopped shallot	

1. Place the mustard in a bowl and with a wire whisk gradually, a drop at a time to start, beat the oil into the mustard until mixture has consistency of mayonnaise.

2. Beat in the vinegar, shallot and sugar.

3. Cut stems from cleaned mushrooms. Slice mushrooms thinly. Pour the sauce over and season with salt and pepper. Toss and chill.

Yield: 6 servings

CHICKEN IN RED WINE

2 three-pound chickens,
  cut into serving
  pieces
  Salt and freshly
  ground black pepper
  to taste
1 cup softened butter

1 teaspoon dried
  tarragon
½ teaspoon dried basil
2 tablespoons chopped
  parsley
2 tablespoons finely
  chopped shallots
  Dry red wine

1. Preheat oven to 400 degrees.

2. Place the chicken in a shallow baking dish. Season with salt and pepper.

3. Mix together the butter, tarragon, basil, parsley and shallots and smear over the top of the chicken. Pour red wine down the side of the dish until wine extends halfway up the chicken.

4. Bake, uncovered, 40 minutes, or until browned and done.

Yield: 6 to 8 servings

Note: Mrs. Knauth prepares the dish completely, lets it sit in the refrigerator until cocktail time and then bakes the chicken. It will take at least 15 to 20 minutes longer to bake if cold.

Colgate-Dartmouth Tailgate Picnic

✼

Kickoff time is 1 P.M., leaving plenty of time for a tailgate picnic before finding seats in the grandstand. Ward off the damp, chilly air with mugs of steaming leek soup carried in a Thermos flask. Cut thick slices of the chicken loaf, which slides easily from the loaf pan it was made in, onto a tray. Pass the lentil salad and a plastic container of raw relishes. Pour a California Zinfandel or, if you prefer, a chilled Chablis. Fruited cheese pies travel well in their individual tart pans and, if they are the disposable kind, so much the better. Better have lots of strong black coffee.

Leek Soup*
Tarragon Chicken Loaf*
Lentil Salad*
Raw Relishes
Fruited Cheese Pies*
California Zinfandel or Chablis

———————◆•◆———————

LEEK SOUP

¼ cup butter
4 cups thinly sliced
(about 8 medium-
size) leeks
2 potatoes, peeled and
thinly sliced
1 carrot, thinly sliced
1 rib celery, thinly
sliced
1 quart chicken broth
Salt and freshly
ground black pepper
to taste

⅛ teaspoon grated
nutmeg
2 tablespoons quick-
cooking oats
½ cup light cream
2 tablespoons chopped
parsley
4 slices bacon, cooked
until crisp, and
crumbled

1. Heat the butter in a heavy kettle or casserole and sauté the leeks in it until golden. Add potatoes, carrot and celery and cook 4 minutes longer.

2. Add chicken broth, salt, pepper, nutmeg and oats. Bring to a boil, cover and cook 1 to 1½ hours, or until vegetables are very soft. At this point the soup may be put through a food mill or left as is.

3. Stir the cream and parsley into the sieved or unsieved soup, and sprinkle the bacon bits over the top.

Yield: 6 servings

Tarragon Chicken Loaf

1 stewing chicken or fowl (4–5 pounds), cut into serving pieces

1 onion, studded with 2 whole cloves

1 bay leaf

2 carrots, quartered

2 ribs celery with leaves, quartered

2 sprigs parsley

1½ teaspoons dried tarragon, or 1 tablespoon plus 1 teaspoon chopped fresh tarragon leaves

2½ cups chicken broth, approximately

Salt and freshly ground black pepper to taste

½ envelope unflavored gelatin

¼ cup water

½ pound cooked ham, cut into slivers (about 2 cups)

1½ cups coarsely ground celery including inner leaves

3 tablespoons chopped parsley

2 tablespoons chopped chives

1. Two days before the dish is to be served, place the chicken pieces in a heavy casserole. Add the onion, bay leaf, carrots, quartered celery ribs, parsley sprigs, 1 teaspoon dried or 1 tablespoon fresh tarragon and enough broth to come about halfway up the chicken pieces. Season with salt and pepper.

2. Bring to a boil, cover and simmer 30 minutes. Turn the chicken pieces and simmer, covered, 30 minutes longer or until the chicken is tender. Allow the chicken to cool in the broth.

3. Remove the chicken pieces, discard skin and bones, wrap meat in clear plastic wrap and refrigerate.

4. Strain the broth into a clean saucepan and boil, uncovered, until reduced to 2 to 2½ cups. Cool and chill overnight.

5. Next day (one day before dish is to be served) soften the gelatin in the water. Remove fat from top of broth. Heat broth to boiling and stir in the softened gelatin. Set aside. Grind the chicken through the coarse blade of a meat grinder. Season lightly with salt and pepper.

6. Rinse out a 9-by-5-by-3-inch loaf pan with cold water. Arrange

the ham in the bottom. Mix together the ground celery, chopped parsley, chives and remaining tarragon and spread over the ham.

7. Add the chicken. Pour the broth over and press the chicken layer down lightly so that broth comes barely to the surface. Chill overnight. Unmold to serve in slices.

Yield: 8 servings

LENTIL SALAD

1 pound lentils, picked over and washed
5 cups cold water
1 bay leaf
Salt
2 onions, each studded with 2 whole cloves
⅔ cup olive oil
¼ cup wine vinegar
¼ teaspoon dry mustard
¼ teaspoon sugar

1 clove garlic, finely chopped
½ teaspoon worcestershire sauce
Tabasco to taste
Freshly ground black pepper
½ cup finely chopped scallions
3 tablespoons chopped parsley
3 hard-cooked eggs, quartered

1. Place the lentils, water, bay leaf, 1½ teaspoons salt and the onions in a heavy saucepan.

2. Bring to a boil, cover and simmer 30 minutes or until lentils are tender but still retain their shape. Drain off excess liquid, remove onions and bay leaf and place lentils in a bowl.

3. Meanwhile, combine the olive oil, wine vinegar, mustard, sugar, garlic, worcestershire, Tabasco and salt and pepper to taste. Beat well and pour over the hot lentils. Toss gently.

4. Chill the lentils several hours or overnight. Add the scallions and parsley and mix. Garnish with the egg quarters.

Yield: 12 servings

FRUITED CHEESE PIES

3 cups peeled, diced ripe nectarines, peaches, pears, apples, pitted cherries or plums
⅓ cup plus ¼ cup sugar
2 tablespoons flour
2 teaspoons grated lime rind
⅛ teaspoon cinnamon
1–2 drops red food coloring (optional)

2 packages (3 ounces each) softened cream cheese
2 tablespoons lime juice
½ teaspoon salt
½ cup heavy cream
3 eggs, separated
1 unbaked 9-inch pie shell, chilled, or 8–10 pastry-lined 3- to 4-inch tart tins, chilled

1. Preheat oven to 375 degrees.
2. Place the fruit, ⅓ cup sugar, 1 tablespoon flour, 1 teaspoon lime rind, the cinnamon and red coloring in a small saucepan. Heat, stirring gently, until sugar is dissolved. Simmer until fruit is barely tender, about 5 minutes. Cool.
3. In a bowl, beat together the cream cheese, lime juice, remaining tablespoon flour, ¼ cup sugar and lime rind, the salt, cream and egg yolks.
4. Beat the egg whites until stiff but not dry and fold into the cheese mixture.
5. Place the fruit mixture in the bottom of the pie shell or tart pans and top with the cream cheese mixture. Bake the big pie 45 minutes, tarts about 25 minutes, or until lightly browned and set. Cool and serve at room temperature.
Yield: 8 servings

Dinner à la
Portugaise

꒰

Fishing is one of the most revered and important industries along Portugal's long coastline. From fresh sardines grilling over charcoal braziers outside peasant cottages, to the spiny crustaceans served in luxurious Lisbon restaurants and the thick hake steaks in pousada dining rooms, fish is a diet staple and the basis for many tasty meals. Caldo verde, a national dish in Portugal, is a simple vegetable soup, and together with the fish casserole it makes an excellent meal for family weekend dining at any season. In the fall this meal will offer a change of pace after the cold dishes and barbecues of summer. For a more elaborate repast, flame sausage slices with rum in the living room and serve with chilled white port. Add an elegant orange torte with tawny port for dessert and you have a festive meal for entertaining.

Ruth McMillin's Obidos Sausage*
Chilled White Port
Caldo Verde*
Peixe a Natercia*
Vinho Verde Branco
Orange Torte*
Tawny Port

Ruth McMillin's Obidos Sausage

1 pound smoked Portuguese, Polish or
Italian sausage
Hot water

½ loaf Portuguese or
Italian bread
5 ounces dark Jamaica rum, warmed
slightly

1. Preheat oven to 160 degrees. Warm a deep heatproof plate.
2. Place sausage in a saucepan, cover with hot water and simmer
very gently 15 minutes. When cool enough to handle, remove skins
and slice sausage into bite-size pieces.
3. Place on the warm plate and keep warm in the oven until
ready to serve.
4. Cut the bread into small pieces that will wrap around each
slice of sausage.
5. Ignite the rum and pour over the sausage; stir with a wooden-
handled or bone-handled fork until flames die out. Eat sausage on
toothpicks or wrapped in a piece of bread.
Yield: 8 appetizer servings

Caldo Verde

1 quart chicken
broth
1 quart water
1 large potato,
peeled and sliced
1½ teaspoons salt
⅛ teaspoon freshly
ground black
pepper
¼ cup raw rice

4½ cups finely shred-
ded romaine, kale
or spinach leaves
1 cup smoked Portu-
guese sausage slices
(Spanish or Polish
garlic sausage can
be substituted)
1 tablespoon olive oil

1. Place the broth, water, potato, salt and pepper in a kettle.
Cover and cook over medium heat until the potato slices are tender.
2. Mash potato slightly into liquid.
3. Add rice and cook until tender.
4. Bring to a boil. Add shredded greens and sausage. Boil, uncovered, 3 minutes. Add oil and check seasoning.
Yield: 8 servings

Peixe a Natercia (Fish Casserole)

2 sprigs celery leaves
2 sprigs parsley
1 scallion, cut into
　2-inch pieces
½ bay leaf
4 whole black pep-
　percorns
3 cups water
2½ pounds fresh cod,
　hake, halibut or
　other large white
　fish, cut into 2-inch
　pieces

1 tablespoon salt
2 medium-size
　potatoes, peeled
2 tablespoons butter
2 tablespoons oil
3 medium-size
　onions, thinly
　sliced

Sauce

6 tablespoons butter
7 tablespoons flour
⅛ teaspoon ground
　white pepper
2½ cups fish stock
　(from cooking fish
　above)

1 cup heavy cream
4 egg yolks, lightly
　beaten
2 tablespoons chop-
　ped parsley
3 eggs, hard-cooked
　and sliced

1. Tie the celery leaves, parsley, scallion, bay leaf and pepper-corns in a muslin bag and place in a kettle with the water.

2. Bring to a boil and simmer 5 minutes.

3. Add fish, salt and whole peeled potatoes. Bring to a boil, reduce heat and simmer until fish is cooked, about 10 minutes.

4. Lift the fish out with a slotted spoon, remove bones and return them to stock. Cover fish and set aside.

5. Continue cooking potatoes in stock until they are tender. Remove potatoes and reduce stock by boiling until it measures 2½ cups. Strain stock and discard solids.

6. Heat the butter and oil, add the onions and sauté them slowly until they brown slightly (this takes 25 minutes).

7. Preheat oven to 475 degrees.

8. To prepare sauce, melt the butter in a saucepan, blend in the flour and cook 3 minutes. Add pepper. Gradually stir in the fish stock. Cook, stirring, until sauce thickens. Add cream.

9. Add a little of the sauce to the egg yolks, return to the pan and cook to thicken but do not boil.

10. Add parsley and check seasoning.

11. To assemble the casserole, break the fish into small pieces and use to cover the bottom of a buttered 9-by-13-by-2-inch baking dish or other shallow baking dish. Slice the potatoes into ¼-inch slices and add in a layer over the fish. Add a layer of egg slices. Spread onions over eggs and pour sauce over.

12. Bake in upper half of oven 15 minutes or until browned.

Yield: 8 servings

ORANGE TORTE

6 eggs, at room
temperature
1 cup sugar
Grated rind and
juice of 1 large

orange (about ⅓
cup)
Confectioners' sugar

1. Preheat oven to 325 degrees.

2. Beat the eggs until light and fluffy. Gradually beat in the sugar until the mixture is very thick and lemon colored.

3. Fold in the rind and juice and pour into a 15-by-10-by-1-inch buttered jellyroll pan lined with well-buttered parchment paper. Bake 35 minutes or until golden and set.

4. Turn out onto a towel sprinkled with confectioners' sugar and roll up like a jellyroll. Cool but do not chill. Serve in thick slices. The torte holds its shape, but is custardy in texture.

Yield: 6 to 8 servings

Chinese Dinner
for Eight

✥

In San Francisco and New York, shopping for Chinese ingredients is an excuse for a half-day's jaunt to Chinatown with an inexpensive tea-lunch as the bonus. It is a stimulating Saturday excursion to put you in the mood for a Chinese dinner at home. In other cities and suburbs, there is likely to be an Oriental store where you can buy celery cabbage, fresh bean curd, hoisin sauce and the other simple ingredients needed for the menu below. These shops have been encouraged by the recent proliferation of schools teaching Chinese cooking. But, this menu to serve eight family-style can be prepared without learning to lift a cleaver. A good sharp French chef's knife will do an adequate shredding and chopping job. Preparing crispy walnuts with hoisin sauce requires patience and time to remove the last bitter specks of nut skin, but the results are worth it. Main dishes can be prepared ahead up to the point indicated, and to limit trips to the kitchen for last-minute preparation, it is suggested that the dinner be served in three parts.

———————◆•◆•◆———————

PART I

*Crispy Walnuts with Hoisin Sauce**
*Shrimp Apples**

NOTE: The walnuts, shrimp apples and spicy lamb and leek are specialties of the Shun Lee Palace Restaurant in Manhattan.

PART II

*Seaweed Soup**
*Spicy Lamb and Leek**
*Bean Curd Vegetable Dish**

PART III

*Poached Sea Bass**

AND

Loquats and Lichees
Blend of Chrysanthemum and Dragon Teas

———————◆•◆———————

CRISPY WALNUTS WITH HOISIN SAUCE

9 *ounces shelled walnuts*
Boiling water
2 *tablespoons hoisin sauce*
1½ *tablespoons sugar*
3 *tablespoons dry sherry*
1½ *teaspoons mono-sodium glutamate (optional)*

⅛ *teaspoon sesame oil*
3 *tablespoons chicken broth*
½ *teaspoon cornstarch mixed with 2 tea-spoons water*
3 *cups peanut or vegetable oil*

1. Cover the walnuts with boiling water and let soak 10 minutes. Drain and cover with boiling water again, soak 10 minutes, drain and cover with boiling water. Remove the walnuts one at a time and with the help of a toothpick remove the brown skin. This is a tedious job but is necessary in order to avoid a bitter end product.

2. Combine the remaining ingredients except for the oil and set aside. In a wok or skillet, heat the oil to 280 degrees. Add the peeled walnuts and stir-fry about 5 minutes.

3. With a skimmer or slotted spoon, remove the walnuts and set aside. Drain off all but 1 tablespoon of the oil.

4. Pour in the sauce ingredients and cook, stirring, 20 seconds over high heat. Add the walnuts and stir-fry another 20 seconds. Transfer to a serving plate. Cool before serving.

Yield: 3 to 4 appetizer servings

Note: This dish can be prepared several days ahead.

SHRIMP APPLES

14 ounces shrimp, shelled, deveined and finely chopped	1 egg white
	¼ teaspoon baking powder
⅓ cup sliced water chestnuts (fresh or canned), peeled, drained and finely chopped	1 tablespoon corn-starch mixed with 1 tablespoon water
	1 teaspoon red food coloring
2 tablespoons dry sherry	½ cup sesame seeds
¼ teaspoon salt	½ small green pepper, cut into 12 pieces, each 1 inch long by ¼ inch wide
¼ teaspoon mono-sodium glutamate (optional)	4 cups peanut oil

1. In a bowl, combine the shrimp and water chestnuts. In a second bowl, mix the sherry, salt, monosodium glutamate, if used, the egg white, baking powder and the cornstarch mixed with water. Add to the shrimp mixture and mix well with the hands.

2. Chill the mixture 30 minutes or longer.

3. Divide the mixture into 12 balls, each with a slight depression in the top to resemble an apple shape. Place the red coloring in a small bowl, add the sesame seeds and mix well.

4. Roll the shrimp balls in the seeds and stick a piece of green pepper into the top of each to resemble the stalk of the apple. Refrigerate to hold for cooking.

5. In a wok or a deep saucepan, heat the oil to about 300 degrees. Add the shrimp balls and cook slowly until the balls come to the surface and are cooked through, about 8 minutes.

Yield: 3 to 4 servings

Note: This dish can be prepared several hours ahead through step 4.

SEAWEED SOUP

2 cans (16 ounces each) chicken broth
Water
4 sheets jee choy (paper cabbage), a seaweed

1 egg, lightly beaten with chopsticks
1 scallion, finely chopped

1. Place broth and 2 cans of water in a saucepan and bring to a boil. Shred the seaweed into 1-inch strips and add to the broth. Simmer 3 minutes.

2. Bring the soup to a fast boil and slowly add the egg alongside of a chopstick while making a circle around the pot with it. This forms tiny egg strips. Add scallion and serve.

Yield: 8 servings

Note: This dish can be prepared ahead through step 1.

SPICY LAMB AND LEEK

10 ounces boneless, well-trimmed leg of lamb (12-ounce steak cut from the top of the leg, boned and trimmed), shaped into a slab of even thickness and well chilled or partially frozen
1 egg white
Cornstarch
Water
3 dried black mushrooms
¼ cup dry sherry
2 tablespoons soy sauce
1 teaspoon sugar

½ teaspoon monosodium glutamate (optional)
⅛ teaspoon ground white pepper
1 tablespoon Chinese chili sauce or paste
½ teaspoon white vinegar
1½ tablespoons chicken broth
3 cups peanut oil
¼ large, sweet red pepper, thinly sliced
½ cup sliced bamboo shoots
1 leek, cut into matchstick-size pieces

1. Cut the chilled or partially frozen lamb into strips ¼ inch wide and about 2 inches long. Add the egg white to the lamb and mix well with the fingers.

2. Mix 1 tablespoon cornstarch with 1 tablespoon water and add to the lamb; mix again. Set the mushrooms to soak 15 minutes in warm water to cover.

3. Mix 1½ teaspoons cornstarch with 1½ teaspoons water. Combine with the sherry, soy sauce, sugar, monosodium glutamate, if used, the white pepper, chili sauce, vinegar and broth in a bowl and mix well. Set aside.

4. In a wok or skillet, heat the oil to 400 degrees. Add the lamb mixture and stir-fry about 20 seconds. With a slotted spoon or skimmer, remove the lamb and set aside. Drain off all but 1 tablespoon of the oil.

5. Drain the soaked mushrooms and cut into eighths. Add the mushrooms with the sweet red pepper, bamboo shoots and leek pieces to the wok and stir-fry 15 seconds.

6. Return the lamb to the wok and pour the sauce over. Stir-fry 15 seconds over high heat.

Yield: 3 servings

Note: This dish can be prepared ahead through step 4.

Bean Curd Vegetable Dish

1 *wong nga bok (Chinese celery cabbage)*	2 *tablespoons soy sauce*
1 *pound bok choy (Chinese white cabbage)*	2–3 *tablespoons peanut oil*
4 *ribs celery*	*Salt*
½ *pound snow peas*	*Sesame oil to taste*
4 *squares dow foo (pressed bean curd)*	1 *carrot, finely slivered into 1-inch lengths*

1. Sliver the cabbages, celery and snow peas into very thin strips 2 inches long. Store separately in plastic bags in the refrigerator. Soak the bean curd in soy sauce overnight and sliver like the vegetables.

2. Bring all ingredients to room temperature. Heat the peanut oil in a hot wok. Add vegetables and bean curd and stir-fry 2 minutes. Salt lightly and add sesame oil. Serve on a round platter and garnish with carrot slivers.

Yield: 8 servings

POACHED SEA BASS

Water
1½ teaspoons salt
  2 sea bass (1–1½ pounds each), cleaned but with heads and tails left on
  6 preserved, sweet cucumbers, slivered into matchstick-size pieces
  6 thin slices fresh ginger, finely slivered, about 1 tablespoon

  2 scallions, with green tops, slivered into matchstick-size pieces
  3 tablespoons imported soy sauce
  3 tablespoons peanut oil
  ½ teaspoon sesame oil (optional) Chinese parsley (also called coriander or cilantro)

1. Place enough water in a fish poacher to cover the fish, add the salt and bring to a boil. Lower the fish into the poacher on the rack. Bring back to the boil, cover, shut off the flame and let stand 15 to 20 minutes or until fish are opaque throughout.

2. Drain fish and place on hot platter. Scatter pickle, ginger and scallion pieces over fish. Pour soy sauce over. Heat the oils and pour over. Garnish with parsley.

Yield: 8 servings

Note: This dish can be prepared ahead through step 1.

Poker Party
Ham-in-Rye

Though most poker players are happy with sandwiches, beer and apple pie, try a variation on that theme: a ham-in-rye loaf to serve with German mustard, apple slaw and beer. I guarantee there will be reorders for hunting and fishing trips coming up later in the fall. The ham-in-rye carries well without refrigeration. Apple cake à la mode will be a winner, too, and there may be enough cake left over for tomorrow's lunch boxes.

*Ham-in-Rye**
*Apple Slaw**
Beer
*Teddie's Apple Cake**

HAM-IN-RYE

1 package dry active yeast	1½ tablespoons caraway seeds
¼ cup lukewarm water	1 canned ham (3 pounds), at room temperature
2 cups scalded milk	
2 tablespoons butter	Cornmeal
2 teaspoons salt	1 egg white, lightly beaten
2 tablespoons sugar	
3 cups rye flour	1 tablespoon water
3½ cups unbleached white flour, approximately	

1. Dissolve the yeast in the warm water.

2. Pour the milk over the butter, salt and sugar placed in a bowl. Stir to melt the butter. Let cool to lukewarm.

3. Stir the dissolved yeast into the cooled milk mixture. Stir in the rye flour, enough of the white flour to make a fairly stiff dough and the caraway seeds.

4. Turn onto a lightly floured board and knead until the dough is smooth and elastic, about 10 minutes.

5. Place the dough in a clean, greased bowl; lightly grease the top of the dough, cover the bowl and let dough rise in a warm place until doubled in bulk, about 1 hour. Place the ham on a platter, cover and let warm in the same place as the bread dough for an hour.

6. Punch the dough down, cover it and let stand 5 minutes.

7. Mark the dough in thirds. On a lightly floured board, press or roll out the center third into a rectangle big enough to set the ham on and to draw up the sides. The other two thirds are still attached, but left thick.

8. Place the ham on the thin, rolled-out center piece of dough, draw up the thin sides of the dough around the ham and overlap the 2 thick ends over the top of the ham, pinching to seal. Shape the dough-covered ham into a neat round and place on a greased 10-inch pie plate sprinkled with cornmeal.

9. Cover with clear plastic wrap or a cloth and let rise in a warm place until doubled in bulk, about 45 minutes.

10. Preheat oven to 425 degrees.

11. Brush the loaf with the egg white mixed with the water. Bake 10 minutes, reduce oven heat to 375 degrees and bake 50 minutes longer or until done. Serve hot, or cool on a rack and serve at room temperature.

Yield: 6 to 8 servings

APPLE SLAW

5 cups finely shredded green cabbage

1 cup finely shredded red cabbage

2 unpeeled red apples, cored and diced

⅓ cup finely chopped sweet red onion

½ cup seeded, diced green pepper

1½ teaspoons plus 1 tablespoon sugar

½ cup dry white wine

⅓ cup lemon juice

1 teaspoon salt

¼ teaspoon freshly ground black pepper

3 tablespoons oil

4 hard-cooked egg yolks, mashed

½ cup heavy cream, whipped

2 tablespoons Dijon or Düsseldorf mustard, or to taste

1 cup chopped walnuts

1. Place the green and red cabbage, apples, onion and green pepper in a large bowl. Sprinkle with 1½ teaspoons sugar and pour wine over mixture. Chill.

2. Meanwhile, combine the lemon juice, remaining tablespoon of sugar, the salt, black pepper, oil and egg yolks. Mix well.

3. Stir in the cream and mustard. Pour over the chilled greens, add the walnuts and toss. Chill.

Yield: 10 servings

TEDDIE'S APPLE CAKE

1½ cups oil
2 cups sugar
3 eggs
3 cups flour
1 teaspoon salt
1 teaspoon cinnamon
1 teaspoon baking
   soda
1 teaspoon vanilla

3 cups peeled, cored
   and thickly sliced
   Delicious apples
1 cup chopped
   walnuts
1 cup raisins
   (optional)
   Vanilla ice cream
   (optional)

1. Preheat oven to 350 degrees.

2. Beat the oil and sugar together in electric mixer while assembling the remaining ingredients or until mixture is thick, creamy and nongrainy.

3. Add the eggs and beat until the mixture is creamy.

4. Sift together the flour, salt, cinnamon and baking soda. Stir into the batter. Add the vanilla, apples, walnuts and raisins and stir to blend.

5. Turn the mixture into a buttered and floured 9-inch angel-food tube pan. Bake 1¼ hours or until done. Cool in the pan before turning out. Serve at room temperature, with ice cream if desired.

Yield: 8 servings

Bring a Main-Dish Casserole to Serve Twelve

Members of a group who get together on a Saturday night at some-one's home share the work and take turns bringing different parts of the meal. The common interest of the group members may be as diverse as square-dancing, planning a campaign for the next elec-tion or going to the theater, but a satisfying meal that doesn't break anyone's budget is the key to continued success of bring-a-dish evenings. The menu below is designed with that in mind, and if the group runs to two dozen or more, pass out two or more copies of each recipe. One sure thing: no two finished dishes will look exactly the same when they come from different kitchens, but they will all taste good.

Stuffed Raw Mushrooms°
Barbecued Eggplant and Pine Nut Appetizer°
Chicken with Giblet Rice°
Fresh Corn Pudding°
Tossed Salad
Sour Cream–Apple Turnovers°

STUFFED RAW MUSHROOMS

6 ounces softened
   cream cheese
1 teaspoon softened
   butter
¾ teaspoon anchovy
   paste
½ teaspoon lemon
   juice

⅛ teaspoon cayenne
   pepper
2 dozen tiny raw
   mushroom caps
2 tablespoons chopped
   chives

Cream the cream cheese, butter, anchovy paste, lemon juice and cayenne together. Pipe the mixture through a small star tube into the mushroom caps and garnish with the chives. Alternately, the mixture can be spooned into the caps.

Yield: 2 dozen hors d'oeuvres

BARBECUED EGGPLANT AND PINE NUT APPETIZER

2 medium-size egg-
   plants
2 tomatoes
⅓ cup lemon juice
1½ teaspoons salt
   Freshly ground
   black pepper to
   taste
2 cloves garlic, finely
   chopped

½ cup olive oil
¼ cup pine nuts
¼ cup finely chopped
   scallions, including
   the green part
3 tablespoons chop-
   ped parsley
   Small squares of
   pumpernickel or
   flat bread

1. Prick the eggplants all over with a fork and place over hot coals on a barbecue grill, turning frequently until all sides are scorched. A skewer inserted through each eggplant makes turning easier.

2. Wrap the eggplants in aluminum foil and cook over the coals until soft. Spear the tomatoes on a skewer, or fork, and cook over the coals until skins wrinkle.

3. Peel the eggplants and tomatoes and place in a bowl. Mash with a fork or potato masher.

4. Beat in the lemon juice, salt, pepper, garlic, oil and pine nuts.

Chill. Sprinkle with the scallions and parsley and serve with the pumpernickel squares or flat bread.

Yield: 8 servings

CHICKEN WITH GIBLET RICE

2 tablespoons oil
2 tablespoons butter
3 frying chickens (3 pounds each), cut into serving pieces
4 carrots, quartered
2 onions, thinly sliced
1½ cups dry red wine
3 teaspoons salt
½ teaspoon freshly ground black pepper

1 cup canned beef gravy
1 tablespoon tomato paste
1 cup chicken broth
2 bay leaves
1 tablespoon chopped fresh tarragon, or ½ teaspoon dried
1 tablespoon chopped parsley
Giblet rice (recipe below)

1. Heat the oil and butter in a large, heavy casserole and sauté in it the chicken pieces, a few at a time, until brown on all sides. Set chicken pieces aside.

2. To the oil remaining in the casserole, add the carrots and onions. Cook, stirring, 5 minutes.

3. Pour in the wine and bring to a boil, stirring to loosen all browned-on particles. Add the salt, pepper, beef gravy, tomato paste, broth, bay leaves, tarragon and parsley. Bring to a boil, stirring.

4. Return the chicken to the casserole, cover and simmer 20 minutes. Stir to bring chicken pieces from the bottom to the top, cover and simmer 20 minutes longer.

5. Transfer the chicken pieces to a warm serving dish and keep warm. Strain the liquid and return to the casserole. Boil rapidly, uncovered, until the sauce is slightly thickened. Pour over the chicken and serve with giblet rice.

Yield: 10 to 12 servings

Giblet Rice

Giblets, necks and
wing tips from 3
chickens
5 cups water
2 small onions
Salt and freshly
ground black pep-
per to taste

1 bay leaf
2 tablespoons butter
1½ cups raw long-
grain rice
1 tablespoon chopped
parsley

1. Place the gizzards, necks and wing tips in a saucepan. Add the water, 1 onion, the salt, pepper and bay leaf. Bring to a boil, cover and simmer 15 minutes. Add livers and hearts and simmer 10 minutes longer.

2. Strain liquid and reserve. Discard necks and wing tips; chop giblets and reserve.

3. Chop remaining onion and sauté in butter until tender. Add rice and cook, stirring, until translucent.

4. Pour in reserved liquid, cover and simmer 20 minutes. Add giblets and parsley. Reheat.

Yield: 8 to 10 servings

FRESH CORN PUDDING

¼ cup butter
⅓ cup flour
1½ cups light cream
2 eggs, separated
1 teaspoon salt
1 teaspoon Dijon
mustard
Cayenne pepper to
taste

2 cups corn kernels
cut from the cob
2 teaspoons worces-
tershire sauce
1 tablespoon chop-
ped parsley
1 cup buttered
bread crumbs

1. Preheat oven to 350 degrees.

2. Melt the butter in a saucepan, stir in the flour and gradually blend in the cream. Bring to a boil, stirring.

3. Beat the egg yolks lightly and add with the salt, mustard, cayenne, corn, worcestershire and parsley.

4. Beat the egg whites until stiff but not dry and fold into corn mixture. Turn into a greased casserole. Top with crumbs and bake 30 minutes, or until lightly browned.

Yield: 6 servings

Sour Cream–Apple Turnovers

Pastry

2 *cups flour*	¼ *cup sugar*
½ *teaspoon salt*	½ *cup sour cream*
¾ *cup butter*	

Filling

2 *tablespoons flour*	4 *tart green apples,*
½ *cup sugar*	*peeled and thinly*
¼ *teaspoon cinnamon*	*sliced*
	¼ *cup butter*

1. To prepare pastry, sift the flour and salt into a bowl. With a pastry blender or 2 knives, cut in the butter until mixture resembles coarse oatmeal. Mix in the sugar and sour cream.

2. Roll out the dough on a lightly floured pastry cloth or board into a rectangle about 18 by 9 inches. Fold lengthwise into thirds. Wrap in aluminum foil and chill 2 hours.

3. Preheat oven to 375 degrees.

4. To prepare filling, combine the flour, sugar and cinnamon and toss with the apples.

5. Roll out the chilled pastry on a lightly floured pastry cloth or board to a thickness of ⅛ inch. Cut into 4½-inch rounds.

6. Place a tablespoon or two of apple mixture in the middle of each round. Dot with the butter. Moisten the edges, fold over and pinch with a fork to seal.

7. Place on ungreased baking sheet and bake 20 minutes or until golden and done.

Yield: 12 to 14 turnovers

Persian Treat

✣

One-pot dishes that can be served in the casserole they are cooked in are a boon to the person who wants to cut down on the number of pans, dishes and plates to scrub on an activity-filled weekend. Almost every country has several such dishes, and one of the more unusual is the group of vegetable and meat combinations from Iran called *khoresh*. The recipe given here is based on lamb and can be made with either eggplant or celery added. The *khoresh* can be made ahead and reheated, covered. One or two carefully chosen Middle Eastern accessories on the table can pinpoint the origin of the menu, which is suitable for a buffet or a seated dinner.

Jennifer Manocherian's Eggplant Khoresh*
Persian Rice*
Cucumbers in Yogurt
Orange Cake*
Turkish Coffee

———————— •❖• ————————

JENNIFER MANOCHERIAN'S EGGPLANT KHORESH

1 cup butter
2 onions, sliced
1 leg of lamb (7 pounds), boned, fat and gristle removed, and cut into 1-inch cubes
1 can (6 ounces) tomato paste

Water
¼ cup lemon juice
Salt and freshly ground black pepper
1 medium-size egg-plant, unpeeled and cut into ⅓-inch-thick slices

1. Heat ½ cup of the butter in a heavy casserole. Add the onions and then the lamb cubes. Cover the casserole and cook on medium-high heat about 20 minutes or until the meat has changed color from pink to brown. Do not stir.

2. Add the tomato paste, 1 paste can of water, the lemon juice and salt and pepper to taste.

3. Bring mixture to a boil, cover and simmer 1 hour.

4. Meanwhile, sprinkle the slices of eggplant with salt and let stand 30 minutes. Rinse off salt and pat slices dry.

5. Heat ¼ cup of the remaining butter in a heavy skillet and quickly brown in it the eggplant slices, a few at a time, on both sides. Add remaining butter as needed. Drain on paper towels.

6. Preheat oven to 300 degrees.

7. Transfer the meat cubes to a casserole or baking dish so that it is ⅔ full. Top with the eggplant slices, pour the sauce from the meat over and bake 40 minutes.

Yield: 6 to 8 servings

Note: For a celery *khoresh*, omit the eggplant slices. Sauté 6 cups diced celery and 1 large bunch fresh coriander or parsley, chopped, in the other ½ cup butter for 15 minutes. Add to the meat mixture in step 2, cover and simmer 1½ hours, or until meat is tender; no baking is needed.

Persian Rice

2 cups raw long-grain rice, preferably Basmatti rice, if available	4 tablespoons salt
	¾ cup butter
	1 Idaho potato, peeled and cut into ¼-inch slices
Water	

1. Early in the day, wash the rice in several changes of cold water. Drain and place in a bowl with cold water to cover. Stir in salt. Let rice soak until about 1½ hours before serving.

2. Drain off the soaking water into a large, heavy kettle. Add another 3 quarts of cold water. Bring to a boil, add rice and boil rapidly 5 minutes. Drain.

3. Melt butter with 2 tablespoons water. Place potato slices in a single layer in the bottom of a heavy kettle. Pour over slices about half the butter mixture, enough to cover bottom of the kettle.

4. Spoon the rice on top of the potato slices, forming a pyramid shape. Pour remaining butter mixture over.

5. Turn the heat to medium-high and cook about 5 minutes, or until steam starts to rise. Lower heat to medium-low; cover rice with a folded turkish towel and a heavy cover.

6. Steam 45 minutes. Check to see that the potato slices are brown. If not, remove cover and turn up the heat briefly to brown.

7. Mound the rice into a serving dish and garnish with the potato slices.

Yield: 6 servings

ORANGE CAKE

1 cup soft butter
1½ cups sugar
3 eggs, separated
2 cups flour
1 teaspoon baking powder
1 teaspoon baking soda
1 cup sour cream

Grated rind of 1 orange
½ cup chopped walnuts
¼ cup orange juice
⅓ cup orange-flavored liqueur
Slivered almonds, lightly toasted

1. Preheat oven to 350 degrees.

2. Cream the butter with 1 cup of the sugar. Beat in the egg yolks.

3. Sift together the flour, baking powder and baking soda. Stir into butter mixture alternately with sour cream. Stir in the rind and walnuts.

4. Beat the egg whites until stiff but not dry and fold into the batter. Pour batter into a greased 9-inch tube pan. Bake 50 minutes, or until the cake tests done.

5. Mix remaining sugar with the juice and liqueur. Spoon over hot cake and let cool in the pan. Sprinkle with almonds before serving.

Yield: 10 servings

Family Menus for Fall Weekends

During crisp fall weekends when the family gathers around the table for leisurely meals and a chance to catch up on the week's activities, there is a need for menus that won't wreck the budget or take an inordinate amount of preparation and worry about the exact time everyone is going to be ready to eat. Below are two menus that fill all these requirements.

*Lima Bean Soup**
*Rice and Sausage Casserole**
Tossed Salad
*Deep-Dish Pear Pie**

AND

*Spaghetti with Nut Sauce**
Garlic Bread
Escarole Salad
*Almond Custard Pudding**

LIMA BEAN SOUP

1 cup large dry lima
 beans
6 cups water
 Ham bone or 2
 ham hocks
2 tablespoons oil
1 onion, finely
 chopped
1 clove garlic, finely
 chopped
1 rib celery, finely
 chopped
½ green pepper, finely
 chopped

½ teaspoon summer
 savory
½ teaspoon chervil
1 teaspoon chopped
 parsley
½ teaspoon grated
 lemon rind
1 cup chicken broth
 or water
 Salt and freshly
 ground black pepper
 to taste

1. Pick over and wash the beans and place in a bowl with the water. Soak overnight.

2. Next day, transfer beans and liquid to a kettle, add the ham bone or ham hocks and bring to a boil. Cover and simmer until the beans are tender, about 1½ hours.

3. Remove ham bone or hocks. Discard fat and bone, chop ham very finely and reserve. Remove fat from the top of the bean mixture and force mixture through a food mill or blend in an electric blender. Return to the kettle. Add the ham to the kettle.

4. In a skillet, heat the oil, add the onion and garlic and cook until tender. Add the celery, green pepper, savory, chervil, parsley and lemon rind and cook 2 minutes. Add the broth or water, the salt and pepper.

5. Bring to a boil and add to the bean mixture. Reheat and check the seasonings.

Yield: 6 servings

RICE AND SAUSAGE CASSEROLE

3 *Italian sweet sausages, cut in ½-inch slices*
1 *Italian hot sausage, cut in ½-inch slices*
1 *bunch scallions*
¼ *pound mushrooms, sliced*
1 *clove garlic, finely chopped*
1 *pound cooked smoked ham, cubed*
2 *tablespoons flour*

3 *tablespoons butter*
1½ *cups raw rice*
1 *cup dry white wine*
Water
2 *tomatoes, skinned and chopped*
1 *bay leaf*
Tabasco to taste
Salt to taste
1 *pound shelled, deveined raw shrimp*
1 *cup toasted walnuts, coarsely chopped*

1. Sauté the sausage slices in a heavy casserole or deep heavy skillet until they are cooked through, stirring occasionally.

2. Slice the scallions with some of the green part and add with the mushrooms and garlic to the casserole or skillet. Cook, stirring, 3 minutes.

3. Dredge the ham in the flour. Add the ham and butter to the casserole or skillet. Cook, stirring, 2 minutes.

4. Add the rice, wine, ½ cup water, the tomatoes, bay leaf, Tabasco and salt. Bring to a boil, cover and simmer gently 15 minutes.

5. Add the shrimp and walnuts. Add another ¼ cup water if mixture is dry. Cover and cook 5 to 10 minutes, stirring occasionally, until the rice is tender and shrimp cooked.

Yield: 6 servings

DEEP-DISH PEAR PIE

Pastry

1 *cup flour*
⅛ *teaspoon salt*
⅓ *cup butter or shortening*

3 *tablespoons water, approximately*

Filling

4 medium-size ripe
pears (Bartlett,
Bosc or Comice)

2 medium-size tart
green apples

¾ cup light brown
sugar

1½ tablespoons quick-
cooking tapioca

¼ teaspoon salt

½ teaspoon cinnamon

¼ teaspoon grated
nutmeg

½ teaspoon grated
lemon rind

1 tablespoon lemon
juice

3 tablespoons butter

1. To prepare pastry, place the flour, salt and butter or short-ening in a bowl. With the finger tips or a pastry blender, work the butter or shortening into the flour until mixture resembles coarse oatmeal.

2. Stirring with a fork, add enough of the water to make a dough that barely clings together. Wrap in wax paper and chill.

3. To prepare filling, peel, core and slice the pears and the apples into a large bowl. Add the remaining ingredients except for the butter. Turn into a 9-inch-square glass baking dish.

4. Preheat oven to 450 degrees.

5. Roll out the chilled pastry to a 10-inch square. Dot filling with remaining butter, and place pastry over the filling. Turn under the excess pastry and make a decorative edge. Make steam holes. Bake 10 minutes. Reduce oven heat to 350 degrees and bake 40 minutes longer, or until pastry is golden and done and fruit is tender. Serve warm or cold.

Yield: 6 servings

SPAGHETTI WITH NUT SAUCE

½ cup olive oil
½ cup salad oil
2 cups toasted
  walnuts
½ cup freshly grated
  Parmesan cheese
1 tablespoon chopped
  fresh oregano, or 2
  teaspoons dried
1 tablespoon chopped
  fresh chervil, or 2
  teaspoons dried

¼ cup chopped onion
1 clove garlic
½ teaspoon salt
¼ teaspoon freshly
  ground black pepper
2 tablespoons chopped
  Italian parsley
1 cup cooked, sliced
  zucchini
1 pound spaghetti,
  cooked al dente and
  drained

1. Combine all the ingredients except the spaghetti in the container of an electric blender and blend until smooth. Pour sauce into a saucepan and heat to just below the boil.

2. Place spaghetti in a deep platter. Pour hot sauce over and toss.

Yield: 4 servings

ALMOND CUSTARD PUDDING

⅓ cup almond paste
  (see note)
1 cup grated
  Muenster cheese
3 cups ½-inch, day-
  old bread cubes,
  crusts removed
3 eggs
¼ cup sugar
½ teaspoon salt

1 teaspoon grated
  orange rind
3 cups milk, scalded
3 tablespoons melted
  butter
2 tablespoons light
  brown sugar
¼ teaspoon cinnamon
1 package (16 ounces)
  thawed frozen
  strawberries

1. Preheat oven to 350 degrees.

2. With the fingers, crumble the almond paste. Mix with the cheese. Alternate layers of bread cubes with the cheese mixture in a buttered 11-by-7-inch baking dish.

3. Beat the eggs lightly with the sugar, salt and orange rind. Gradually stir in the milk and pour over the layered ingredients.

4. Combine the butter, brown sugar and cinnamon and sprinkle over the pudding. Set the baking dish in a roasting pan with 1 inch hot water in it. Bake 40 minutes or until set. Serve warm with the berries.

Yield: 4 to 6 servings

Note: Almond paste is sold in cans in many supermarkets and specialty food shops. To make at home, combine ½ cup very finely ground blanched almonds with ½ cup confectioners' sugar, ¼ teaspoon almond extract, pinch salt and just enough lightly beaten egg white to make mixture hold together.

Supper Before,
or After,
Friday Night Class

❧

The fish shop you pass on the way home can be the source of umpteen ingredients for quick and easy-to-fix main dishes. On the nights you are dashing to class, PTA or an exercise class, the meal should not be heavy with starches and yet it must also satisfy those who are staying home. Let them eat the bread and also the pie that was tucked into the freezer the night before or early in the morning. The pie goes together in 10 minutes flat and leftovers can go back into the freezer for a late-evening snack. The chowder is ready to serve in 30 minutes from the time the bacon hits the pan.

Fish Chowder*
Hot French Bread
Tossed Salad
Arnie's Frozen Lime Pie*

FISH CHOWDER

6 slices bacon, diced
1 cup finely chop-
ped onions
1½ cups fresh or bot-
tled clam juice
2½ cups water
1½ cups diced carrots
2 cups diced
potatoes
1½ teaspoons salt
Freshly ground
black pepper to
taste
1 can (1 pound)
tomatoes, including
juice

½ teaspoon rosemary
¼ teaspoon thyme
½ cup diced celery
2 pounds fresh or
thawed frozen gray
sea trout, sea bass,
cod, halibut or
striped bass fillets,
cut into 1½-inch
slices
2 cups half-and-half,
light cream or milk

1. Sauté the bacon pieces until crisp. Remove the bits, drain on paper towel and reserve.

2. Sauté the onions in the bacon drippings until tender.

3. Add the clam juice, water, carrots, potatoes, salt, pepper and tomatoes. Bring to a boil and simmer, covered, 15 minutes or until the vegetables are almost tender.

4. Add the rosemary, thyme, celery and fish. Simmer, covered, about 10 minutes or until fish flakes. Add the half-and-half, cream or milk and bring to simmer point while stirring. Do not allow to boil. Sprinkle with reserved bacon bits.

Yield: 6 servings

ARNIE'S FROZEN LIME PIE

1 cup graham cracker
crumbs
¼ cup melted butter
1 teaspoon sugar
2 eggs, separated

1 can sweetened
condensed milk
½ cup lime juice
Grated rind of 1
lime

1. Mix together the crumbs, butter and sugar and turn into an 8-inch pie plate. Press against the bottom and sides of the plate to make an even pie shell. Chill while making the filling.

2. Using a wooden spoon, beat the egg yolks with the sweetened condensed milk. Do not use an electric mixer. Gradually stir in the lime juice and rind.

3. Beat the egg whites until stiff but not dry and fold into the lime mixture. Pour into the pie shell and freeze until firm. Allow the pie to set at room temperature 10 to 15 minutes before serving.

Yield: 4 to 6 servings

Mycological Morsels

Mycologists are a great group of naturalists, and it is well worth wangling an invitation to tag along on one of their mushroom-gathering forays. The exercise is stimulating, the countryside beautiful and the diverse backgrounds and interests of mushroom fanciers encourage discussion of many topics besides fungi. And, there's the bonus of collecting—perhaps sulphur mushrooms to make mushroom balls and a tasty snack to serve over toast points, or morels to put into flaky piroshki to enjoy as appetizers or accompaniments to bowls of hearty borscht for Sunday night supper. All three mushroom treats can be made with store-bought mushrooms, but they will not be quite the same.

Check the local phone directory under Mycological Society and only gather edible fungi under the watchful eye of an expert. When in doubt, discard.

Francis Neale's Sulphur Mushroom Balls*
Marion Bush's Piroshki with Morels*
Mrs. David Morris's Sulphur Mushroom Snack*

FRANCIS NEALE'S SULPHUR MUSHROOM BALLS

2 pounds diced or sliced sulphur or store-bought mushrooms
Boiling water (optional)
½ cup butter
1½ pounds softened cream cheese
½ whole nutmeg, grated

3 tablespoons apple butter
½ cup dry sherry
½ cup imported soy sauce
Juice of half a lemon
2½ cups chopped pecans toasted in butter
1½ cups ground toasted almonds

1. If sulphur mushrooms are used, they should be simmered in boiling water to cover until tender, 5 to 20 minutes.

2. Heat the butter in a skillet and sauté the mushrooms in it 5 minutes or until tender. Place in a bowl, add the cream cheese, nutmeg, apple butter, sherry, soy sauce and lemon juice and mix well. Cover and refrigerate overnight.

3. Stir in the pecans and form mixture into 1-inch balls. Roll the balls in the almonds and serve cold or wrap in foil and heat briefly in oven preheated to 375 degrees.

Yield: About 5 dozen balls

MARION BUSH'S PIROSHKI WITH MORELS

Pastry

4½ cups flour
1½ cups shortening
1 teaspoon salt

9–12 tablespoons water

Filling

¼ cup butter	2 teaspoons lemon
3 cups chopped	juice
morels or store-	⅛ teaspoon grated
bought mushrooms	nutmeg
1 cup finely chopped	1 cup sour cream
onions	2 tablespoons fresh
1 teaspoon salt	snipped dill weed
Freshly ground	Water
black pepper to	
taste	

1. Preheat oven to 400 degrees.

2. To prepare pastry, place the flour, shortening and salt in a bowl and, with the fingertips or a pastry blender, work in the shortening until mixture is the consistency of coarse oatmeal.

3. Add the water a little at a time until it makes a dough, using as little as possible.

4. Melt the butter in a skillet and briskly sauté the morels or mushrooms and the onions for about 4 minutes. Add the salt, pepper, lemon juice and nutmeg. Cook 1 to 2 minutes.

5. Remove from the heat and stir in the sour cream and dill. Mix well.

6. Roll out the pastry to a thickness of ⅛ inch and cut into 2-inch circles. Place ½ teaspoon mushroom mixture in center of each round. Brush edges with water, fold in half and seal by pinching with fingers or fork.

7. Place seam side up on ungreased pastry sheets. Press down slightly to form ovals with seam on top. Bake 20 to 30 minutes or until golden and done.

Yield: About 10 dozen

Mrs. David Morris's Sulphur Mushroom Snack

2 tablespoons unsalted
butter
1 tablespoon finely
chopped onion or
shallot
2 cups cleaned sul-
phur mushrooms
cut into bite-size
pieces, or store-
bought mushrooms,
stems left on, and
quartered
1 cup chicken broth
(optional)
1 clove garlic, finely
chopped
¼ cup sour cream
1 teaspoon salt
2 tablespoons chopped
parsley

1. Melt the butter in a skillet and sauté the onion in it 1 minute. Add the mushrooms and stir until butter is absorbed.

2. If using sulphur mushrooms, add the broth and cook 15 minutes or until tender.

3. Add the garlic, sour cream and salt. Stir over low heat until well blended. Sprinkle with parsley and serve warm.

Yield: 4 to 6 servings

Dinner for Eight

Special guests are coming Saturday night and everything must run smoothly and the dinner taste extra good. One couple's hobby is cooking and there will be the man from the office who bagged the partridge on a hunting trip and expects them to be superb, and the Waltons who regularly visit every three-star restaurant in Europe. Surprise them all with a sophisticated, yet not too elaborate, menu served in a leisurely manner with the best wines you can afford.

The Store Shrimp and Fennel Appetizer*
Muscadet or Sancerre
Partridge à la Vigneronne*
Straw Potatoes
Vegetable Casserole*
California Pinot Noir or Côtes du Rhone
Endive Salad
Cheese Tray
Crusty Rolls
Lemon and Strawberry Sherbet*
Sour Cream Cookies*
Sauternes
Espresso
Cognac

THE STORE SHRIMP AND FENNEL APPETIZER

Court bouillon

1 cup dry white wine
1 cup water
1 cup clam juice
½ lemon, sliced
3 sprigs parsley
3 celery rib tops with leaves

1 large onion, studded with 3 whole cloves
1 bay leaf
6 peppercorns
Salt to taste

Salad

3 pounds shrimp
1 clove garlic
1 whole stalk celery, finely chopped
3 ribs fennel, very finely chopped
4 shallots, finely chopped

Juice of 1 lime
1 large can pitted black olives, roughly chopped
½ cup chopped fresh basil

Vinaigrette

1 clove garlic
2 small shallots, finely chopped
Kosher salt
1 package bouillon powder
1 teaspoon Dijon mustard
Juice of 2 lemons

1½ cups oil (a mixture of corn and olive oils to taste)
3 tablespoons French red wine vinegar
Freshly ground black pepper to taste
2 limes

1. Place all the court bouillon ingredients in a large kettle and bring to a boil. Add the shrimp and cook 3 to 4 minutes. Clean and devein the shrimp, leaving the tail shells on.

2. Rub a bowl with the garlic and discard. Add celery, fennel, shallots and lime juice and toss well. Add the shrimp, black olives and basil.

3. To prepare dressing, mash the garlic and shallots with 1 teaspoon kosher salt until they form a paste. Add the bouillon powder and mustard and mix well.

4. Add the lemon juice and gradually beat in the oil. Stir in the vinegar and pepper.

5. Pour the dressing over the shrimp mixture and marinate 1 hour. Season with kosher salt to taste. Cut the limes into thin slices. Cut the slices in half and use to garnish.

Yield: 10 appetizer servings

Note: Leftover shrimp with fennel makes a delightful salad or sandwich filling.

PARTRIDGE À LA VIGNERONNE

8 small partridge	partridge giblets
Salt and freshly	with water, season-
ground black pepper	ing and onion
16 slices bacon	2/3 cup champagne or
1/4 cup bourbon or	dry white wine
cognac	3 cups seeded
2/3 cup game stock	Emperor grapes
made by boiling	

1. Wash the birds and pat dry. Season the cavity and outside of birds with salt and pepper. Wrap the bacon over breasts and legs; secure with string while trussing the birds.

2. Brown the birds on all sides in two heavy, enameled skillets, turning with wooden spoons. This takes about 25 minutes. Add the bourbon or cognac and set aflame.

3. When the flame dies down, add the game stock and champagne. Cover and cook gently, 15 to 20 minutes longer, or until the birds are tender.

4. Remove the birds to a warm platter. Remove trussing. Add the grapes to the skillets and cook, stirring, 3 minutes. Pour drippings and grapes over birds.

Yield: 8 servings.

Note: This recipe can be used for squab or Cornish game hens.

Vegetable Casserole

¼ cup butter
2 large onions, chopped
2 cloves garlic, finely chopped
1 cup chicken broth
1½ cups sliced carrots
2 potatoes, diced
1½ cups unpeeled eggplant cubes
½ cup peas
½ cup lima beans
½ cup green beans cut into 1-inch lengths
½ green pepper, cut into strips
¼ head green cabbage, cut into 4 slices
½ small head cauliflower, broken into flowerets
1 small zucchini, sliced
Salt and freshly ground black pepper to taste
1 apple, cored and diced
½ cup olive oil, heated

1. Preheat oven to 350 degrees.

2. Melt the butter, add the onions and garlic and sauté until tender but not browned. Add the broth and bring to a boil.

3. Meanwhile, arrange the carrots, potatoes, eggplant, peas, lima beans, green beans, green pepper, cabbage, cauliflower and zucchini in a large, shallow casserole.

4. Season with salt and pepper. Add the apple, hot onion mixture and hot oil. Toss lightly to mix.

5. Cover tightly and bake 30 minutes or until the vegetables are tender. Serve hot or lukewarm.

Yield: 6 to 8 servings

Note: The choice of vegetables is flexible and can be adjusted to use seasonal specials.

Lemon and Strawberry Sherbet

1½ cups water
¼ teaspoon salt
1½ cups sugar
¾ cup light cream
¾ cup lemon juice
¾ teaspoon grated lemon rind
3 egg whites
1 cup mashed, sweetened strawberries

1. Place water, salt and 1¼ cups of the sugar in a saucepan and bring to a boil. Boil 5 minutes. Cool.

2. Stir in the cream, lemon juice and rind and pour into freezer tray(s). Freeze until firm. Turn mixture into a bowl and beat until smooth.

3. Beat the egg whites until soft peaks form. Gradually beat in remaining sugar until mixture is stiff and glossy. Fold into lemon mixture. Fold in strawberries and return to freezer tray(s). Freeze until firm.

Yield: 8 servings

SOUR CREAM COOKIES

1 *cup butter*	2 *teaspoons grated*
¾ *cup sugar*	*lemon rind*
1 *egg yolk*	2¾ *cups flour*
⅓ *cup sour cream*	½ *teaspoon salt*
¼ *teaspoon lemon*	¼ *teaspoon baking*
extract	*soda*

1. Preheat oven to 375 degrees.

2. Cream the butter and gradually beat in the sugar until the mixture is light and creamy.

3. Beat in the egg yolk, sour cream and lemon extract.

4. Stir in the rind. Sift the flour with the salt and baking soda and blend into the butter mixture. Form the cookies through a cookie press onto an ungreased baking sheet. Bake 10 to 12 minutes or until golden.

Yield: 8 dozen small pressed cookies

Cooking the Catch

The greatest compliment to give an enthusiastic, amateur fisherman, who is out before dawn with high hopes and lures ready, is to invite guests to share his catch. But wait until the fish is being cleaned at home or there may be disappointment all around. Fish tastes best the day it is caught and needs little embellishment and few accompaniments to make it a feast. Keep a bottle of Chablis or Reisling on hand to chill for the occasion and it will be an instant party.

*Cream of Cauliflower Soup**
*Stuffed Striped Bass**
*Carrot and Cucumber Mélange**
Sliced Tomato Salad
*Ginger-Apple Cream**
or
Bananas Baked in Rum

CREAM OF CAULIFLOWER SOUP

¼ cup butter
3 shallots, finely chopped
2 ribs celery, finely chopped
½ tart apple, peeled and diced
1 teaspoon curry powder, or to taste
¼ cup flour
4 cups chicken broth

1 small head cauliflower, broken into small flowerets and thinly sliced
1 egg yolk, lightly beaten
1 cup light cream
Salt and freshly ground white pepper to taste
2 tablespoons chopped parsley

1. Melt the butter and sauté in it the shallots, celery and apple until tender and golden. Sprinkle with the curry powder and flour and cook, stirring, 2 minutes longer.

2. Gradually stir in the broth. Bring to a boil and add the thin slices of cauliflower. Cook, covered, until cauliflower is tender, about 10 minutes. At this stage the soup may be forced through a food mill for a completely creamed product or the cauliflower can be left in the slices if preferred.

3. Combine the yolk and cream and gradually stir into the sieved, or unsieved, soup mixture. Reheat while stirring, but do not allow to boil. Sprinkle with parsley.

Yield: 4 servings

STUFFED STRIPED BASS

1 striped bass (4 pounds)
¼ cup diced salt pork or butter
2 tablespoons finely chopped shallots
½ cup sliced mushrooms
1 pound shrimp, shelled, deveined and roughly chopped

½ cup fine soft bread crumbs
1 tablespoon chopped parsley
¼ teaspoon thyme
Salt and freshly ground black pepper to taste
2 tablespoons melted butter
2 tablespoons lemon juice

1. Preheat oven to 400 degrees.
2. Clean the fish but leave the head on.
3. Sauté the salt pork in a skillet until the bits are crisp. Or melt the butter in a skillet. Add the shallots to the drippings or the butter and cook until tender but not browned.
4. Add the mushrooms and shrimp and cook quickly until the shrimp turn pink and mushrooms wilt, about 5 minutes. Add the bread crumbs, parsley, thyme, salt and pepper. Stuff the fish with mixture and secure with skewers or sew to close.
5. Place the fish in a greased baking dish. Brush with the melted butter, season with salt and pepper and sprinkle lemon juice over all.
6. Bake about 35 minutes or until fish flakes easily.

Yield: 4 servings

Note: Bluefish, sea bass, scrod or haddock can be substituted.

Carrot and Cucumber Mélange

2 cucumbers, peeled, halved and seeded Boiling salted water	¼ cup water Salt and freshly ground black pepper to taste
1 bunch carrots, scraped and cut into 2-inch pieces	1 teaspoon sugar
2 tablespoons butter	1 tablespoon chopped parsley

1. Cut the cucumbers into 2-inch lengths and blanch in boiling salted water 1 minute. Drain.
2. In a small heavy pan, combine the carrots, butter, water, salt, pepper and sugar. Cover and simmer about 10 minutes or until the carrots are crisp-tender.
3. Add the cucumbers and cook, uncovered, stirring occasionally, until extra liquid has been evaporated and vegetables are just tender. Sprinkle with parsley and serve.

Yield: 4 servings

GINGER-APPLE CREAM

3 pounds McIntosh apples, peeled, cored and chopped
3 tablespoons butter
1 teaspoon grated lemon rind
3 tablespoons honey
2 tablespoons water
Lemon juice
1 tablespoon unflavored gelatin
3 tablespoons dark rum
3 tablespoons chopped crystallized ginger
⅓ cup chopped walnuts or pecans
1 cup heavy cream, whipped
1 Red Delicious apple

1. Place the chopped apples in a heavy saucepan with a tight-fitting cover. Heat slowly, stirring occasionally, until apples are quite tender. Check to make sure they are not sticking on the bottom of the pan. McIntosh apples have sufficient moisture in them so that no added liquid is needed.

2. Beat in the butter, lemon rind and honey and continue to cook, uncovered, stirring until the mixture is very thick.

3. Combine the water and 2 tablespoons lemon juice. Soak the gelatin in the mixture. Stir into the hot apple mixture and continue stirring to dissolve. Allow the mixture to cool to room temperature.

4. Stir in the rum, ginger and nuts and chill until mixture just starts to thicken further.

5. Fold in the whipped cream and spoon into a serving bowl or individual glasses. Chill well.

6. Cut the unpeeled apple into quarters, remove core and slice apple very thinly. Brush cut surfaces with lemon juice to prevent browning. Use slices for garnish.

Yield: 6 servings

Last Brunch of the Season

✕

September. October. Chilly mornings. Autumn sunshine. Time for a last weekend get-together outdoors before the boat is lifted out of the water, the country house is closed and the winter winds whistle. The brunch menu here is hearty enough to overcome any hint of autumn chill. Make the casserole and biscuits at home and reheat in the galley or on a camp stove or hibachi on the beach.

*Rum Eye-Opener**
*Spinach and Cheese Casserole**
*Flaky Biscuits**
Raw Relishes
Fresh Fruit Compote

RUM EYE-OPENER

2 ounces freshly
squeezed orange
juice
½–1 ounce lime juice

1–2 teaspoons sugar
2 ounces light rum
Ice cubes
Tonic or soda water

Place the orange juice, lime juice and sugar in a tall glass. Stir to dissolve the sugar. Add the rum, ice cubes and enough tonic or soda water to fill the glass.

Yield: 1 serving

SPINACH AND CHEESE CASSEROLE

1½–2 pounds kielbasa
  (Polish sausage)
  Hot water
3 bags (10 ounces
  each) fresh spinach
  or 2½–3 pounds
  loose fresh or 3
  packages (10
  ounces each) frozen
½ teaspoon grated
  nutmeg

4 cups (about 1
  pound) shredded
  Cheshire or mild,
  natural yellow
  Cheddar cheese
2 tablespoons flour
1 teaspoon worces-
  tershire sauce
¾ teaspoon dry
  mustard
1 cup beer or ale

1. Heat through or cook the sausage in hot water to cover, depending on whether sausage is ready-to-eat or uncooked. Slice either variety into ½-inch-thick chunks and sauté in a skillet until lightly browned on both sides. Discard the fat drippings.

2. In the bottom of a shallow 8-cup baking dish, arrange kielbasa slices, skin removed if desired, reserving a few for garnish.

3. Cook the spinach in the water clinging to the washed leaves if fresh, according to package directions if frozen. Drain, pressing out all excess moisture with a wooden spoon. Stir in the nutmeg.

4. Spread the spinach over the sausage.

5. Meanwhile, place the cheese, flour, worcestershire, mustard and beer or ale in a heavy casserole or in the top of a double boiler over simmering water. Heat, stirring, until the cheese melts and forms a smooth sauce. Bring to a boil and pour over the spinach. Garnish the dish with reserved sausage slices.

6. Run under a preheated broiler to brown the cheese.

Yield: 8 servings

Note: If it seems easier, the sausage, spinach and cheese sauce can be served separately and each person can assemble his own.

FLAKY BISCUITS

2 cups flour
3 teaspoons baking powder
½ teaspoon salt
½ cup powdered skim milk
¼ cup wheat germ (optional)

½ cup butter
2 eggs, lightly beaten
½ cup milk, approximately
2 tablespoons light cream

1. Place the flour, baking powder, salt, powdered milk and wheat germ in a bowl and, with finger tips or pastry blender, blend in the butter until mixture resembles coarse oatmeal.

2. Make a well in the center of the blended mixture and add the eggs and ⅓ cup of the milk. Stir, adding more milk if necessary to make a soft, slightly sticky dough.

3. Turn the dough out onto a floured board and knead briefly until dough holds together.

4. Roll out the dough into a rectangle about a ½ inch thick. Fold in thirds lengthwise. Roll out again; fold into thirds. Repeat the rolling and folding 4 more times—a total of 6 rollings and foldings.

5. Preheat oven to 450 degrees.

6. Roll out to a thickness of ½ inch and cut with a cookie cutter into rounds. Place on an ungreased baking sheet, brush tops with cream and bake about 10 minutes or until browned and done. Serve piping hot.

Yield: 1 dozen 2½-inch biscuits

Note: These biscuits are rich enough to stand reheating.

Bicentennial Celebration Dinner

The 200th anniversary of our nation is cause for many celebrations during 1976, and we should use American-grown bounty and recipes that were enjoyed by our ancestors. The menu below uses some foods popular in Colonial times, a soup with a French name that was created at the Ritz Carlton Hotel in New York City by the great Louis Diat and a modern, lighter version of a traditionally spicy dessert. Pour the ale or the American wine and share a celebration feast.

*Vichyssoise**
*Stuffed Loin of Pork**
Baked Sweet Potatoes
*Butternut Squash and Cranberry Bake**
Cole Slaw
Pickles
Hot Biscuits
*Chilled Spice Mousse**

VICHYSSOISE

4 leeks, white parts only, thinly sliced	1 quart chicken broth
	Salt to taste
1 medium-size onion, chopped	3 cups milk
	2 cups heavy cream
¼ cup butter	Chopped chives
5 medium-size potatoes, thinly sliced	

1. Sauté the leeks and onion in the butter in a deep kettle. Add potatoes, broth and salt. Bring to a boil, cover and simmer 30 minutes or until potatoes are very tender.

2. Puree the mixture through a food mill or in an electric blender. Return mixture to the kettle.

3. Add the milk and 1 cup of the cream and bring to a boil. For an extra-smooth soup, pass the mixture through the food mill or electric blender a second time. Chill.

4. Stir in remaining cream and serve in chilled soup bowls, sprinkled with chives.

Yield: 8 servings

STUFFED LOIN OF PORK

1 center cut loin of pork (6–8 pounds), boned	1 hard-cooked egg, chopped
	1 cup soft bread crumbs
Salt and freshly ground black pepper to taste	1 Golden Delicious apple, peeled, cored and diced
½ pound lean sausage meat	Grated rind of 1 orange
1 clove garlic, finely chopped	2 tablespoons chopped parsley
1 cup finely chopped onions	1 cup dry white wine, approximately

1. Preheat oven to 325 degrees.

2. Spread out pork, fat side down, and season with salt and pepper. In a skillet, fry the sausage meat until it loses its pink color.

3. Add the garlic and onions to skillet and cook 5 minutes longer or until the onions are tender. Stir in the remaining ingredients, except for the wine, and add salt and pepper to taste.

4. Spread the mixture over the pork, leaving a 1-inch margin clear around the sides. Roll up in jellyroll fashion and secure with string.

5. Place the rolled roast in a small shallow roasting pan. Pour 1 cup wine over pork and roast 30 minutes to the pound or until cooked through, basting several times with the wine and drippings. Add more wine if the pan becomes dry.

Yield: 6 to 8 servings

BUTTERNUT SQUASH AND CRANBERRY BAKE

1 large butternut squash, or 4 cups cooked mashed squash	Salt and freshly ground black pepper to taste
Boiling salted water (for uncooked squash)	1 tablespoon grated onion
3 tablespoons melted butter	2 tablespoons sugar
	¾ cup raw, halved cranberries
	⅛ teaspoon grated nutmeg

1. Slice and peel the squash and remove seeds. Cube the squash. Add to boiling salted water to cover and cook, covered, until tender, about 8 minutes. Do not overcook. Drain well and mash.

2. Preheat oven to 400 degrees.

3. Beat the hot mashed squash with 2 tablespoons of the butter, the salt, pepper, onion and sugar. Stir in the cranberries. Turn into a casserole or baking dish, sprinkle with nutmeg and remaining butter and bake 45 minutes.

Yield: 6 to 8 servings

Chilled Spice Mousse

2 envelopes unfla- vored gelatin	½ teaspoon cinnamon
¾ cup water	⅛ teaspoon allspice
1 cup lemon juice	½ teaspoon almond extract
8 eggs, separated	3 tablespoons orange- flavored liqueur
½ teaspoon salt	
2 cups sugar	1½ cups heavy cream, whipped
¼ teaspoon grated nutmeg	

1. Soften the gelatin in the cold water. In the top of a double boiler, combine the lemon juice, egg yolks, salt, 1 cup sugar, the nutmeg, cinnamon and allspice.

2. Cook, while stirring over boiling water, until mixture is slightly thickened. Do not allow to boil.

3. Stir in the gelatin mixture until dissolved.

4. Pour the mixture into a large bowl and cool. Stir in the almond extract and liqueur.

5. Beat the egg whites until foamy and gradually beat in the remaining sugar until stiff peaks are formed.

6. Fold the egg white mixture and the cream into the gelatin mixture and pour into a serving dish or 2-quart soufflé mold fitted with a greased collar. Refrigerate several hours or until firm.

7. If soufflé dish is used, remove collar before serving.

Yield: 8 servings

Preserving the Harvest

Combining forces with others to buy fresh produce from a farm stand to preserve in jams, jellies, pickles and relishes means extra savings because you'll be buying by the bushel instead of the pound. Peeling all those peaches and tomatoes won't seem half so tedious if or more work together on a miniature production line and the day's activities will provide many jars for the store cupboard and for holiday gifts. Working with food builds appetites, but no one wants to stop long enough for a formal meal. A big kettle of soup on the back of the stove is the answer, and at the end of the day a slice of strudel that came out of the freezer, with coffee and a dash of anisette, can mark the end of the project.

*Peach and Pear Chutney**
*Grape Relish**
*Tomato and Apple Chutney**
*Plum Chutney**
*Lamb and Zucchini Soup**
*Gilda Latzky's Strudel**

Peach and Pear Chutney

1½ pounds ripe peaches
1½ pounds pears, peeled, cored and sliced
1 cup cider vinegar
¼ cup chopped onion
¼ cup raisins
1½ teaspoons pow- dered ginger
¼ teaspoon mustard seeds
¼ cup light brown sugar
½ teaspoon celery seeds
½ small fresh chili pepper, finely chopped (optional)

1. Dip the peaches, one at a time, in boiling water for a few seconds. Remove and peel. Pit and slice into a large heavy kettle.

2. Add the remaining ingredients, bring to a boil and simmer, uncovered, until mixture is very thick, stirring to prevent sticking.

3. Ladle into hot, sterilized canning or jelly jars, cover tightly and cool. Store in a cool, dark, dry place. Mellow 1 week before serving.

Yield: About 4 half pints

Grape Relish

5 cups seeded grapes
5 cups peeled, cored and sliced tart apples
1 cup raisins
4 small white onions
1 large clove garlic
1 tablespoon salt
2 cups light brown sugar
½ cup lemon juice
1 tablespoon dry mustard
2 tablespoons grated horseradish
2 tablespoons finely chopped preserved ginger
½ cup cider vinegar

1. Put the grapes, apples, raisins, onions and garlic through the coarse blade of a meat grinder.

2. Put the ground mixture in a large kettle and add remaining ingredients. Bring to a boil and simmer, uncovered, until mixture is very thick. Stir to prevent sticking. Spoon into hot, sterilized can-

ning or jelly jars; cover tightly. Cool. Store in a cool, dark, dry place. Allow to mellow 10 days before using.

Yield: About 6 half pints

TOMATO AND APPLE CHUTNEY

2 pounds ripe
tomatoes

2 pounds tart green
apples, peeled,
cored and sliced

2 onions, sliced

2 cups cider vinegar

2 teaspoons powdered
ginger

2 dried chili peppers,
crumbled

1 teaspoon mustard
seeds

1 cup light brown
sugar

½ cup raisins

1. Plunge tomatoes into boiling water for a few seconds. Remove, peel and slice into glass or ceramic bowl.

2. Add apples, onions, vinegar, ginger, chili peppers and mustard seeds. Stir to mix, cover and let stand in a cool place overnight.

3. Next day, transfer to a kettle, add the brown sugar and raisins, bring to a boil and simmer, uncovered, until thick. Pour into hot, sterilized canning or jelly jars. Cover tightly, cool and store in a cool, dark, dry place. Allow to mellow for 10 days before serving.

Yield: About 6 half pints

PLUM CHUTNEY

3 pounds Italian
purple plums

1½ pounds tart apples,
peeled, cored and
sliced

1 tablespoon pow-
dered ginger

1 tablespoon whole
allspice

1 tablespoon mustard
seeds, roughly
crushed

1 teaspoon whole
cloves

3 small fresh chili
peppers

1 teaspoon salt

2 cups cider vinegar

2 cups light brown
sugar

1. Wash and pit the plums and place in a kettle with the apples. Add the ginger. Tie the allspice, mustard seeds, cloves and chili peppers in a muslin bag and add to kettle.

2. Stir in the remaining ingredients, bring to a boil and simmer gently, uncovered, until mixture is very thick. Stir frequently to prevent sticking. Remove muslin bag.

3. Ladle into hot, sterilized canning or jelly jars, cover tightly, cool and store in a cool, dark, dry place. Allow to mellow 2 weeks before serving.

Yield: About 5 half pints

LAMB AND ZUCCHINI SOUP

2 tablespoons oil
1 pound boned lamb shoulder, cut into ¾-inch cubes
3 leeks, thinly sliced
2 large carrots, diced
2 white turnips, diced
2 cloves garlic, finely chopped
1 bay leaf
1 cup lentils, picked over and washed

6 cups lamb stock, made from bones, or chicken broth
Salt and freshly ground black pepper to taste
3 medium-size zucchini, sliced
1 teaspoon rosemary
2 tablespoons fresh mint, or 1 teaspoon dried

1. Heat the oil in a heavy casserole, add the lamb and brown on all sides. Add the leeks, carrots, turnips and garlic and cook 3 to 4 minutes, stirring occasionally.

2. Add the bay leaf, lentils, stock or broth and the salt and pepper. Bring to a boil, cover and simmer 1 hour or until meat and lentils are tender.

3. Add the zucchini and rosemary, cover and simmer 10 minutes or until zucchini is barely tender. Stir in the mint.

Yield: 6 to 8 servings

GILDA LATZKY'S STRUDEL

Dough

1¾ cups strudel flour, sifted twice before being measured

¼ teaspoon salt

1 large egg

1 teaspoon melted butter

1 teaspoon cider vinegar

⅓ cup lukewarm water

1 cup melted unsalted butter

¾ cup soft bread crumbs

Filling

1 cup plus 2 tablespoons vanilla-flavored confectioners' sugar (see note)

3 tablespoons softened butter

2 large egg yolks

¼ cup golden raisins

Grated rind of ½ lemon

12 ounces very dry cottage or pot cheese

11 ounces softened cream cheese

1. To prepare dough, sift the flour and salt into a bowl.

2. Make a well in the center and drop in the egg, 1 teaspoon butter and the vinegar. Using your hands, gradually mix in the water to form a cohesive mass, adding a drop or two extra water if absolutely necessary.

3. Turn the dough onto a lightly floured board and knead until the dough is elastic, smooth and blistery on the surface. This will take from 10 to 20 minutes depending on kneading skill.

4. Throw the dough against a hard wood or marble surface for about 5 minutes to develop the gluten in the flour to maximum elasticity. Shape into a ball, cover with the bowl and let rest 30 to 45 minutes.

5. Meanwhile, heat ½ cup melted unsalted butter in a small skillet, add the bread crumbs and brown lightly. Set aside.

6. To prepare filling, combine 1 cup confectioners' sugar and the remaining ingredients. Mix well. Set aside.

7. Place the dough on a floured muslin-covered or cloth-covered large table. Roll as thin as possible with a rolling pin. Brush lightly with melted butter, preferably using a goose-feather brush.

8. Lift the dough over the wrists and knuckles with palms facing down and gently stretch it until it is about doubled in size.

9. Place dough back on the cloth and start stretching with the upturned finger tips, starting from the center and working out to the edges.

10. Move around the table as you work at stretching so that the motion is in an even circular direction. Continue to stretch dough until it is as thin as onion skin. Ignore any small holes that may appear. Lift the dough off the table occasionally to let air circulate underneath.

11. The stretched dough should measure at least 4 by 5 feet. With scissors, trim off any thick outer edges.

12. Preheat oven to 425 degrees.

13. Sprinkle bottom third of dough with ½ cup of the bread crumbs. Spread filling in a narrow strip over the bread crumbs.

14. Brush remaining dough lightly with melted butter and sprinkle with remaining bread crumbs. Roll the pastry around the filling, jellyroll style, using the cloth to help the movement. Do not roll too tightly.

15. Place crosswise in a jellyroll pan lined with parchment paper or, if dough is too long, cut into 2 pieces and set them side by side.

16. Brush with melted butter and bake 25 to 35 minutes or until golden, brushing with remaining butter twice during baking. Allow the strudel to cool for 20 to 30 minutes before serving. Dust with confectioners' sugar, if desired. To reheat for serving later, place in a 350-degree oven for 10 minutes.

Yield: 12 to 14 servings

Note: Vanilla-flavored confectioners' sugar is made by placing a vanilla bean in a jar of the sugar and letting it stand several days or weeks.

INDEX

Kir, 23
Kisses, 37
Krinkles, Fanny Pierson Crane's spice, 38

Lacy granola cookies, 148
Lamb
    clay-roasted stuffed leg of, 64
    eggplant khoresh, 297
    kebabs, 119, 177
    and leek, spicy, 285
    shanks, Provençale, 111
    shishkebab, 216
    spiced ground, 121
    stuffed crown roast of, 24
    and zucchini soup, 332
Leek
    soup, 274
    spicy lamb and, 285
Leftovers, Thanksgiving, 261–264
Lemon
    fluff, 215
    ice cream, 115
    –lime chicken, 186
    loaves, 59
    mousse, Bert Greene's, 5
    pie, frozen, 62
    soufflé, frozen, 62
    and strawberry sherbert, 316
Lentil
    salad, 276
    and sausage casseroles, 80
Lima bean(s)
    chicken with fresh corn and, 218
    soup, 301
Lime
    chicken, lemon–, 186
    pie, Arnie's frozen, 307
Liver
    beef, 233
    chicken, 197
    paste, 170
Lobster, 190

Macaroni salad, fish and, 234
Macédoine of vegetables, 192
Maksatahna, 170
Maple ice cream, 57
Marinated cod and shrimp, 194
Marlborough tart, Lee's, 141
Marmalade bars, orange, 103
Mayonnaise, herbed, 191
Meat
    See Beef; Chicken; Duck; Ham;
    Lamb; Meatloaf; Mincemeat; Part-
    ridge; Pork; Sausage; Steak; Tur-
    key; Veal
Meatloaf,
    cold fruited, 224
    stuffed, 8
Meringue(s), 133
    pie, orange, 121
Middle Eastern flat bread, 118
Mincemeat coffeecake, 58
Miso soup, 99

Morels, Marion Bush's piroshki with, 310
Mousse
    Bert Greene's lemon, 5
    chilled spice, 328
    chocolate
    –torte, Maida Heatter's, 70
    two-tone, 61
    frozen, Izarra, 16
    raspberry, 192
    smoked salmon, à la Caravelle, 19
Muffin(s)
    appetizer, shrimp, 136
    apricot–whole wheat, 212
    high protein, Pearl Gordon's, 167
Mushroom(s)
    appetizer, 55
    balls, 310
    chowder, 164
    cream sauce, 82
    escabèche with, 68
    morels, 310
    salad, 271
    snack, Mrs. David Morris's sulphur, 312
    stuffed raw, 293
    sulphur, 310, 312
    over toast points, stewed, 63

No-bake chocolate almond snowballs, 149
Noodles
    with anchovy sauce, 133
    dilled rice and, 15
    homemade, 153
    See also Pasta
Nut
    custard, honey and, 80
    sauce, spaghetti with, 304
    squares, chocolate, 102
    See also Almond; Filbert; Pea-
    nut; Pecan; Pine nut; Pistachio;
    Walnut

Oeufs en gelée, 270
Onion–cheese tarts, 51
Open house punch, 35
Orange
    cake, 299
    cookies, 74
    (or grapefruit) peel, candied, 104
    marmalade bars, 103
    meringue pie, 121
    torte, 28
Oyster
    beignets with horseradish sauce, 23
    bisque, 253

Pancake, Reuben's apple, 112
Parfait, blueberry, 216
Partridge à la Vigneronne, 315
Passover sweetmeats, 102–105
Pasta
    cannelloni, 41
    and fettucine, 194
    macaroni and fish salad, 234
    noodles
    with anchovy sauce, 133

342 *Index*

Spinach (*Continued*)
  sauce with fettucine, 194
  timbales, 130
  torte di spinaci, 113
Split pea soup, 40
Spring vegetable soup, 107
Squid, 223
Squash
  butternut, 327
  with peas and spinach, baked, 25
  zucchini, *see* Zucchini soup
Steak salad, cold, 186
Stock, fish, 20
Strawberry
  fluff, 162
  ice cream, 219
  layer cake, 145
  sherbet, lemon and, 316
  soup, chilled, 203
Striped bass, stuffed, 316
Strudel, Gilda Latzky's, 333
Sultsinat, 168
Sunflower seeds vinaigrette, 88
Swedish-style hamburgers, 117
Sweet and sour bean salad, 207
Sweetmeats
  Passover, 102–105
      See also Candy

Tagliarini with pesto, 229
Tarragon chicken loaf, 275
Tart(s)
  almond, 230
  cheese, 157
      onion–, 51
  fruited cheese pies, 277
  Lee's Marlborough, 141
  William Greenberg's sand, 207
Thanksgiving
  dishes, 252–260
  leftovers, 261–264
Tiens, 165
Timbales, spinach, 130
Tomato
  and apple chutney, 331
  salad, sliced, 219
  sauce, for cannelloni, 43
Torte
  almond, 131
      eight-layer, 139
  blueberry, 201
  chocolate mouse–, 70
  orange, 281
  di spinaci, 113
Tortière de famille, 264
Turkey
  barbecued, 232

breast cordon bleu, 227
croque-monsieur, 261
how to thaw and roast, 253
timetable for cooking, 254
tortière de famille, 264
vegetable soup, 263
Turnovers
  salmon, 137
  sour cream-apple, 296
Two-tone chocolate mousse, 61

Veal
  escalopes, 130
  with peppers, 4
Vegetable(s)
  caldo verde, 279
  casserole, 316
  cold plate, herbed, 239
  coulibiac, 90
  dish, bean curd, 286
  frittata, 217
  kebabs, 176
  macédoine of, 192
  with salsa verde, 60
  soup
      spring, 107
      turkey, 263
  tiens, 165
      See also names of vegetables
Velouté, fish, 20
Vichyssoise, 326

Wafers, sesame seed, 89
Walnut(s)
  cakes, black, 37
  with hoisin sauce, crispy, 283
Water chestnuts, Grace Chu's broccoli
      flowerets with, 64
Watercress
  bean sprout and citrus salad on, 92
  soup, 11
Wheat
  cracked, *see* Cracked wheat
  germ cookies, apple–, 149
  whole, *see* Whole wheat
Whole wheat
  bread, Cornell, 47
  muffins, apricot–, 212

Yakitori, 99
Yogurt granola bread, 78

Zucchini soup
  cold, 226
  lamb and, 332